Monograph 65

THE AMERICAN ETHNOLOGICAL SOCIETY

Robert F. Spencer, Editor

*

SIX
KOREAN WOMEN

The Socialization of Shamans

Youngsook Kim Harvey

West Publishing Company
St. Paul   New York   Los Angeles   San Francisco

COPYRIGHT © 1979 by West Publishing Co.
50 West Kellogg Boulevard
P.O. Box 3526
St. Paul, Minnesota 55165

Printed in the United States of America

Library of Congress Cataloging in Publication Data

Harvey, Youngsook Kim.
    Six Korean women.

    (Monograph—The American Ethnological Society; 65)
    Bibliography: p.
    Includes index.
    1. Shamanism—Korea—Case studies. 2. Women—
Korea—Biography. I. Title. II. Series: American
Ethnological Society. Monographs; 65.
BL2370.S5H36   299'.57   78-27500
ISBN 0-8299-0243-0

To Bob
    Andrew
    Sarah
     and
    My parents

*

CONTENTS

*

PREFACE

This book brings together the life histories of six Korean women who are shamans and thus share in common the social ascription of outcaste status. They vary widely, however, in age and social backgrounds, representing almost the full range of Korean social structure, traditional, and contemporary. All have at one time or another lived as members of patrilineal extended families, though some grew up primarily in nuclear families. Two are of urban origin whereas the other four moved to urban areas from agricultural villages at different stages of their lives. Two had the first-hand experience of living as immigrants, one in Manchuria and the other in Japan. In education, they range from a total illiterate to a college graduate.

The oldest woman was born in 1911 and the youngest in 1937. As a group, they have thus lived during critical periods of transition in Korean culture. The oldest was born a year after the official annexation of Korea as a colony of Japan, a period when Koreans were in a state of shock. The others were born later during the colonial experience, a time of national humiliation, which is reflected in their lives. In one way or another, all had to adjust to the sudden transformations, political and technological, that swept over Korea following World War II. They were then soon engulfed by the chaos of the Korean War in 1950-1953.

These events affected each of the women differently, of course. This book brings together individual subjective accounts of these women's lives: how they came to acquire the role of shaman, the impact it had on their personal lives and the lives of their families, and how their lives enmeshed in Korean society. The accounts that follow are then narratives describing what it has meant to six Koreans to be women of their particular times and circumstances. Because their biographies provide important glimpses and intimate details of Korean society and culture that they have lived through and now share with other Koreans, this book is also an ethnography of Korea in a more general sense.

The fieldwork on which this book is based was carried out in Korea between 1971 and 1973 and was supported by the National Institute of Mental Health, Grant #MH-10469. Chaminade University of Honolulu, of which the author is a faculty member, provided two grants for the initial writing of the manuscript during the summers of 1974 and 1975. The Social Sciences and Linguistics Institute of the University of Hawaii graciously allowed me the use of an office between 1974 and 1976 for completing the manuscript. I wish to acknowledge my deep gratitude to these institutions for their generous support.

In writing this book, I have also had the help of many people. My heartfelt thanks go first to William P. Lebra, Professor of Anthropology, University of Hawaii, who guided, prodded, and otherwise encouraged me throughout the study that has resulted in this book. Next, I wish to thank Edward Norbeck, Department of Anthropology, Rice University; Katharine Luomala, Takie Sugiyama Lebra, Fred Blake, and Alan Howard, all of the Department of Anthropology, University of Hawaii; and Dr. Wen-Shing Tseng, of the Department of Psychiatry, and Dr. James Wright Frierson, of the Department of English, University of Hawaii. These people read the manuscript and made constructive suggestions at different stages of its writing. I am deeply indebted to Freda Hellinger for typing and otherwise assisting in the preparation of the manuscript.

In addition, I wish to acknowledge the invaluable help I received while in the field from Professor Kwang Kyu Lee, Assistant Professor of Anthropology, Seoul National University; Professor Chu-Keun Chang, Professor of Hongik College and Specialist with Cultural Project Bureau, the government of the

Republic of Korea; Dr. Kwang-iel Kim, Professor and Chairman, Department of Neuropsychiatry, School of Medicine, Kyŏnghi University; and Mr. Young Bin Min, President of Sisa Publishing Co., all of Seoul. I am most indebted to them for their guidance and counsel as well as to many others too numerous to include here. Responsibility for the book, however, rests with myself alone.

Finally, I wish to thank the six shamans who served as my informants. Their personal courage has been an inspiration for me. I want, also, to express my gratitude and appreciation to Bob, my husband, and to Andrew and Sarah, my children, who endured and coped with the sundry side effects of having a doctoral candidate in their midst for several years.

In romanizing Korean words and names, I have followed the McCune-Reischaur system exclusively, except in those cases where proper names had already been romanized according to a different system and had become established in those forms.

*

1

INTRODUCTION

Several reasons moved me to do a biographical study of female shamans of Korea. The most important was probably the keen personal interest I have always felt in the lives of contemporary professional women of Korea, especially those who combine their professional careers with family life. I come by this interest quite naturally, having grown up in the cross fire of conflict between career-minded modern Korean women and the traditional conservatism inherited from the predominantly Confucian Yi Dynasty (A.D. 1392-1920), which still binds them. Historically, the role of the shaman in Korea has been held mostly by women, and I wondered if these traditional career women experienced conflicts in combining their professional lives with family life. It occurred to me that a study of their lives might reveal some insights into the nature of conflicts they experienced in combining their professional and domestic roles and, further, reveal the strategies they found effective in managing these conflicts.

A second motivating factor was the pervasive force that shamanism has exerted in the life of Koreans throughout their history, making the shaman role an important vehicle through which women have influenced Korean society. I wanted to learn what kinds of women aspired to the shaman role, how it was acquired, maintained, and used, and what impact it had on the

1

women themselves, their families, and more indirectly, on Korean society.

Still another consideration was the ongoing controversy in the literature of anthropology and psychiatry regarding the mental health of shamans. Given the generally influential role that shamans play in the lives of their clients and, therefore, in their societies, it seemed desirable to have the controversy regarding the psychopathology of shamans resolved. Such a resolution seemed particularly important with reference to Korea, where the influence of shamans has long been pervasive. However, individual life histories of shamans, which seemed to be the first type of data to collect toward reaching this aim, are almost nonexistent for Korea as well as for other societies.

An added stimulus to research was personal, the curiosity of a native who comes to appreciate an aspect of her native culture only when removed from it. I left Korea at the age of seventeen, having little systematic knowledge of Korean shamanism. My parents took painstaking care to insulate us from exposure to shamans. My father, a headmaster of a rural school in Hwanghae Province in what is today North Korea, and my mother, one of the teachers in the school, were determinedly modern in their outlook and assiduously shielded their children from all that they regarded as superstitious and detrimental to the modernization of Korea and therefore to their education. They considered shamanistic activities particularly pernicious to our developing minds. Even so, my brother and I managed without difficulty to see clandestinely two or three *kut* ("shamanistic rituals") a year for several years, so prevalent were shamamistic activities in the rural community where we grew up. Because shamanistic activities were both a forbidden topic at home and also extraordinarily dramatic, my childhood experiences of them, fragmented as they were, have always remained vividly imprinted in my mind. However, it was not until I began my graduate studies in psychological anthropology and had a seminar on shamanism that I began to take an active interest in Korean shamanism as a scholarly topic, becoming more interested in it as I progressed in my research.

In its long course of evolution, Korean shamanism seems to have undergone a complete metamorphosis from a male-centered activity intimately involved in the political system of the society to

an activity primarily of and for women, with only the most informal, often underground, connections to the government in modern times.[1] During the proto-historic period, before A.D. 400,
there appear to have been shaman kings. Today, while there
continue to be male shamans, the vast majority of shamans and
their clients are female. Until very recently, male shamans were
expected to practice transvestism as an attribute of their role.

This metamorphic process was apparently accelerated and
became crystalized under the influence of Confucianism during
the Yi Dynasty, the most critical historical period for understanding contemporary Korea. The Yi Dynasty made the eradication of
shamanism an official policy and launched a systematic campaign
of persecution of shamans and their followers. The policy discouraged men, especially of *yangban* ("aristocratic") background,
from becoming publicly involved with shamanism and drove it
underground. In so doing, the government inadvertently made
the shaman role and other roles associated with it more accessible
to women. And since shamanism remained a persistent force in
the life of Koreans in spite of official persecution, it provided its
female specialists with an unexpectedly powerful avenue for making their influence felt in the society.

Indeed, it appears that the Yi Dynasty government coped
with its failure to eradicate shamanism by giving it begrudging
recognition as a belief system suitable only for women and some
men of ignorance. It made the role of shaman one of the four
professional roles officially permitted to women, the other three
being those of *kungnyŏ* ("palace woman"), *ŭinyŏ* ("female physi-
cian"), and *kisaeng* ("courtesan"). The shaman role, however,
differed from these other roles in some noteworthy aspects.

It was, for example, the only role that permitted women
access to all levels and spheres of the society, making it potentially the most powerful role through which women could exert
influence in a society where they had no authority, which belonged first to their fathers, then their husbands, and finally to
their sons. The shaman served royalty as well as commoners,
males as well as females, and had access to both the public and
private domains. It was also the only female professional role for
which there was apparently no formally institutionalized pattern
of recruitment, training, or practice. There was no explicit pros-
cription against shamans marrying, either before or after recruit-

ment, as there was for palace women and courtesans. (It was not entirely clear if female physicians were subjected to this constraint.) In other words, the role of shaman alone apparently offered women of traditional Korea the possibility of combining a professional career with family life.

Since in traditional Korea the only normative role for women had been the domestic one and since the expectations were such that it could not be satisfactorily performed in conjunction with any extradomestic career,[2] it was reasonable to suppose that married shamans must have encountered serious and numerous conflicts socially and personally in maintaining their dual roles. What, I wondered, had these conflicts been and how had they coped or failed to cope with them? It is my contention that the life histories of shamans may yield insights having useful application to modern Korean women, who are seeking in increasing numbers to combine careers with family life. Since modern career women must sustain their efforts to maintain dual roles in a cultural milieu that remains stubbornly conservative in the realm of family life and particularly in the realm of women's role expectations, they might benefit from the experiences of shamans, the pioneers of dual careers for women in Korea.

The controversial theory proposed by some scholars that shamans are psychopathological personalities needs to be noted.[3] In view of this theory, one might ask if the experiences of shamans represent the lives of the "normal" population of women in Korea. Of course, since a shaman is a religious practitioner "who has (1) recognized supernatural powers which are utilized for socially approved ends or goals, and (2) the capacity to enter (and withdraw from) culturally defined trance states (i.e., spirit possession)" (Lebra: manuscript in preparation), one could answer, on that basis alone, whether or not shamans' experiences apply to other women who combine family life with secular professional roles. The theory evokes still other questions that cannot be ignored.

Why, for example, would any society assign to psychopathological personalities such important functions as those performed by shamans? What does the practice say about the society as a whole? Or, having institutionalized a socially useful role for psychopathological personalities, how does the culture maintain them in that role at a functional level? Does the shaman role provide them with a means for achieving social adjustment not attainable otherwise? Are shamans indeed recovered psychotics or psychoneurotic personalities who, through the shaman role, serve their societies as "deputy lunatics" as some scholars have suggested?

Other interpretations of the mental health of shamans have also been offered. Some scholars have found them well within the normal range of personalities for their cultures, whereas others have considered shamans to be supernormal individuals potentially capable of acting as "cultural brokers" and innovators on behalf of the members of their societies. However, in the light of what we know today from both psychiatry and anthropology about early socialization experiences in the formation of adult personality and the life-long process that socialization has been shown to be by behavioral and social scientists, these theoretical disputes become meaningless. They were formulated without adequate information on the life histories of shamans, and have contributed little to an understanding of how personal experiences influenced their recruitment into the shaman role and their performances within it. Moreover, they have not considered the impact of the shaman's role on the subsequent development of their personalities.

Nevertheless, in the case of Korea, it seemed to me for a number of reasons to be particularly important to have these theories re-evaluated on the basis of adequate material on the life histories of shamans. Shamanism pervades Korean life and nearly all shamans are female. Koreans clearly regard shamans and their families as social deviants—as outcastes. Moreover, Korean folk beliefs hold that shamans have certain psychological predispositions for their role.

Korean folk beliefs regarding shamans do not directly concern the mental health of practicing shamans; however, several beliefs which refer to the psychological and behavioral propensities of recruits to shamanism support the theoretical position that shamans are psychopathological. For example, Koreans believe that spirits in search of human beings to possess and use as mediums tend to gravitate toward those individuals whose *maŭm* ("heart" or "soul") has already been "fractured" and made vulnerable by some psychological distresses. They also believe that all potential shamans experience *sinbyŏng* ("possession sickness") of varying duration, during which time they may behave in ways that can cause them to be mislabeled as insane. Moreover, they believe that recruits can become permanently crazy if shamans officiating at their *naerim-kut* ("initiation rite for shamans") fail to guide properly the entry into and possession of their bodies by their possessing spirits.

If recruits are successfully initiated, Koreans believe that their conjugal and familial relationships will inevitably disintegrate. They believe that possessing spirits are notoriously jealous of shamans' attachments to human beings, particularly their husbands, and will do everything possible to possess them exclusively, as in marriage. Some shamans report dreams of recurring sexual intercourse with their possessing spirits.

These folk beliefs seem to imply that Korean shamans may indeed be "healed madwomen," who, in consequence of successfully assuming the shaman's role, become social deviants.

Could it be that Korean culture has developed patterns of systematically mobilizing the psychological insights and strengths of individuals, who, through traumatic personal experiences, have achieved psychological conditions suitable (through the role of shaman) for counseling others in the resolution of conflicts? Could it be also that Korean culture has assigned to shamans the additional function of serving their society as "deputy lunatics" by depriving them of the usual support system available to women through the family and kin group? And for those shaman families that remained together and shared the social ostracism of the shaman, could there have been hidden gains? Was the institutionalization of the shaman role specifically for women a way of allowing females an indirect means of exerting influence and thus compensating them for their position of inferiority to males in authority and decision-making?

The answers to these and other questions that arise require knowledge of the history of Korean shamanism as well as detailed information on the life histories of modern shamans.

Even a cursory review of Korean history points to a long tradition of shamanism. Some historians push it back to the neolithic period, though without any specific archeological evidence (P.K. Sohn and others 1970: 15). W.J. Joe (1972: 11), a culture historian, suggests that shamanism evolved from the animistic beliefs of the *Mumun* people, the makers of pottery without surface designs, who are believed to have lived in Korea during the Bronze Age.[4] Still others suggest a similarly early presence, noting, in one instance, that the term, *ch'ach'aung*, meaning the clan patriarch and shaman, was used in Silla before A.D. 400 (W.K. Han 1079:7-8 and C.K. Chang 1974:65). They noted, in another instance, that the legendary heroes of Korea have shamanistic traits and that the gold crowns worn by early Silla kings bear a striking similarity to the headgear worn by the shamans of Siberia (P.C. Hahm 1967:12-13). Three gold crowns of the type referred to have been excavated from Silla tombs in Kyŏngju and are thought to date from A.D. 500-600. Unfortunately, the sources cited do not specify how the crowns were dated (P.K. Sohn and others 1970-5 and 337 and W.J. Joe 1972:138-139).

These differences in scholarly opinions as to the earliest date of shamanism in Korea are not likely ever to be settled. No such differences of opinion divide the scholars concerning the presence and importance of shamanism during the Three Kingdom period, beginning about A.D. 400 (Clark 1961[1929]:175-177; P.C. Hahm 1967:13; W.K. Han 1970:52; Hulbert 1969[1906]:404-410; W.J. Joe 1972:43-44; and C.K. Chang 1974:65). In fact, the claim that shamanism is the only indigenous religion of Korea and that it has been the enduring core of Korean religious thought since the Three Kingdom period recurs with the regularity of a refrain throughout the writings of scholars of this subject, who also consistently point out that Buddhism and Confucianism failed to displace shamanism even though they became the official religions of the Koryo Dynasty (A.D. 918-1392) and the Yi Dynasty (A.D. 1392-1910).[5] They claim further that shamanism has remained a potent political force, and this claim is well supported by writings of historians and religious scholars as well as the traditional literature of Korea.

Citing accounts given in *Samguk-sagi* and *Samguk-yusa*, the two earliest Korean sources on the proto-history of the Three Kingdom period, C.K. Chang (1974:65) points out that female shamans took part in the defense of the Kokuryo Dynasty (37? B.C. -A.D. 668) against the Sui and T'ang Dynasties of China,[6] and adds that shamans were retained in the palace and given the official title of *sŏn'gwan* during the Koryo Dynasty, when the official religion was Buddhism. In volume 59 of *Yijosillok*, the official history of the Yi Dynasty, Prince Yonsan, the tenth ruler

(A.D. 1494-1506), is described as possibly suffering from the possession sickness of a recruit to shamanism (B.Y. Rhi 1970:39).

In *The True History of Queen Inhyŏn*,[7] a classic in Korean literature, Queen Inhyŏn, the wife of King Sukchong (A.D. 1674-1720), is glorified for her virtues. However, the king's concubine, Chang Hibin, is condemned for being under the sway of shamans in her employment at the palace, providing an excellent account of the influence shamans sometimes exerted in the making and unmaking of rulers during the Yi Dynasty (C.U. Kim 1974: 179-234 and H.S. Koh, 1975). Additional evidence of shamans' influence at the top levels of the Yi Dynasty government is given by Hulbert, who, in describing the annual embassy sent to Peking until 1894, writes:

> . . . before it started the attendants and underlings held a great *kut*. It would have been beneath the dignity of the envoy to have anything to do with such a superstition, but there is every reason to believe that a good part of the cost was defrayed by him. . . . The ceremony was in the shape of a pantomime, in which one of the *mudang* personated the envoy and another the Minister of State (1969[1906]:419-420).

Queen Min, the last queen of the Yi Dynasty, who was murdered by the Japanese in 1895, tried to organize Korean shamans into a centralized, national group and, having elevated her favorite shaman, Yi Chi Yong, to the rank of Princess, attempted to force "grave old Confucian statesmen to do her reverence" (Clark 1961 [1929]: 177).

Palmer (1967a:5-6), writing on the problem of identification with Korean tradition by Christianity, acknowledges shamanism as the most powerful religious force among the Koreans and observes that new religions, whether imported or generated from within, have historically failed to survive among the Koreans unless shamanistic traits were incorporated on a large scale. According to P.C. Hahm (1967:51), Wanggŏn, the founding king of the Koryo Dynasty, was a devout Buddhist who made it the official state religion; but the Buddhism he practiced was much Koreanized, with great emphasis on "geomancy and shamanistic-animistic rituals" (See also W.K. Han 1970:52 and Palmer 1967a:5-6.) Apparently, Confucianism also became Koreanized, especially with reference to ancestor worship, for Clark (1961([1929]:118) writes: "The funeral ceremonies include a

lot of exorcising of spirits and the like which are more a proper
part of the Shamanistic worship. . . ." Christianity proved no
exception; as it is practiced in Korea, it is highly "shamanized"
(See, for example, T.G. Kim 1967).

   Ch'ŏndoism,[8] a native religion that originated and flourished
in nineteenth century Korea, displayed many shamanistic traits.
The founder's experiences of the call to religious leadership were
most distinctly shamanistic in character. Some felt that many of
his rituals, especially his use of the talisman and incantation, were
appropriated from shamanism (W.J. Joe 1972:415-417 and W.K.
Han 1970:356). According to M.H. T'ak (1971), who has studied
religions founded by women in contemporary Korea, twenty-five
of thirty such religions were started by women who had formerly
been shamans.

   In his introduction to the Royal Asiatic Society's special issue
on new religions of Korea, Palmer summarizes his views of the
influence of shamanism upon the new religions:

> Shamanism is the primitive ethos of the Korean people. It is the
> basic instinct of the masses, especially in the countryside. All
> Korean religious ideas and ceremonies are influenced by it, and
> at some point coalesce with it. All successful religious move-
> ments in Korean history have drawn upon strong Shamanistic
> underpinnings. And such is certainly true of the New Religions
> (1967:5).

   Many foreign observers of Korea during the late nineteenth
century Yi Dynasty found the shamans and their rituals and
associated practices among the most conspicuous features of the
society. Bishop (1970[1897]), an early Western observer of the
twilight years of the Yi Dynasty, devotes three chapters to
shamanism in her book, *Korea and her Neighbors*.

   Hulbert, who first came to Korea in 1886 as a missionary
educator and who later served as the Korean king's emissary to
Washington, D.C., (1905-1906) and to the Hague Peace Confer-
ence (1906-1907), wrote in his book, *The Passing of Korea*:

> As a general thing, we may say that the all-around Korean will
> be a Confucianist when in society, a Buddhist when he
> philosophises and a spirit-worshipper when he is in trouble.
> Now, if you want to know what a man's religion is, you must
> watch him when he is in trouble. Then his genuine religion will
> come out, if he has any. It is for this reason that I conclude that

the underlying religion of the Koreans, the foundation upon which all else is mere superstructure, is his original spirit-worship. In this term are included animism, shamanism, fetichism and nature worship generally (1969 [1907]:403-404).

The pervasiveness of shamanism in Korean life and history is nowhere more dramatically evident than in the nationwide and systematic persecution launched by the neo-Confucian government of the Yi Dynasty throughout its long reign. It periodically barred shamans from the capital and, in 1413, confiscated books from shamans and burned them.[9] In addition, shamans were designated ch'ŏnmin ("outcastes") by government decree (P.C. Hahm 1967:38 and 111, and C.K. Chang 1974:66). Despite such persecution, shamanism persisted in Korea not only among the common people but also in the palace of the king himself.

During their period of colonization in Korea (1910-1945), the Japanese continued the policy of persecuting shamans (C.K. Chang 1974:66. See also Rutt 1964:214, for indirect evidence of Japanese oppression of shamanism in Korea.) At the same time, many Japanese researchers were attracted by Korean shamanism. These include Akamatsu and Akiba who collaborated in 1938 on the two volumes of Chōsen fuzoku no kenkyu [A Study of Korean Shamanistic Beliefs and Practices]; Chijun Murayama,[10] who wrote four studies, Chōsen no miko [Korean Shamans], 1930 (cited in Akamatsu and Akiba 1938:25), Chōsen no kishin [Korean Spirits], 1929, Chōsen no semboku to yogen [Korean Fortune-telling and Prophecy], 1933, and Buraku-sai [Religious Festivals and Rituals in Korean Villages], 1937 (cited in Knez and Swanson 1968:56-58); Izumi, who published Chōsen no shamanizumu [Korean Shamanism] in 1970, based on material collected largely before 1945; and Akiba, who wrote a doctoral dissertation on Korean shamanism for Tokyo University in 1943 and published Chōsen fuzoku no genchi kenkyū [A Field Study of Korean Shamanism] in 1950.

The two-volume work by Akamatsu and Akiba remains a classic today among Korean scholars of shamanism.[11] Both the colonial policy of persecution of shamanism and the scholarly research on the subject (which could not have been conducted without governmental approval and encouragement even by Japanese scholars) testify, if only by implication, to the significance of shamanism in the life of the Koreans, as the Japanese perceived it.

The present Korean government has mounted a renewed campaign to eradicate shamanism from Korea. Police raids on shamanistic ceremonies are a commonplace occurrence, and a primary objective of the government-sponsored *saemaul-undong* ("New Village Movement") is to eliminate traditional religious practices, which are in the main shamanistic in nature. Government newsreels designed to disseminate information on public health single out the shaman as a target of ridicule and attack. However, unlike earlier governments, the present regime makes a distinction between shamanism as an unscientific system of knowledge and shamanism as a part of the Korean cultural heritage. It encourages the people to identify themselves with the cultural aspects of shamanism and has designated as a national cultural treasure Kuksa-dang, a shamanistic shrine in Seoul used by some of my shaman informants (C.K. Chang 1965). It has also designated as national cultural treasures several living authorities on chants, ceremonies, and dances of shamans.

As it was with the earlier Japanese researchers, shamanism is very prominent today as the focus of serious scholarly interest among Koreans from such diverse disciplines as psychiatry, religion, culture, history, literature, the performing arts, and anthropology. For example, seven articles appearing between 1962 and 1973 in twenty-four issues of *Neuropsychiatry*, the official publication of the Korean Neuropsychiatric Association, are on shamanism. *The Journal of Cultural Anthropology*, published by the Korean Association of Cultural Anthropology, has fifteen articles on shamanism out of a total of forty-six in its first four volumes, 1968-1971. The *Bibliography on Family and Religion in Korea* (1945-1970), published by East Asian Cultural Studies (Tokyo), has forty entries on shamanism.

The number of clients that successful shamans see in the course of a day and the comparatively high levels of income that many shamans enjoy today are additional indicators of the strength and prevalence of shamanism in modern Korea. There also exist various census statistics on shamans, which are more or less reliable.

Palmer (1967a: 118), citing Yi Saeng-Baek (1960) as his source, estimates the number of practicing shamans in the first years of the twentieth century as 12,390. The population of Korea for 1909 was 13,091,000 (Grajdanzev 1944:73), making one out of every 1,057 Koreans a shaman. Clark (1961[1929]:219), who queried the head of a shamans' guild in the city of P'yongyang as to the number of practicing shamans in that city of 100,000 was told there were 300. That is, the ratio of shamans and the population was 1:330.

Regrettably, K.I. Kim (1972c:127-63) does not say how he arrived at his figures, which are the most recent, but he states: "Today the number of shamans is roughly estimated to be 100,000 in South Korea. This figure is applicable to be one shaman per 314 of the general population." C.K. Chang (1974:60), who expresses some skepticism of the accuracy of the figure, nonetheless quotes the head of Kyung-Shin Hoe, an organization of shamans and fortune-tellers, as claiming 48,980 official members in the organization and estimating the number of shamans and fortune-tellers throughout the nation as 208,424 in 1973. Even assuming that only half the estimated total, or 104,212 persons are shamans, it gives a ratio of one shaman per 316 members of the population, using 32,905,000 as the total population of South Korea in 1973 (Bureau of Statistics, Economic Planning Board, Republic of Korea, as reported in its 1975 Korea Statistical Yearbook:35).

Among the most carefully collected, though not necessarily the most accurate, census statistics on shamans are probably those published in *Chōsen Sōtokufu no Chōsa* (The Korean Government-General Investigation),[12] dated August, 1930 (cited in Akamatsu and Akiba 1938:25). These statistics were compiled under the direction of Chijun Murayama, who was in charge of the Department of Archives in Chōsen Sōtokufu (The Korean Government-General). His census of 12,380 shamans did not include either the *p'ansu*, the blind fortune-teller, or the family shaman, hereditary family priestesses (*ibid*:25). According to K.S. Ch'oe (1970:137), the census was collected through the network of police stations. He points out that the strong regional variation in the number of shamans is much more a function of the placement of police stations than actual regional differences in the distribution of shamans throughout Korea. Since police stations were generally located in *ŭp* ("town") or *myŏn* ("county") level only, it is doubtful that the census statistics include as accurate a counting of shamans in the villages as they do of shamans in towns and cities. Notwithstanding, Murayama's 1930 census of shamans gives us a ratio of one shaman per 1,616 population. The total population of Korea in 1930 was about tewnty million.[13]

Still another interesting indication of the prevalence of shamanism comes from Clark (1961 [1929]: 179), who, citing Gifford as his source, states that the Koreans spent two and a half million dollars during the year 1900 for the services of shamans. The estimated national revenue from rice production for 1910 was ¥ 92.9 million (Granjdanzev 1944) or roughly $46.5 million.[14] The total cotton goods imported during 1896 was valued at $3,338,545 and the total export from Korea for the same year, at $4,728,700 (Bishop 1970 [1897]: 465-466).

Although there are indications of past and present prevalence of shamanism in Korea, for a variety of reasons it proved a difficult task for me to locate shamans who might serve as informants for my study. Because of the present government's policy of persecution, shamans and their clients maintain a very low profile, sometimes carrying out their religious activities in hiding. Understandably, shamans do not advertise their practice through the usual channels available to other practitioners in the field of health; rather, they depend entirely on word-of-mouth advertising. In fact, they view with considerable suspicion clients who walk in "off the street" without known intermediaries or other acceptable social identity. Certainly, the shamans that I tried to get to know by walking in "off the street" and asking to have my fortune told as a way of becoming acquainted ultimately denied me anything beyond the cursory transaction necessary for divination. They had no way of inferring my identity with any real sense of security as I brought no go-between with me. Some even refused to accept me as a client, voicing suspicion that I was from the Ministry of Education, that is, an agent of the government.

In one instance, I came close to being assaulted for refusing to leave the scene of an ongoing *kut*, though my companions, my father and my husband, a Caucasian American, and I were in a crowd of about thirty or forty people. The presence in my party of a Caucasian and an apparently learned man who looked as if he might be an official of the government so inhibited the shamans that they refused to continue the ceremony unless we left. When my father tartly remarked that if they believed in what they practiced they should not feel so constrained, the shamans, both of whom happened to be male, became angry. In subsequent attempts to meet shamans I went alone, but the earlier incident served as additional evidence that the shamanistic subculture in

Korea operates in a climate of fear and suspicion with regard to
the authorities.

It quickly became evident that I needed first to identify
people who could and would be willing to introduce me to shamans they knew personally. In less than a month, I was able to
obtain introductions to about fifteen shamans.

On learning the nature of my request, about half of the
shamans refused, giving a variety of reasons. A few said that even
their children did not know their full life histories, and they did
not want to divulge them to a stranger, however noble the purpose. One shaman was afraid that my frequent visits to her home
might "give me away to my son-in-law." She insisted that her
son-in-law of almost ten years did not know of her shaman role.
She lived with her daughter and son-in-law and contributed
economically to the household but managed, she insisted, to
conceal the source of her income from her son-in-law by confin-
ing her shamanistic activities only to *kut* held in shrines or the
homes of her fellow shamans. Another shaman, a young woman
only very recently initiated, was similarly afraid that my visits
might arouse the suspicion of her neighbors and lead subsequently to an investigation and discovery of her role by her
husband, who spent almost all of his time with his concubine.
She was, she explained, seeing all her clients in the home of her
"adoptive mother," the shaman who officiated at her initiation
kut. I eventually decided on five shamans from this group; seven
were actually willing but two lived in areas which posed transportation problems for me. The sixth informant I met during my
second summer of fieldwork.

Even with these shamans who agreed to serve as informants,
rapport was established slowly. They were most vexed that I was
interested in them as individuals rather than as religious
specialists who could give me information on various aspects of
shamanism. Three of them had had previous exposure to Korean
scholars (males) studying shamanism, and one much-interviewed
shaman concluded aloud to me that my insistence in getting her
life history illustrated how utterly ignorant I was of shamanism.
She stated that everyone knows individuals who become shamans have been so predestined and that they suffer a series of
afflictions until they realize they have been called to become
shamans. Why should anyone want to know the biography of any

shaman? she asked, and she immediately launched into a long
discourse on the historical development of shamanism in Korea.
It was also difficult at first to disengage adult male members of the
households of the shamans from dominating my visits with their
"knowledge" of shamanism and shamans.

When I finally succeeded in half convincing my informants
that it was indeed their life histories that I was interested in, I
began to share with them my own life history as a way of putting
them at ease. I explained that I had left Korea as a young girl and
had now returned to learn more about women of Korea, among
them shamans. Some still thought I might be a reporter for a
newspaper or a magazine, doing research for an exposé. I made
myself more vulnerable by sharing with them the information
that I had an American husband and two half-American children,
both generally unacceptable to Koreans. I tried to make them
understand why I returned to school at my age and how my
husband and children felt about it as well as the general attitude
of Americans towards women who returned to academic life after
marriage and family. I explained to them why I was interested in
knowing how they came to be shamans, how they felt about it,
and why. When they finally accepted me, it was expressed as a
willingness to be helpful. One informant put it this way: "Well, as
one working woman with a family to another, the least I can do is
give you what you need before you have to go back. I still don't
understand how you could possibly want to study me, or any
other shaman, for that matter."

Between 1971 and 1973, I spent approximately nine months
in field research, three months each year over the three-year
period. The sixth informant was interviewed over a two-year
period. During the period of my fieldwork, five of the informants
were practicing their profession in Seoul; the sixth one had stopped practicing but she too had practiced in Seoul.

Field data were collected predominantly in the homes of the
informants in loosely structured interviews, with members of the
household and/or clients often present. Although I held some
private interviews with each informant, as when we travelled
alone together to and from *kut* held outside the shamans' homes,
exclusively private sessions were nearly impossible to arrange, for
the general patterns of Korean social life do not permit the individual much privacy. This difficulty may be regarded as charac-

teristic of interviews with most Korean informants. Since I had grown up with this experience, the presence of others during interviews did not interfere significantly with elicitng information; moreover, the situation provided opportunity for *in situ* observation of the shamans' interactions with family members and clients as well as with other shamans.

For recording interviews, with the consent of the informants, I used a cassette tape recorder. Otherwise, I recorded information in a notebook which I carried with me at all times. In taking pictures, I always secured prior permission and confined my activity to the limits agreed upon.

The process of eliciting information was structured to the extent that I used the life-history approach as my primary technique, but the interactional process itself was generally very informal and spontaneous. I also developed a detailed questionnaire to guide me in planning my interviews and in chronologically organizing the material obtained. The questionnaire had several parts: early and late childhood socialization; the history of marriage including marital relationship after becoming a shaman; the history of recruitment as shaman; and the ensuing enactment of the role. I also made a two-part survey on other aspects of the informants' experiences. The first part was intended to elicit information indicating the informant's familiarity with traditional Korean cultural patterns; the second part was intended to reveal the informant's attitude on a variety of controversial social issues such as whether young people should marry in the face of parental opposition or whether one should move one's parents' grave site in accordance with a geomancer's instruction, and so forth. My purpose was to use the information obtained by this survey to cross-check, for internal consistency, the information elicited in the interview sessions. The only parts of the questionnaire that I brought into a directed interview were those dealing with census, genealogy, and the survey mentioned above.

To further supplement my interview data, I engaged in participant-observation throughout the period of my fieldwork by attending the informants' sessions with their clients,[15] their performances in *kut* of various kinds, and by visiting and interacting with their families, relatives, friends, and hangers-on. The data collected by these means constitute an important secondary source of information for this study.

2

WANGSIMNI-MANSIN

BRIEF CHRONOLOGY OF WANGSIMNI-MANSIN'S LIFE

1911	Born, the first and the only daughter of three children
1917	Devastated by overheard remarks denigrating shamans and their offspring
1918	Younger brother born
1921	Attended the Bible school at a neighborhood Protestant church run by missionaries
	Learned to read Korean
	Started to read the Bible diligently; began to attend the church service as well
	Mother often the chief target of the minister's sermons; urged to convert mother to Christianity
1923	Received baptism
	Quit church shortly afterward; no longer able to tolerate attacks on mother and prejudice against herself
	Enrolled in the elementary school established and operated by the same church
1924	Second younger brother born

1927	Quit school just prior to graduation; could not tolerate social prejudice
1927	Went into a depressed state; refused to eat ritually-used foods
1929	Married to the son of another shaman under special conditions
	Assisted husband in his business
1930	Became bored; began to assist mother-in-law in her shamanistic activities
1931-1933	Her failure to conceive became an issue; husband expressed relief which shocked her
1932	Began to lead a "double life" to conceal her increasingly active involvement in mother-in-law's professional activities; husband continued to object to any involvement in his mother's professional life
1945	Began to hallucinate actively and frequently; declared by mother-in-law and others as possessed
	De facto assumption of many pivotal functions of her mother-in-law's *mudang* role, including seeing clients in her absence
1946	Traumatic confrontation with husband over her involvement in his mother's professional activities; given ultimatum to give up involvement or face divorce
	Simultaneously, mother-in-law growing more dependent on her to perform some of her professional duties
	Promised husband she would curtail involvement but found it almost impossible to keep promise
1947	Began to find physical intimacy with husband repulsive; renewed consensus by others she was suffering from *sin-byŏng* and destined to become a *mudang*
1951	Mother-in-law died
1951	Husband destroyed all shamanistic paraphernalia of his mother and forbade Wangsimni-mansin to see any clients
1951-1957	Tried to live "normally" but found it boring in the extreme; began to visit mother more frequently and assist her in her professional role

	Severe quarrels with husband over visit to natal household; marital relation increasingly strained and deteriorating
1957	Husband suffered first stroke; post-hospitalization recovery very poor
1957-1958	Husband acquiesced to entreaties by mother-in-law and wife to let them perform a *kut* for his recovery; results efficacious
	Husband renewed objections to her involvement in her mother's professional activities
1959	Husband had second stroke; his grain business continued to dwindle
1959	Husband voluntarily gave permission for her to receive his mother's ghost and become a *mudang*
1960	Officially initiated by her mother
1961	Husband died
1963	Sold all belongings and moved back to natal household; began to work as an assistant and partner to her mother

WANGSIMNI-MANSIN

Addressed as either ŏmŏni ("mother") or sŏnsaeng-nim ("teacher") by other shamans, Wangsimni-mansin is the most tradition-bound of the six shamans in this study.[1] A frail-looking woman in her late fifties, she exudes an aura of legitimacy that is absent for the most part from the other shamans I have met. She conveys this quiet air of legitimacy by the humble and effortless manner in which she observes traditional etiquette. Her careful and formal speech, the completeness of her attire in spite of the humid climate, and a myriad of other trivia set her apart from the other shamans and ordinary housewives of her age. In her presence, one is reminded of court ladies in historical novels of the Yi Dynasty or, at the least, of the legendary model eldest daughters-in-law of great yangban ("nobility") families. There is a quality of timelessness about her face, as though, on reaching perhaps forty, she had arrested time permanently.

She assumed the shaman role publicly a little over ten years ago. When her husband died, she moved back to her natal household as she had no children and it made her professional partnership with her mother, also a shaman, more convenient.

Her mother, now in her mid-eighties, has been a shaman since about age eight or nine. Though addressed as *halmŏni* ("grandmother") by everyone, she is as diminutive as a child. She is a classic beauty, with finely chiseled features in a perfectly oval face. Wangsimni-mansin, though very attractive herself, compares poorly with her mother in beauty. Halmŏni boasts that she still has her own teeth, much to the chagrin of her daughter whose false teeth sometimes clack noisily as she talks. But Halmŏni is not without complaints of old age: her eyes water and dim her vision and her ears are not so sharp as they used to be. She is now in semi-retirement, but it is her legendary fame as a shaman which sustains their clientelle even now.

Halmŏni claims to have been born of a high-ranking court official of the Yi Dynasty. When, at age eight or so, she became possessed by the spirits and it became apparent to her parents that she had been predestined to become a *mudang*, they expelled her from the family to avoid social humiliation and loss of their *yangban* status. They placed her with a peasant family just outside the capital and provided for her future generously. She thinks she was about eleven or thirteen when she began to receive paying clients.

Although her foster parents had assured her of her *yangban* origin, she confesses that she had always been a little skeptical. Her doubts were completely removed, however, during the Korean War, 1950-1953. Soon after General MacArthur's landing in Inch'ŏn in September 1950, two elderly gentlemen called on her and inquired how she had fared during the three-month siege by the North Korean Army. They claimed to be her brothers. As they were well-known and well-placed public figures who would not have risked public association with a shaman for the lark of it, Halmŏni says she accepted their claim. When a second evacuation of the capital seemed inevitable, the same gentlemen reappeared and offered to take her and her family with them. Though she was happy to have her brothers' long-delayed recognition, she did not evacuate with them.

In addition to her claim of *yangban* origin, Halmŏni has enjoyed the even more glamorous distinction of having been a palace shaman during the declining years of the Yi Dynasty. More astonishing, she claims that she is currently serving a particular, unnamed royal princess living in one of the palaces in Seoul.[2]

Wangsimni-mansin and Halmŏni live in an old-fashioned house, hedged in tightly by houses that seem to have sprung up hodge-podge in the urban sprawl. My guess is that the house had been originally an isolated one outside the city limits of Seoul, perhaps on the edge of a village long since gone.

Inside, the house has the same kind of agelessness that characterizes Halmŏni and Wangsimni-mansin. The furnishings, including dinnerware and serving tables, are of another period. The television, the stereo set, the electric fan, and the telephone on a lace doily seem unreal in the setting, but these two women seem impervious to the contradictions in their surroundings. They mix and match the old and the new with no apparent sense of unease. They served me Maxwell House coffee, percolated, with a choice of Pet condensed milk or Pream, on my first visit to them. No doubt, these items had been purchased or given to them from the American G.I. blackmarket.

The coffee tray was faultlessly set with matching egg-shell china and ornately designed silver spoons of the size used with espresso coffee in America. The sugar came in lumps served with a pair of tiny silver tongs. But the coffee was not served by a servant, as it is likely to be in a more "westernized" Korean household with servants; instead, it was brought to the door by a servant but served to me by Halmŏni's daughter-in-law.

A forty-year-old woman with her hair bobbed and set in a modern permanent and always dressed in knee-length Western dresses or a blouse and skirt, Halmŏni's daughter-in-law further underscores the contrasts already noted between the old and the new. She and her chronically unemployed husband live in a wing of the same house with their children. They are totally dependent on the two shamans for their support. Her husband, an urbane man in his late forties, is college-educated and that, according to his mother, has been responsible for his unemployment. There is a dearth of jobs suitable for a man of his qualifications in Korea.

On my first visit, Halmŏni's son came into the women's quarters briefly to meet me and extend the household's official hospitality. Apparently, they are accustomed to hosting people interested in shamanism. He mentioned a long series of names some of which I recognized from my bibliography on shamanism. When I explained to him that I was not so much interested in shamanism as a belief system as I was in his mother and sister as women who happened to have become shamans, he listened politely but without interest. It was apparent that he dismissed me as a serious student of shamanism.

Halmŏni and Wangsimni-mansin too were confused by my insistence that I was more interested in learning what it had meant to them to be shamans than in shamanistic beliefs or practices. When her son left, Halmŏni remarked that even if I were not interested in shamanism, I could scarcely hope to understand shamans as persons without seeing them at work. In a coaxing tone of voice, she invited me to attend the forthcoming *Yongsin-kut* on the Han River,[3] a rite conducted only every three years. I accepted and asked if I might spend the rest of the day with them. She was delighted and ordered lunch for me. Wangsimni-mansin also expressed her approval. After the first few appointed visits, I was told I could visit them whenever I wanted; they suggested, however, that I might want to telephone ahead to make sure that they were home.

Halmŏni and Wangsimni-mansin see absolutely no one without prior arrangements through intermediaries. (It took me nearly two weeks to secure an appointment with them, and my sponsor was one of their oldest and richest patrons.) Their clients are generally from the middle and upper classes who pay two to three times the standard rate for the *chŏm* ("divination"). Clients on their first visit are received in the all-purpose receiving room, but established clients, who nearly always bring gifts, are first taken to a small shrine-room to offer their gifts and light incense sticks at the altar of the spirits. They are politely queried as to the well-being of everyone in their households and given refreshments before consultation.

The main shrine or *tang* where they perform most of their *kut* is not open to visitors in general. It sits on a raised platform and measures about twenty feet by forty feet. The platform in effect makes the *tang* a concealed second story within a house which, from the outside, appears to be a single story structure. The space beneath the *tang* is used for storage. The stairway to the *tang* is concealed behind a short door that leads out of the storeroom on the far side. When I commented that the passage to the *tang* must be terribly inconvenient for carrying food and other items needed for *kut*, Wangsimni-mansin said, "Yes, but it cuts down on the noise." There are no windows or any other form of opening to the outside from the *tang*.

Wangsimni-mansin and Halmŏni, both seemingly passive old ladies, have strong passions which can animate them quickly. They talk excitedly about the need to develop a shamanistic doctrine. While, interestingly, they consider it presumptuous to aspire to equalize shamanism with Confucianism, they would like to see shamanism elevated to the level of other legitimate religions such as Buddhism, Taoism, and Christianity. It is this ambition, they told me, that motivates them to help researchers of shamanism. They deeply resent the social stigma attached to shamans and their practices. Shamanism, they contend, is the only truly native Korean religion and, as such, it deserves more understanding and respect from the people. They point out that even during the Yi Dynasty when shamanism was officially banned, there had been palace shamans. They take their professional role very seriously; apparently, Wangsimni-mansin also takes herself quite seriously.

On a subsequent visit, I asked her to fill out the family census sheet for me. Noticing that she had put down only her mother and herself, with herself as the household head, I asked about her brother and his family. Ordinarily, he would have been considered the household head. She answered sharply that her brother was there only temporarily. In actuality, however, he and his family had been living with them for the past five years. She also refused to enter the servant family of three who live with them. After learning her name, I realized that one of the two name plates above the front door was hers. It is most unusual for a woman to put her name plate up on the front door, for generally only the name of the male household head appears there.

Wangsimni-mansin was born in 1911, the first of Halmŏni's three children and the only daughter. Halmŏni was nearly twenty-six at the time, regarded as a very late age for a woman to be having her first child. Halmŏni was thrilled with her daughter. Halmŏni was already at the peak of her shamanistic career, having been "appointed" a palace shaman for some time by then. She was financially very comfortable, and she showered her daughter with all the comforts and luxuries her resources could command. Halmŏni says, "Nothing was too good for her."

Because of the demands of her shaman role, Halmŏni could not give much time to Wangsimni-mansin's direct care, but she made sure that her daughter received constant personal attention from her wet nurse whom Halmŏni fed well, as well as from the other servants. Halmŏni's foster parents oversaw Wangsimni-mansin's care as they did the general management of the household. Looking at her now gray-haired daughter, Halmŏni says that she had doted on her daughter and was restless whenever she was away from her.

Neither Halmŏni nor Wangsimni-mansin mentions her father spontaneously in their recollection of this period. It is as though there had been no father. On direct probing, I learned that he was an educated man, in the tradition of the Yi Dynasty, from an impoverished *yangban* family that had seen better days. He managed his wife's tenant farmers and otherwise looked after her financial and public affairs, such as paying taxes. He was a kindly gentleman who never belittled his wife for her shaman role and who generally kept quietly to himself.[4] Halmŏni laughs as she confesses that she cannot recall what her husband's reaction to their daughter's birth was.

He maintained his aloofness from his daughter as she grew older. It is difficult to discern at this point whether or not his aloofness was an indication of lack of interest or simply a way of managing his dependent relationship with his wife who was the de facto household head. If he had any criticisms regarding the excessively indulgent manner in which his daughter was being brought up, as if she were a boy, he did not express his feelings to anyone apparently. He simply did not interfere.

From her own observations of daily life around her, Wangsimni-mansin had little opportunity to infer the inferior social status of women to men. Although her father was deferentially and correctly treated by the women in the household, he remained essentially removed from the hub of the household activities which were focused on her mother and her professional role. He remained almost exclusively in the male quarters. Her foster grandfather spent much more time in the women's quarters, but he did not command the respect generally accorded senior male members of a household, for he had been hired by Halmŏni's parents to look after her. Although Halmŏni addressed him as father and his wife as mother, there was always a tacit understanding among them that they were Halmŏni's employees.

At the same time, Wangsimni-mansin was exposed daily to the professional activities of her *mudang* mother and the unambiguously central and decision-making role that her mother performed, both as a *mudang* and as the mistress of her household. Since nearly all of her mother's clients were women, she grew up in a predominantly female social milieu with a minimum of intrusion by males of any consequence, including her father.

Although Halmŏni was preoccupied with her professional activities most of the time, she was sensitive to the child-care she had delegated to others. She recalls that she used to "strain her nerves" over it—*sinkyŏng manhi ssŏssŏ*.[5] If she heard her daughter cry, she demanded to know why her caretakers had made her cry, for it distressed and distracted her while she was engaged with her clients. As a result, Wangsimni-mansin's caretakers did everything necessary to satisfy her every whim. No one disciplined her; everyone strove to keep her mollified at all times. As Halmŏni puts it, "She grew up not knowing *nunch'i*"—that is, without the necessity of learning to detect signs that give cues and insights into other peoples' minds.

When Wangsimni-mansin was about seven, her mother gave birth to her brother, but the event does not appear to have affected her significantly. According to Halmŏni, her brother's care was delegated to others as hers had been, but to different persons so that there was no serious change in Wangsimni-mansin's routine. However, Wangsimni-mansin did sulk and pout over the attention her mother gave to her younger brother, Halmŏni recalls. On such occasions, Halmŏni herself did whatever was expedient to placate her daughter, for she could not have a child's prolonged cry or temper tantrum interfere with or disturb her professional activities with clients.

Halmŏni remembers being anxious about protecting her daughter from the stigma and ostracism of being a shaman's daughter. She kept her isolated within the household as much as possible. This was achieved easily, for no kinsmen or neighbors called on them for social visits. Consequently, Wangsimni-mansin spent most of her first seven years almost exclusively in the company of female adults and a handful of male adults who were servants.

Beginning at about age six or seven, Wangsimni-mansin recalls, both her mother and caretakers began to scold and correct her behavior, saying, "You mustn't do that, or else people will say you haven't been taught any better because your mother's a *mudang*." She remembers being vaguely bothered by their implied threat and feeling that somehow her mother's importance must be spurious. The veiled threat was nonetheless sufficient to make her an apt and determined pupil of proper etiquette and other desired attributes of the Korean female.

One day, however, the veiled threat was made devastatingly explicit. During her mother's absence, she lost her temper with a servant and went into a tirade. She was quickly given her own way, but she also overheard the retreating servant mutter, "Sure enough, *mudang*'s offspring can't be helped; their seed is bad." It was like having a gourd full of cold water poured over her exposed heart to hear that, Wangsimni-mansin remembers.[6] By her own account, she lost all of her self-conceit and arrogance. She felt herself and her entire household held in suppressed but utter contempt by their own servants. Even worse, she says, she felt estranged from her mother and distrustful of servants and people. She became withdrawn and watchful. Somehow she could not talk to her mother about the incident.

She remembers also longing terribly for friends at about the same time; they lived away from the main village and she had no age-mates nearby. She developed the habit of hanging about the gate of her house, watching children go by and sometimes venturing to ask where they were headed.

When she was about ten, a Christian Protestant mission established a church and a normal school[7] in the vicinity and recruited actively for potential converts and students, especially among girls and women. Some of the girls her age from the main village started to attend the Bible school because the church taught them how to read Korean. Wangsimni-mansin decided that she wanted to attend also. At first her mother objected strenuously. Though she did not tell her daughter so, she knew that she was the primary target of attack by the minister. Finally, she gave in to her daughter's nagging when her husband remarked that it would not be harmful for girls of the day to learn to read. It would make women more fit for male company, he said.

She loved learning to read; she found it magical. It gave her freedom from the constrictions of the female domain of her household and gave her access to some of the books in her father's room, especially the novellas written in the vernacular, that is, completely in Korean. She began to attend the Church services as well and to read the New Testament diligently. But her initial enchantment and attachment to the Church and the Bible school turned into a quiet anger which, she says, sat in her chest like a weight. The minister and Bible school teachers attacked her mother and her professional activities as the doings of Satan himself and thanked God for her presence in their midst. They fervently urged her to repent not only for herself but for her mother as well. They were, she recalls, determined to alienate her from her mother and her professional role, and to bring the mother to the Christian faith through her.

Their relentless proselytism apparently had the effect of alienating her from them instead. For two years, Wangsimni-mansin recalls, she agonized in her young heart, trying to choose a side. In the meanwhile, she was insufferably antagonistic to her mother and difficult for others in the household to manage. Finally, at twelve, she quit the church, shortly after she was baptised. She could no longer tolerate their vilification of her mother or their lack of charity.

Notwithstanding, she was unwilling to give up "book learning" which she thoroughly enjoyed. She says she liked the competition in the classroom as much as the knowledge of books and the company of girls her age. So, she prevailed on her mother to enroll her in the normal school after she quit the church.

Wangsimni-mansin continued to attend the normal school operated by the church for four years until she was sixteen, quitting it just before graduation. As she grew older she became inescapably and painfully aware of discrimination directed against her by her classmates and most of the teachers as well because of her mother's shaman status. She also found it increasingly more difficult to countenance her supposedly Christian mentors' lack of charity toward her and the general social rejection she met in the school. None of her classmates responded to her overtures toward them, and she did not have a single good friend during her school years.

She realized that she was helpless to change the discriminatory attitude of others toward her and her family. With that realization, she says, she lost the courage to attend school any longer and withdrew to the relative safety of her mother's subcultural world of shamans and their followers. Still, she recalls, she desperately wanted somehow to escape the stigma of being a shaman's daughter. She vowed that she would never become a shaman herself.

Following her withdrawal from school, she went into a prolonged depressed state.[8] She sulked, refused to talk with anyone, and went into a frenzy whenever she was served food that had been used for *kut* or other shamanistic rituals. Since most shamans and their families eat the ritual foods used in ceremonies as their regular meals, this must have created special demands on the cook. Gradually, she decided to accept her fate as a *mudang's* daughter and make the best of the "sunny spot' that was indisputably hers in her mother's world. She says she got bored with her own sulking—*chiruhaesŏ* ("got tedious").

Halmŏni says she knew what was happening to her daughter and was heartbroken to see her dispirited resignation to being a *mudang's* daughter. There was nothing she could do about that, but she decided to spare her daughter anymore social rejection on that account. She decided to look for a son-in-law from a similar background. She found an acceptable candidate in the son of a fellow shaman. After the usual negotiations involved in arranging a marriage, Wangsimni-mansin was married at eighteen, a bit late by the standards of the time.

One of the conditions of the marriage was that Wangsimni-mansin was to be excused from assisting her shaman mother-in-law in any of her professional activities, including the preparation of the ritual foods. Another related condition was that she and her husband were to live in a modified neolocal residence to facilitate faithful observance of the first condition. Both her mother and mother-in-law-to-be agreed that Wangsimni-mansin should be sheltered as much as possible from following the fairly common pattern of daughters-in-law succeeding their deceased mothers-in-law in the *mudang* role. Halmŏni gave a proper wedding ceremony and Wangsimni-mansin rode to her husband's house in a *kama* ("palanquin"), accompanied by her father.

In the two-year interval between school and marriage, Wangsimni-mansin learned some of the skills and knowledge needed in the anticipated domestic role after marriage; however, she remained generally lackadaisical about them. Neither did she show any greater interest or responsibility in her second younger brother, born when she was about thirteen.

Halmŏni had striven to make a marriage in which her daughter would have an edge of advantage over her husband and had succeeded. Since the groom's mother was a shaman also, her own shaman role could not become a point of social discord or a source of humiliation to her daughter. Also, as she was a well-known shaman, having access to some members of the royal family, her daughter's mother-in-law was not likely to be abusive of her daughter; after all, they moved in the same social network of shamans among whom Halmŏni enjoyed the highest prestige. She would be mindful of her own need to remain on good terms with Halmŏni. Since the groom despised being the son of a shaman and was trying to be a self-respecting merchant, her daughter should be able to get sympathy for her own sentiments. Furthermore, she had demanded and gotten special conditions of marriage which would protect her daughter from involvement in any shamanistic activities, as Wangsimni-mansin had found these distasteful.

Although Wangsimni-mansin had been inadequately prepared for the domestic role, it did not pose a serious problem because of the special relationship that existed between her mother and mother-in-law and also because there were servants who could compensate for her lack.

Wangsimni-mansin remembers that she had agreed to the marriage, for she could not think of anything else to do with herself. Avoidance of marriage was not a preferred or even a thinkable alternative in those days.

Wangsimni-mansin says her husband was a quiet man, rather small in build, and often given to melancholy. He was kind to her; he made few demands on her and was easily pleased. He operated a grain store in a section of the house that faced outward onto a thoroughfare. The store was attached to what would normally be the *sarang-bang*, the male receiving room. It had two interconnected rooms and a small kitchen. She and her husband were secluded in this part of the house, as stipulated in her marriage contract, so that she could avoid the shamanistic activities that took over the main part of the house every day.

Wangsimni-mansin found her marriage an agreeable enough change from her life at home, but, as the newness of it wore off, she felt restless with boredom. One could read the same novellas but so many times, she says. She began to assist her husband in keeping the accounts of his business but that too did not take up enough of her time. As a result, much to the chagrin of her husband and herself, she began to spend more time with her mother-in-law in the main part of the house where she assisted her in her shamanistic practices. She sometimes accompanied her mother-in-law on the latter's visits to Halmŏni. As a result, Wangsimni-mansin saw much more of her natal household than was customary for young brides.

Wangsimni-mansin got along well with her mother-in-law, who made no excessive demands or otherwise caused her much grief. Compared to the other women in the household or even clients, Wangsimni-mansin was much better educated; consequently, she was much admired by them, especially for her ability to do bookkeeping for her husband's business. Thinking back, Wangsimni-mansin says that she had no special difficulties during the first year or so of her marriage except for her growing sense of oppressive boredom.

As her boredom increased, she hoped more and more that she might become pregnant so that she would have something to do. Apparently, she or her husband was infertile and so she never became pregnant. As the years wore on, her failure to conceive troubled her mother and mother-in-law terribly. There was discussion as to what might be done to correct the condition. As concern over her failure to conceive mounted, her husband openly expressed his personal relief that she could not bear a child. He had no desire to have a son who had two shamans for his grandmothers; he had always felt that he hadn't functioned as a whole man in the society of men because he had been born the son of a *mudang* and did not wish a similar fate for his heir.

Although she understood her husband's feeling, his unexpected and anomalous reaction to her infertility completely confused her. If she were not to be a mother and a wife, what was she to be? How was she to spend her empty hours, especially since he objected to her involvement in her mother-in-law's and mother's professional activities? She felt frustrated by the boredom of her domestic role and broke her own conditions of marriage by participating in her mother-in-law's professional activities with increasing frequency, until within a short time she tacitly assumed charge of all supportive activities within her mother-in-law's compound. Her husband was furious and demanded that she abide by their marriage agreement. She tried but found she could not cope with her empty days. She began to slip into her mother-in-law's compound surreptitiously, behind her husband's back but with a tacit nod from her mother-in-law. She had begun her "double life" within her own household. They had been married about three years at the time.

Wangsimni-mansin is not sure when her attitude toward *kut* began to change. She still finds it incredible that she could have changed so drastically in her reactions. Before her marriage, she had hated with a passion all the cacophony created by *kut* performances in her natal household. She used to wonder, even during the first year or so of her marriage, why both her mother and mother-in-law persisted in their shaman role when it brought them so much social ostracism. She says:

> I used to feel so frustrated that my mother did not seem to see the simple option of just slipping out of the *mudang* role. It took me nearly four decades and my own experience with spirit possession to really understand my mother. When I became possessed by the spirits, I felt elated. I felt like the only human being in all the world. . . . All the rest were below me somewhere.

Continuing with her recollection of events which led to her becoming a shaman, she told me:

> Long before I had any indication of supernatural notification, I found myself feeling excited by the rhythm of the *changgu* ("drum"). I don't remember how I came to feel that way. . . . All I know is that I used to have to be brought back to myself. . . ., it happened more and more often. When I heard the *changgu*, I seemed to forget everything instantly and lose all sense of inhibition. I wanted to dance and chant to it. It is this helpless sense of being swept up and away in a weightless sort of a way that makes you dance and be a *mudang* in spite of everything else. When you are in that state of mind, you cannot think of anything else. . . . Even now, just talking about it to you makes the temperature rise in me. . . . You can see how people who are possessed by spirits can go insane if they are improperly initiated. . . . You have no way of making use of the feelings that take hold of you. . . .

When you start doing your own *kut*, you just feel your spirits
stealing into you and taking over; the sensation is incomparable.
. . . You just know that you've got the spirits in you . . . that
you don't have to worry because it's them inside you, not you.
. . . You're just a medium and you feel marvelous. Otherwise,
how could any one do the things a *mudang* does in her sober
mind? You lose all sense of embarrassment . . . all inhibition . . .
you are suffused with the feeling, "I'm the number one, the
best—there is none else like me in the whole world!"

By the time she was in her mid-thirties, she began to "hear"
the *changgu* calling her to dance at odd hours of the day and night.
She would stop whatever she was doing and begin to dance to the
"drum in my ears." When she began to have these auditory
hallucinations, everyone about her declared that she had been
possessed by the spirits. She did other strange things, though of
course they make very good sense when retrospectively regarded. For example, she accumulated a *mudang*'s full comple-
ment of ritual costumes; not even her mother-in-law knew about
it.

Her husband had come to accept his wife's clandestine participation in his mother's and her mother's professional activities,
but because he had refused to go into his mother's quarters
especially when any shamanistic activities were going on, he had
not known of her hallucinatory behavior, or, for that matter, the
extent of her active participation in some of the shamanistic practices. It was only when he discovered her costumes and other
shamanistic paraphernalia in their room that he became alarmed.
Sitting with a drawn match by the pile of stuff he had found, he
called in his wife and demanded an explanation. He threatened to
put a match to the whole collection. Wangsimni-mansin remembers him saying:

> It could not be helped that I was born the son of a *mudang*, but I
> am not going to sit by while I become the husband of one as
> well. That's something I can help. . . . If I marry a hundred
> times more, I shall not marry a *mudang*. Either you cut out all
> this nonsense or you can go home to your mother and stay
> there. I don't want to see your face.

Wangsimni-mansin became alarmed, as she had never seen
her husband so agitated before. She was frightened by him and
begged for forgiveness. She promised to give everything away to

her mother if he but would spare the match. She continues with what followed:

> After that encounter with my husband, I couldn't do any work for a long time. I just couldn't keep my mind on what I was doing. . . . I kept hearing the *changgu* . . . I had to struggle to suppress the urge to get up and dance to the beat of it. . . . Whenever I had to fight to block the sensation of spirits entering me, I got very restless. . . . Somedays, I just let go and even saw some clients if my mother-in-law was not available. Some of my prophecies came true but others did not, and that bothered me a lot. If my prophecies weren't fulfilled, how was I different from the insane women who went around babbling things? I thought I should put everything away and forget about the spirits and becoming a *mudang*. . . . But I felt inexorably drawn to the 'doings' of a *mudang*. . . .

Halmŏni was very upset by these developments. She had after all spent her life trying to keep Wangsimni-mansin from becoming a shaman. Her mother-in-law, on the other hand, was not at all displeased. While she never actively urged the role upon her, she did everything she could to tacitly and covertly help her daughter-in-law perform more and more of the functions involved in her own shaman role. Even when she learned that her daughter-in-law was seeing some of her clients in her absence, she did not say anything. Rather, she increasingly depended on her daughter-in-law: she left her in charge of all of her professional and domestic matters when she had to be away. Without her mother-in-law's help, Wangsimni-mansin says, she could not have managed the "double life" she led between her own and her mother-in-law's compound.

She was about thirty-six, Wangsimni-mansin recalls, when everyone—perhaps with the exception of her husband—acknowledged that she had been "gotten hold of by the spirits." In any event, as her spirit possession occurred more frequently, Wangsimni-mansin began to feel an increasing revulsion toward her husband. She could barely tolerate physical intimacy with him. The possessing spirits hoped to alienate her from her husband, the more securely to possess her themselves. She explains that this is the surest sign of spiritual possession and assures me that every genuine possession-type shaman will report this as part of her experience in becoming a *mudang*. There is a common suspicion among Koreans that some possession-type shamans are charlatans who fake spiritual possession.

When Wangsimni-mansin was about forty, her mother-in-law died. No sooner than his mother's funeral was over, Wangsimni-mansin's husband rid the entire house of every article of shamanistic paraphernalia and ordered her to refuse his mother's old clients who continued to call. She was angry over his unilateral decision because she had expected to hold an initiation rite and succeed her mother-in-law in the *mudang* role. Halmŏni advised her to listen to her husband; she did not have her mother-in-law to help her now.

She repressed her own wishes and tried to live "normally" as her husband wished but found it tedious in the extreme. She became so agitated with boredom that she began to visit her mother frequently. After each visit, there was a quarrel with her husband. He suspected, correctly, that she was helping her mother in her practice. For five or six years following her mother-in-law's death, she and her husband lived in a state of strained tension. Then one day her husband suffered a stroke from which he made a very poor recovery even though he had been hospitalized in one of the most expensive and famous modern hospitals in Seoul.

Terribly discouraged by his slow recovery following his discharge from the hospital, Wangsimni-mansin's husband finally succumbed to his wife's and mother-in-law's entreaties that they be allowed to hold a *kut* for him. After the *kut*, he made an almost miraculous recovery. But as soon as he began to feel well again, he also began to object even more strenuously than before to Wangsimni-mansin's now more open participation in her mother's shamanistic activities. He then suffered a second stroke. Following his second stroke, he called her to his bedside and told her that he was being punished by the gods for refusing the spirits who had possessed his deceased mother a successor. He told her he no longer objected to her becoming a *mudang*—that it must all be his karma. He asked only that she should not practice her profession in his house. Perhaps she could go in partnership with her mother, he suggested.

Subsequently, Wangsimni-mansin was officially initiated into the *mudang* role in a *kut* performed by her own mother. Halmŏni confirmed that her daughter's possessing spirits were those who had been her mother-in-law's *momju* ("master" or "guardian spirits") and who now needed a new place to go, that is, a new person to act as their medium. Wangsimni-mansin was forty-nine at the time. She says, "After more than ten years of struggle to resist the role, I finally became a *mudang* at my husband's urging." At the time, she had been married for over thirty years, had been practicing the role of *mudang* more or less surreptitiously for about thirteen years, and had been suspected of having had her first experience with *sinbyŏng* twenty years or so ago.

When her husband died about a year after her initiation, Wangsimni-mansin sold her husband's grain store (which incidentally had been losing money for several years) and the house and moved back with her mother where she now functions as a general assistant to Halmŏni and where I met them both.

The joint practice proved an ideal arrangement for them. Her mother had a prosperous and well-established clientele which in some instances went back two or more generations to the very beginning of her shamanistic career as a child *mudang*. Wangsimni-mansin, on the other hand, could assist her aging mother, already in her seventies at the time, in the more physically strenuous aspects of her practice, especially in the performance of *kut*. I have observed that Halmŏni usually presides over the opening and closing ceremonies, while Wangsimni-mansin conducts the rest. Both mother and daughter now firmly accept the popular folk belief that the role of *mudang* runs in the family, although not necessarily lineally. They point to the history of Wangsimni-mansin's acquisition of the *mudang* role as evidence of the validity of the folk belief.

Since Wangsimni-mansin has already inherited her mother-in-law's possessing spirits, Halmŏni and Wangsimni-mansin believe that when Halmŏni dies, someone either in Wangsimni-mansin's or Halmŏni's patrilineage will probably inherit her possessing spirits and role. Or, equally possible, they will be inherited by Halmŏni's present daughter-in-law. They think it also likely that one of Halmŏni's granddaughters will succeed her.

In view of this anticipation on the part of the mother-daughter team, it is interesting that the two women are working on a history of shamanism in Korea with the help of Halmŏni's son. They not only believe that shamanism is the only truly indigenous religion but firmly believe that the first Korean *mudang* was a princess of the Silla Kingdom. They explain the outcaste social status of *mudang*, begun in the Yi Dynasty and continuing to the present, as the result of commercialization of their religious functions by the *mudang* themselves.

3

NAMSAN-MANSIN

BRIEF CHRONOLOGY OF NAMSAN-MANSIN'S LIFE

1927 or 1928[1]	Born
1928-1930(31)	Two younger sisters born and dead within a year of their birth
1932(33)	Grandmother died
1933(34)	Mother gave birth to a daughter who also died within the year of her birth
1934(35)	Mother gave birth to another daughter; this one survived her infancy and grew up a healthy child
1938(39)	Namsan-mansin enrolled in school
1941(42)	Severe attack of malaria; "cured" after shamanistic rite
	Quit school
1942(43)	Got a job in a factory and lived in the workers' dormitory
1945	Married
1946	Gave birth to her first son
1948	Gave birth to a daughter, stillborn
1949	Gave birth to a second daughter

1951   Second daughter died

                Namsan-mansin became mysteriously ill

1954   Namsan-mansin diagnosed by shamans as suffering from
                sinbyŏng

                Namsan-mansin fled from husband's house to avoid the
                shaman role

1954   Namsan-mansin worked as a domestic servant

                Namsan-mansin tried peddling

                Namsan-mansin moved to Kangwon Province and met Mr.
                Kim, her second and current husband

1956   First daughter with Mr. Kim born

1958   After first business failure by Mr. Kim, they moved to Seoul
                where they bought a bakery

                Their son was born

1960   Their second daughter was born. Namsan-mansin made
                the decision to be self-sufficient—not to depend on her
                husband

                Namsan-mansin joined a *kye* ("mutual credit association")
                to obtain working capital

1960-1961   Namsan-mansin had strange dreams and began to behave
                oddly, such as talking irrationally. (She views this retros-
                pectively as a supernatural signal for her to become a
                shaman.)

                She went into her own wholesale business

1962-1963   She leased a store for her business

1964   She bought a house

                Namsan-mansin financed her husband's venture in a con-
                struction business which thrived for a very brief time and
                then plunged them into bankruptcy

                Namsan-mansin leased out their house on *chŏnse* and
                rented a room

                Her six-year old son wandered often; he was lost once for
                over a week. She consulted a shaman and learned that Mr.
                Kim's first wife and their daughter were both dead

Namsan-mansin became ill about the same time; during illness, made prophecies which came true

Experiencing difficulties in her wholesale business due to shortage of working capital

1965   Gave birth to her third daughter and abandoned her within the month

1965   Mr. Kim's "dead daughter" from his first marriage appeared in Namsan-mansin's dream. The dream was interpreted as a supernatural call to the shaman role for Namsan-mansin

Namsan-mansin and her husband experienced intense conflicts between them during this period

1966   They moved to a new location to avoid people who asked Namsan-mansin to perform shamanistic functions but she continued to provide such services to few friends without charge

Intense conflicts with husband continued. She began to disappear without a word to husband for several days at a time

1967   Unable to stay in her wholesale fruit business, she went on the road as an itinerant peddler once again but refused to give up the lease on the store space

1969-1970   Namsan-mansin returned from one of her itinerant journeys acting strange and secretive

Namsan-mansin secretly subleased her store space for $500 and disappeared with it

Mr. Kim considered mass suicide with the children but did not follow through

On the advice of a shaman from his hometown, Mr. Kim set up an altar in his room for his ancestral ghost in the hope of getting his wife to return home

With the deposit money he collected when he moved out of their rented room to a friend's place, rent free, Mr. Kim considered going into business but instead decided to spend the money to look for his wife first

1971   Mr. Kim located his wife in January and demanded money. She gave him the money and followed him home

The family was again reunited and moved into a room in their own house

To Mr. Kim's chagrin, Namsan-mansin sat home, staring into space for six months

None of Mr. Kim's schemes for getting work materialized and he had to sell everything of value to feed the family

Namsan-mansin had hallucinatory experiences

1971   In July when there was nothing more to sell in their posses-
              sion, Namsan-mansin suggested that she assume the sha-
              man role and her husband consented

1972   I met Namsan-mansin in June

1973   My last visit with her in August

NAMSAN-MANSIN

Namsan-mansin gets her name not from her place of birth, as many shamans do, but from the mountain at the foot of which she practices. It is a well-known redlight district. There, she rents a room about eight by eight feet from an old-fashioned inn which is partially shaded throughout the day by the towering new Tokyu Hotel,[2] located diagonally across the street and over a bridge. She has the only room in the inn that faces outward toward the street. All the others face the enclosed courtyard where both the communal water pump and toilet are located. A dangerously narrow ledge connects her room with the front gate of the inn. Access to the room from the street is by an unevenly laid, almost perpendicular stone stairway at the top of which there is a narrow entryway, measuring perhaps three by eight feet. This doubles as the kitchen. A pair of faded plastic mats shields the kitchen paraphernalia from both the sun and the gaze of passersby in the busy street below.

Namsan-mansin lives here with her second husband, a man of rugged good looks in his fifties, and their three teenage children. He is an unemployed contractor who fled from a large port city in North Korea during the war. His son from his first family lives nearby but has little to do with them; he is thoroughly ashamed of his stepmother.

Namsan-mansin calls her husband *yŏnggam*, the Korean equivalent of the American expression "the old man." She does not add the honorific suffix, *-nim*, at the end. In fact, she observes hardly any of the linguistic etiquette expected of a wife in conversation with her husband. Given her unmistakable dialect of Ch'ungch'ŏng Province, reputed to be the last bastion of Korean traditionalism, her rough speech strikes one as unusual even for a woman of the lower class. Her husband does not address her conventionally either. He refers to her as *chŏ-ch'in'gu* ("that friend there"), an expression more commonly used among male companions to refer to a third party among them. Unlike the other husbands of shamans, Mr. Kim, Namsan-mansin's husband, is eager to talk about his wife's possession experiences and other behavior patterns that preceded her assumption of the shaman role. Yet, he takes apparent care to conceal from his friends the fact that his wife is a shaman.

Because his presence tends to inhibit his wife's clients, Mr. Kim leaves the room early, often as soon as he has had breakfast. Before he leaves, he invariably asks his wife for transportation money—a euphemism for personal spending money for almost any purpose. He spends most of the day in air-conditioned coffee houses with his cronies. Usually, he eats supper in marketplaces or other similarly cheap places. Generally, he gets home between 9:30-10:00 P.M. By then, the last of his wife's clients have left to avoid being caught by the midnight curfew.[3]

Namsan-mansin's eldest child, an attractive but shy girl of seventeen, works as an usher in a cinema. As cinemas operate continuously from about 11:00 A.M. until about 9:00 P.M. or later, she too is gone from the tiny, oppressively hot, and faintly malodorous room most of the day. She dropped out of school in the eighth grade. This does not seem to concern Namsan-mansin or her husband; it is not unusual for girls from poor families to drop out of school in Middle School. In fact, many do not enter Middle School.[4] Unlike her father and younger siblings, she refused to talk about her mother's professional role or of its effects on her. During a six-month period, spanning two years, I talked with her only once. If on her return home, she saw me still in the room, she would go into a beauty parlor across the street and visit with the girls there. According to her mother, she does the same if she sees any clients still in the room when she returns home from work.

Namsan-mansin's fourteen-year-old son is also a school dropout. Namsin-mansin and her husband are quite vexed by this, as they had spent a sizable sum of "palm-greasing" money to get him into a particular Middle School.[5] She calls him mad, crazy, insane, and other things. When I commented that both her daughter and son had dropped out of school about the same time when her "possession" behaviors were peaking, she brushed it aside, saying, "No relationship there." Her husband, however, indicated that his children had suffered greatly from other children's taunts about their "crazy" mother.

The boy has no specific occupation. When he has no errands to do for his mother, he hangs about the tiny room trying vainly to make himself small. When there are no clients, he listens to a pocket radio or plays with his younger sister, aged twelve. Occasionally, he plays solitaire and responds loudly to various signs of his fortune. When he gets hungry, he gets up and walks past a large pot in the kitchen from which he quietly retrieves a boiled potato. Sometimes his younger sister joins him in this activity. I never saw anyone in the family have a regular meal for lunch.

Namsan-mansin's second daughter is big for a twelve-year-old. She too is a school dropout, in a manner of speaking. When she finished grammar school, her parents did not enroll her in a Middle School; they explain that she would probably have dropped out as her brother and elder sister had done before her. She protests, saying she did not even get to go to her graduation. It is not clear if she really finished the sixth grade or not.

When there are no clients about, Namsan-mansin's younger daughter acts quite "babyish" with her mother until brusquely pushed aside. She occupies her time with small errands for her mother, such as fetching cold sodas for clients and buying incense sticks and candles as these are needed. From each such errand, she holds back a small amount of money. Namsan-mansin gives her a sidelong look of disapproval but does not demand the money.

The girl is keenly interested in her mother's shamanistic activities. At times she gets so engrossed in watching her mother that her mouth sags open and her face grows motionless in an awestruck expression. She is very proud of her mother's showy nylon and synthetic-silk costumes worn during the *kut* performance.

When properly dressed, Namsan-mansin looks quite attractive for a woman in her mid-forties. Unlike the other shamans, she wears her hair bobbed and permanent-waved, a style she had adopted as a merchant before assuming the shaman role. She is fretful that her hair is taking so long to grow because she would like to wear it in the traditional style customary for shamans. She is not sure that her *momju* ("guardian spirits") care but thinks it signifies her novice status to all the other shamans who use the same shrine at Samgak Mountain. She is very sensitive about being an uninitiated shaman. When I first met her in 1972, she had been practicing for only about eight months but had joined several *kye* (an informal but institutionalized credit union) in order to finance her initiation *kut*.

Whether because she is a relatively inexperienced shaman or not, she is certainly eager to talk about herself. By the standards of other shamans I have observed, she is also a little too anxious in welcoming her clients. She is not as assertive as the others are: I never saw her intimidate her clients into additional payments by embarrassing them, a very common strategy among seasoned shamans. She also accepts the lowest "donations" for services rendered.[6]

On the street where Namsan-mansin lives, several different kinds of diviners depend on the uncertainties and anxieties of its inhabitants—bar girls, streetwalkers, beauty and massage parlor operators—to earn their living. Looking out from her room, one can see the shingles of five different kinds of diviners: geomancer, prognostic diviner of physical ailments, diviner for auspicious dates for any undertaking, diviner of marriage suitability, and diviner for missing persons. Namsan-mansin would not mind hanging out a shingle herself, but she has never heard of shamans doing that. So she refrains. But she enjoys one distinction which has so far eluded her neighborhood competitors. She is the only one there (and the only shaman of my knowledge) who enjoys a foreign clientele. My intermediary was in fact a German woman who herself had been introduced to Namsan-mansin by two American women. Apparently the Americans are regular customers who come every month or so, although I never met them.

According to Namsan-mansin, she has also had some Japanese
male tourists for clients. However, the bulk of her clientele is
made up of displaced peasants who eke out a confused and
precarious existence on whatever work they can find on a day-
to-day basis. One may describe Namsan-mansin as an urban
ghetto shaman who has the unique distinction of having a foreign
clientele.

The eldest of seven daughters born to a farmer of above
average means in either 1927 or 1928, Namsan-mansin could
easily calculate the exact year of her birth by conversion of the
twelve-year zodiac cycle, but she is uninterested. She is satisfied
enough to know that she was born in the year of the dragon
which, according to folk belief, destines girls to a harsh life, and
that her life has proven the old belief.

Namsan-mansin's father was an only son for the third consecutive generation in his branch of the lineage, born long after all
such hope had been given up. His mother was forty-eight years
old at the time, and her postpartum recovery was difficult and
protracted. As a result, he was raised as much by his sister who
was twenty-three years his senior and had returned home at
twenty a childless widow, as he was by his mother. Consequently, Namsan-mansin's aunt had an unusually binding emotional
hold on her father. Unlike most widows returned to their natal
homes to live out a life of servitude under their adult, married
brothers and their wives, Namsan-mansin's aunt became a verit-
able second mother to her father and, when he married, a second
mother-in-law to her mother.

As the first born of her father, Namsan-mansin was, to quote
her, "disgracefully and shamefully" welcomed by her grandmother, aunt, and father, although she was only a girl. They
almost completely appropriated her from her own mother. Except
during feeding and sleeping at night, her mother had little to do
with her from the very beginning. Namsan-mansin was the wonder and the miracle of the household, and her grandmother, aunt,
and father spent endless hours indulging her and vying with one
another for access to her. Quoting her mother, Namsan-mansin
says that she never had a chance to have a good cry as a baby, for
her every wish was anticipated and she was mollified almost
before she could show displeasure.

Namsan-mansin's mother gave birth to two more daughters

in quick succession, but both died within a year of their birth. For all practical purposes, therefore, she was an only child during most of her childhood and was all the more precious to her father, aunt, and grandmother. She does not mention her mother.

According to Namsan-mansin, there is a family legend that the soles of her feet did not touch ground until she was fully five years old and even then only because she threw such horrendous temper tantrums at being so restricted. Although her grandmother was past seventy, she insisted on carrying Namsan-mansin on her back wherever she went. She could not be persuaded to take Namsan-mansin off her back even to use the outhouse so that, out of fear of danger to both, her aunt used to accompany them to the outhouse.

When Namsan-mansin was old enough to eat solid food, she was sometimes fed from the father's table by the grandmother. Otherwise, she ate with her grandmother, getting always the choicest morsels of food while her aunt and mother ate inferior food later.

Namsan-mansin feels that she was deprived of the free give-and-take relationship other village girls had with one another. By the time they were five, six, or seven, many of them were carrying younger siblings on their own backs as they played together, while she was carried on the back of her grandmother or aunt until after age five. She recalls screaming at that age to be taken off the back of her grandmother or aunt so she too could play with the girls. Usually she had to be content with being a spectator. She speaks vividly of the longing she used to feel to join the other girls at hopscotch and other games. The girls sometimes interrupted their games to adjust the straps that held their bouncing siblings on their backs and admired a new toy or hat that Namsan-mansin had. Her father was the only one in the village to bring home such presents from the market town nearby.

When Namsan-mansin was about five, her grandmother died, but as her aunt had been her "understudy" for such a long time, her death scarcely caused a ripple in the general operation of the household or in its established patterns of interaction.

Namsan-mansin was hardly troubled by the usual childhood diseases and, after about five, enjoyed much greater freedom of movement as she grew too heavy to be carried about for any length of time. But her newly gained freedom and pleasure with the company of peers were short-lived. As she approached seven, her peers began to withdraw from her—the boys because of the strict rule of sexual segregation and the girls because of the increasing demands by their mothers and grandmothers to help with housekeeping tasks indoors. Thus, after a brief interlude, which Namsan-mansin calls the most fun-filled period of her life, she was once again without companions. Unlike them, she was never asked to do anything around the house, although when she was six or so her mother had given birth to another daughter. This daughter also died in the first year of her life.

When Namsan-mansin was a little over seven, her mother gave birth to yet another daughter. This one survived her infancy without difficulty and was a healthy child. Though Namsan-mansin was old enough and lonely for company, she was neither asked nor wanted to look after her sister. She does not think she was particularly jealous of the baby; she remained so much the favorite child with her father and aunt that her younger sister was left entirely to her mother's care.

The long succession of female births caused tremendous pressures to be brought upon her father to take a concubine, lest his particular branch of the lineage be terminated. While he readily promised his lineage elders that he would do so, he never acquired a concubine. Since he could well have afforded a second wife and her mother was in no position to complain, everyone wondered why he did not. Namsan-mansin is not sure, but thinks it had to do with the circumstances of her aunt's widowhood. As Namsan-mansin relates the story:

> My aunt's husband took a concubine because she remained barren several years after the wedding. Well, the concubine got pregnant right away and began to drain my uncle of his wealth. Then, just before the baby was due, she disappeared, having stolen everything of worth. My uncle was so heartbroken over her desertion that he sold part of his farm to search for her. He never found her but got sick on the road and came home to die shortly afterwards.

By the time Namsan-mansin was seven, she had several names by which she was known. Although her father had recorded her name as Chungdung in the family genealogy, he preferred to call her Onyŏn, as did her aunt. Her grandmother and mother, on the other hand, called her Kkotsun-i, a more

common girl's name meaning "an agreeable flower." It was later
sinicized as Hwasun when she entered school. She says that
while she had answered to her several names without much
thought, it had struck her as interesting that she had so many
names. Most of the girls in the village were known merely as
ch'ŏttchae ("number one"), *tultchae* ("number two") and so forth.

Namsan-mansin was absolutely untrained in any of the
domestic tasks normally expected of girls during this period. She
never cooked, washed, swept the floors, or waited on anyone.
Her account of childhood gives a picture of a very spoiled child
who presented serious disciplinary problems to her elders.

> As a child, I was terribly impetuous. If I wanted new clothes,
> there was no rest for anyone in the household, including my
> father. He could not even perform the ancestral rites. I would
> get out his *turumagi* ("overcoat") and drag it all over the place
> whining and screaming alternately until I had my new clothes
> for the holidays. . . . I should have had a brother. I was a
> thoroughly spoiled brat, and I had a temper that everyone
> dreaded. . . . If I didn't get my way, I put on such a temper
> tantrum that everything had to halt until I was appeased. My
> father and aunt, because I was their treasure, and everyone else
> because they were afraid of my aunt, strained their nerves to
> anticipate my every demand before they did anything else. . . .
> At *chesa* ("ancestral rite") or the New Year's celebration,
> everyone moved in dread of my outbursts and made sure I was
> not in any way crossed, lest I disrupt them and embarrass them.
> . . . I also couldn't bear losing. Sometimes I forced my cousins to
> stay up all night until I had won at games when they came for
> overnight stays during holidays. Competition and winning,
> they are the keenest interests of my life to this day.

As she grew older, she had increasingly fewer contacts with
peers who had little time for play. The boys of course would have
nothing to do with her. When she was eleven, she succeeded in
persuading her father to enroll her in the same school in a nearby
town that some of the village's more privileged boys went to. The
only girl from her village to attend school in those days, she
completed three years of the elementary grades before dropping
out because of poor health. While in school, she excelled in both
academic subjects and sports, though she preferred sports. Occasionally she even beat the boys at some events. She explains that
not having to stay home during peak periods on the farm, as

many students did, was a great advantage in staying at the head of the class. She found the strict discipline at school a new experience but she did not mind it because, as she put it, "I rarely did anything wrong." However, she remained a disciplinary problem at home by her own account.

Namsan-mansin thinks that her neighbors had always been a little wary of their daughters playing with her because she had "learned nothing"—that is, was not brought up properly. When she started school and tried to play with the boys who also went to school from her village, village grandmothers and mothers actively discouraged their children from associating with her. As a result, her life in the village grew even more solitary than before. She recalls with some bitterness that even some adults in the village avoided her. Most of the peasants in the village considered sending daughters to school a foolishness guaranteed to contaminate them with modern ideas and render them unfit for suitable marriage.

Namsan-mansin thinks that she would have continued school until graduation if she had not been debilitated by recurring malarial attacks. She had had her first bout with malaria when she was eight years old, but it had not been severe. When she was eleven, she was again attacked by malaria, which thereafter recurred every summer. The severest and longest attack came when she was thirteen. Her family did not spare its resources in seeking remedies; her father even obtained quinine, a difficult substance to acquire in rural areas. When she failed to respond, her father resorted to Chinese herbal medicine, as he had done before. Nothing was effective. Desperate, her father finally consented to her mother's pleas to have a curing *kut*. Though her recovery was not immediate, she recovered within a short period and never again suffered from malaria. However, when the fall school term began, she was too weak to walk to school four kilometers away. She quit school and idled about the house until fully recuperated from the effects of malaria.

Once recovered, though, she felt restless and bored again. She had heard that jobs were available in defense factories in town, for which the Japanese were already recruiting able-bodied young girls from rural areas of Korea. She harassed her initially reluctant father until he finally gave permission to work in a textile factory. Her aunt and mother were mortified, she says.

She moved into a dormitory for women employees and went home on weekends, as she worked only half a day on Saturdays and was off on Sundays. According to her:

> . . . I really preferred staying in town and joining the other girls in different activities, especially recreational ones. The work was pretty hard but very interesting to me. It was very different from farmwork which I had never done but which I nevertheless disliked a lot. I loved working and living with other girls my age.

She does not recall what they were paid. Though it could not have been very much, most of their pay went directly to their families, leaving them with a small allowance. A favorite pastime among them was going downtown and spending their little money on personal items that appealed to them. As she acquired a real liking for her life at the factory and dormitory, she went home less frequently. Whenever she failed to go home on weekends, her father came to town the following Saturday, because "he had to have a look at his favorite child." Namsan-mansin looks back upon the three years she spent at the factory as an idyllic period. The idyll came to an abrupt end towards the close of the third year, however.

In February 1945, home on a rare visit, Namsan-mansin went to call on a relative. When she entered the kitchen to chat with the daughter-in-law, she greeted her with a coy smile, saying, "You must be happy since you received the *saju* ("a person's birth date and hour")." Since Namsan-mansin did not know what a *saju* was, she was unable to respond. But when she learned that it signified marriage, she rushed home in a rage, taking everyone by surprise, for they had not intended to let her know about it at the time. Her mother finally showed it to her. Namsan-mansin recalls:

> I was surprised to see it was so "nothing looking," . . . I tore open the red wrapping and saw there were some papers inside with writings and strands of blue thread. Throwing the pieces up in the air, I declared that no one was marrying me off. . . .

She heard her mother weeping and mumbling in the kitchen, "I told you she would not want to get married." Namsan-mansin remembers being startled by her mother's assertiveness but never learned why she had been so opposed to her marriage. Though she carried on as before whenever she had wanted her way, neither her father nor her aunt would yield. For once, they stood firm; it was many years later that she learned their reason for such resoluteness.

> There had been rumors toward the end of World War II that the Japanese were conscripting young unmarried Korean girls and sending them to Manchuria as prostitutes for the Japanese soldiers there. . . . One day my father happened to see a trainload of girls bound northward and immediately decided that I had to get married. . . . He told my aunt to find a groom post haste. . . . He was sure I would be conscripted sooner or later even though I was working in a factory. . . . They were so scared they didn't even explore any other possibilities; they grabbed the first offer that came in. By the time I heard about the *saju*, the betrothal had already been carried out—on February 22nd. The wedding date was set also, for the 9th of April. . . .

She returned to the factory as usual, worried, but unconvinced of the inevitability of her marriage. She decided not to go home for more visits, thinking that so long as she remained there she would be safe from marriage. As she mulled over the events, she realized that recently her father had been coming to see her more frequently. On one of his visits, she now remembered, there had been a "shrimp of a guy" lurking nearby, ogling her as though "he would put a hole through me." His odd behavior had angered her so that she had muttered loud enough for him to hear, "What a fucking bastard some people are! The nerve of some people going around staring at perfectly strange virgin daughters of other people!" Her father had roared with helpless laughter at her outburst, though he made a show of scolding her. She guessed that her father must have invited him to come along and have a look at her—that the stranger was probably her future husband.

Some time after her last visit home, her father showed up at the dormitory and announced that she was going home with him, informing her of her release from the factory, which he had already obtained. Unable to stay at the dormitory, she accompanied her father home with loud protests. Upon arrival, she was shown the various dowry items prepared for her, such as a vanity, chests, bedding, and so forth. It was as though they thought she would be appeased by her dowry. They told her that the wedding was four days away. Namsan-mansin felt utterly humiliated and betrayed.

> I had no idea who the groom was or anything like that—only
> that I was going to the household of such-and-such in a village
> not too far away. . . . I was so furious . . . I had liked my job and
> my friends. I was a good worker; my supervisors praised me.
> . . . I was very happy; I had many good friends for the first time
> in my life. . . . Marriage was the last thing I wanted just then. In
> fact, I hadn't even thought about marriage. . . . I determined to
> run away from home that very same day. . . .

As everyone was busy with the wedding preparations,
Namsan-mansin was able to slip away unnoticed. The very next
day, however, she was apprehended by her father and a relative
in Pusan where she had taken refuge. Once home, she was under
constant watch—she could not go even to the outhouse alone.
She was seventeen. She felt that her world had come to an end.
The wedding itself was a "mixed-up affair," she says. She had
destroyed most of her dowry in a fit of anger and had to be forced
through every step of the ceremony. All the while, she plotted to
escape en route to her husband's house twelve kilometers away.

Though it was the custom in her village for the groom to
spend the wedding night in the bride's house, they did not. She
was carried, kicking and screaming, to the palanquin and shoved
inside; the bearers were told to start their journey forthwith. They
did not stop for rest until they had covered at least four kilometers. When the bearers brought out a wine jug a respectable
distance from the palanquin, Namsan-mansin decided to escape:

> I got out of the palanquin, but no one seemed to notice. But
> when I started to walk quickly toward the woods, that "shrimp"
> appeared from nowhere and blocked my way. He told me to get
> back in the palanquin. Small and young as he was, he looked
> determined to act the lord and master. . . .

Even if she had been an eager bride, Namsan-mansin would
not have been the most desirable one, for her upbringing and
personality were incompatible with the traditionally ideal attributes of the domestic role. On the other hand, to those who did
not have such information about her, she was a "good match";
her father was a comparatively well-to-do farmer who was likely
to provide a good dowry. Apparently, her husband's family responded to these surface indicators.

While her father's arrangement of her marriage was in line
with the usual expectations, Namsan-mansin's own anticipatory

socialization for the domestic role fell radically short of the normal expectations. She was not only grossly ignorant of the role attributes and lacking in the necessary skills for their performance, but she was also psychologically unprepared for the role, as she amply demonstrated by her attempted escapes and destruction of her dowry.

Once installed in her husband's house, Namsan-mansin found it impossible to escape, though she plotted constantly. Speaking of her first year of marriage, she says:

> I was in no way prepared for marriage. I didn't know how to cook, sew, or keep house. I had been working for three years and living in a dormitory. What can you learn in such a place? I never had to do much in my ch'injŏng ("natal household") . . . I don't remember any of them (her grandmother, aunt, and mother) ever sitting me down and telling me anything about anything. And I didn't know the first thing about man-woman relations [sex].
>
> At my husband's household, I spent the days crying and begging to be sent back to my natal household. I just didn't like that little husband of mine—whenever he came into a room I got up and left. Soon after our wedding, he got a factory job in town and spent the week there, coming home on Saturday afternoons and leaving early on Monday mornings. . . . When he was home, I alternated between crying and dodging him . . . I could not stand it when he tried to "mount" me. I had no older brother—and when I was working, I had stayed in a girls' dormitory—and I had no notion of such things. . . . I knew of course there was something but didn't really know what to expect. . . .

Four months after the wedding, Namsan-mansin was told that she could go home for a visit. By that time she had built up such a hatred toward her father whom she blamed entirely for her current misery that she did not want to go home. Her parents-in-law insisted that she go. In the end, she went home for a lengthy visit. Her husband visited her there on weekends and finally consummated his marriage. She says, "He finally 'did it' to me there. And it took that one time to get me pregnant. . . . I fought him off for several more weeks after that."

With a wan smile, Namsan-mansin says that life is funny. She had not really disliked her husband; she simply could not tolerate sexual intercourse with him. She adds that her parents-in-law were also kindly people who treated her decently. She simply had not been ready for marriage. She claims that she has never reconciled with her father after her marriage, saying, "I figured he was as good an enemy as I ever wanted when he married me off like that." Then, as if taken aback by her own vehemence, she adds, "It's a folk belief that marriages arranged by *komo* ("father's sister") do not work out well. I don't know why, but it turned out to be true in my case. . . . It was my aunt's go-between who found my husband."

Namsan-mansin found cooking the most difficult of her new tasks. As she puts it, "I could dodge my husband but there was no way I could escape cooking." Though she had watched her mother cook all her life, she had no clear idea of how to go about it, never once having cooked herself. Her rice was always under-cooked, half-burnt, or came out the consistency of gruel. She found routine housekeeping chores equally a source of panic. Although she had seen her mother and aunt polish brass pots and bowls with ashes and straw, it was only after much uncertain experimentation that she could get them to shine.

Her husband's household was not as wealthy as her own and hired few laborers. As a result, her mother-in-law helped out in the fields during busy periods, leaving Namsan-mansin in charge of household chores, including preparation and transportation of lunch to the fields for the workers. She recalls:

> That was hard for me . . . I hardly knew how to cook rice much less the side dishes that went with rice. It makes me cringe even now just to remember it. Whatever domestic skills I know I learned from my mother-in-law, not from my mother or aunt. I sometimes experimented on the sly and taught myself. Cooking for my in-laws and their laborers was really the most challeng-ing and difficult task. . . . And there I was, the kind of a person who could not stand being second best at anything, serving burnt rice and badly seasoned food to strangers!

Sewing was no exception. When first asked to sew her father-in-law's garments, she had to steal one of his old garments and study it. She was too proud to ask anyone for help. "I measured the new cloth against it, and with violently shaking hands cut out the patterns. I was shocked that he could wear the garments I made." She felt self-conscious and ashamed of her ignorance. She says, "I had never been the kind to go asking for help. With each passing day, I just got to hate my father more and more. . . ."

About a year after her marriage, she gave birth to her first child, a son. She knew then that escape was no longer a possibility.

Namsan-mansin did not go home to her mother for her first childbirth, as was the custom, partly because her mother was also pregnant at the time but primarily because she hated her father. Unfortunately, her mother died from postpartum complications, leaving the baby and two younger daughters motherless. After her mother's funeral, Namsan-mansin did not go home for many years.

In the meantime, she attempted to compensate for her woefully lacking domestic training under the generally kind and uncomplaining tutelage of her mother-in-law. She was determined to excel at least in those tasks that had high visibility and achieved considerable success. Her attitude toward her role remained unaltered, however. In fact, she cannot recall having had any strong feelings even about her son. She found no particular pleasure in his birth or him as a baby.

Two years after her son's birth, she had two daughters, a year apart. The first was stillborn, and the second died when she was about two. Namsan-mansin denies that her second daughter's death disturbed her especially, though she acknowledges that her death had been more difficult to accept than that of the stillborn child. She had, she says, become accustomed to having her daughter around for two years, after all. Then she adds, as if to explain something, that infant mortality was very common in those days.

Coincidentally, the onset of the illness which was to plague her for the next four or five years and ultimately diagnosed as *sinbyŏng*, the possession sickness, began immediately after the burial of her second daughter. Asked pointedly if she might have become ill from grief over the child, she discounts the probability:

> Sure, I felt a little empty when the child was gone, but I wasn't particularly unhappy about it. I don't remember pining for her. I just had no appetite at all and couldn't use my left arm too well, that's all. I had no other symptoms. . . . It was a *marŭnŭn-byŏng* (a drying-up sickness, i.e., a debilitating one). I lost lots of weight and began to look like an advanced T.B. case. . . . The pain in my left arm grew worse for no apparent reason until

finally it became paralyzed. I could not use it at all. This went on
for four or more years getting worse as time passed, but I would
get better for a little while in between. . . . I think it must have
been a sickness to make me a *mudang*; only I could not have
thought so at the time.

In the meantime, World War II came to an end, the Japanese
left Korea, and her husband came home to stay and assume the
major responsibility in the management of the family farm. By
contrast, she failed increasingly to function in her role due to
illness. Her prolonged illness alarmed her parents-in-law for she
did not respond to the usual folk remedies, Chinese herbal
medicine, or even modern medicine. Desperate, they repeatedly
engaged shamans for *pyŏng-kut* ("healing ceremony").

> . . . After each *kut*, I'd get better for a while but there was no
> real improvement. I was too sick to care what happened to me or
> to anyone else; I only wanted to die. The fourth year of my
> illness, I was very close to death . . . I must have been, because
> my parents-in-law sold a total of 5 *majigi* (6000 square yards) of
> *already planted* rice paddies right after the transplanting of seed-
> lings. That's a desperate measure for a farmer. They sold it to
> pay for a fifteen-day *kut* for me! Still, there was no improve-
> ment. . . .

The shamans were supposed to be the best in the entire
province, and they said her illness was no ordinary one—that it
was in fact *sinbyŏng*. They advised her parents-in-law to engage
them to perform her *sin-nae-rim-kut* (the initiation rite during
which spirits are officially invited to descend and possess the
victim's body) and to allow her to assume the shaman role. "You
see," Namsan-mansin explains, "if you make such a public
acknowledgement of your possessing spirits, then they will release you from the afflictions which they had been causing you."
Namsan-mansin was not so shocked by the diagnosis—she
had overheard old women in the village say it before—as she was
by her parents-in-law's reaction to it. They were seriously re-
duced in their circumstances as a direct result of her prolonged
illness, and now they counseled her to accept fate and become a
mudang. They argued that the alternative was death for her or
some equally catastrophic consequence for someone in the
household. Namsan-mansin protested; she knew she herself preferred death to becoming a *mudang*:

I was twenty-seven at the time. Sick as I was, who at that age would accept such a fate? I decided that all I needed to do to escape the role of *mudang* was to leave my *sijip* ("one's husband's household"). . . . When I crawled out of the house that night, it was to die, nothing less. . . . But as you see, I did not die . . . and I *did* become a *mudang* after all! . . . it's *p'altcha* ("fate"). How else can you explain it? That was twenty years ago—it took me that long to accept my *p'altcha*.

I learned many years later that my parents-in-law looked for me far and wide for a long time. They were not bad people. They could not have truly welcomed my becoming a *mudang*, but I was a person of their household and they looked for me. Sometimes I think I might have done all right if I had stayed. But I was determined not to become a *mudang* even if it meant giving up my place there and leaving my son behind. I was ready to die, I tell you!

Namsan-mansin cannot understand where she got the strength to make the escape, but she walked all night in the direction of Taejŏn, the nearest big city. She knew that the last place she could or would go to was her natal household. Not only would her parents-in-law have looked there first, but she had not been reconciled with her father.

Namsan-mansin claims total amnesia regarding the recovery of her paralyzed left arm. According to her, she realized one day, with the shock of discovery, that it was no longer paralyzed. She subsequently found a job as a domestic servant in Taejŏn and worked there for about half a year, living in dread of being found. When she had saved a little money, she decided to venture out on her own as a peddler and, with a small stock of merchandise she intended to sell en route, headed on foot for Kangwŏn Province on the east coast of Korea. She was in robust health by then, she says, and was very anxious to put as much distance as possible between herself and her former husband and his household. She thus successfully aborted the first supernatural call to the role of *mudang*. That was in 1954.

Namsan-mansin made unexpectedly good profits on her merchandise as an itinerant peddler en route to the city of Ch'unch'ŏn, Kangwŏn Province, so that on arrival she could set up a small business in notions in the marketplace. It was there that she met Mr. Kim, her current and second husband. In a short time, she set up housekeeping with him and his son. She says he was then the kind of man she would have liked to have married, if he had been willing!

Today, at fifty-six (1972), he still has an engaging smile and carries his tall frame in a remarkably erect posture. He is still a handsome man, if a bit rugged. Although his Hamkyŏng dialect falls with raspy coarseness and uneven inflection on ears more accustomed to the smooth standard Seoul dialect, he has a way with words. He has a seemingly inexhaustible fund of information on every subject or, at least, an opinion on every subject.

Born the youngest of eight children but the second son, Mr. Kim had lived all his life on the outskirts of the port city of Hamhŭng until he evacuated south with the retreating soldiers during the Korean War. Believing the retreat a temporary setback for the South, he and his elder brother brought along only their sons. His wife and daughter remained behind with his parents. Four years later in 1954, he had no way of bringing them out of North Korea or of returning there himself. He and his elder brother were thus living as "war-widowers" with their young sons when Namsan-mansin met him.

Namsan-mansin says she was instantly and strongly attracted to her husband and moved in with him and his retinue without any fanfare. Shortly afterward, she persuaded Mr. Kim to leave his elder brother and nephews to set up housekeeping with her alone. She did not mind his ten-year-old son whom she looked after as best as she could while still tending her own business in the marketplace. She now bought and resold whatever would return a profit, however small. "Short of selling my body and wine in a winehouse," she declares proudly, "I've dealt in everything from cosmetics, used clothing, foodstuffs, stolen P.X. goods, to you-name-it." She realized that she liked her involvement in business and that she had a real knack for making money. She began to contribute her earnings to Mr. Kim's business ventures. Best of all, her health remained sound.

With Namsan-mansin's backing and support—financial, social, and emotional—Mr. Kim was able to concentrate on building up his service contract with the Korean Army into a reasonably prosperous one. Then rather abruptly the business failed for reasons which they say they have never fully understood. Almost penniless, they picked up such remnants of their business as they could and moved to Seoul where they hoped to find better opportunities for business. Once there, they accumulated a small amount of capital in a short time, owing largely to Namsan-mansin's success in the marketplace, and bought a bakery. Shortly after their investment, however, the bakery business collapsed. Neither had ever worked in a bakery, much less operated one. When asked in some detail about the conditions of the bakery at the time of its bankruptcy, Mr. Kim insists there were no ordinary reasons for the failure, adding:

> Of course, at the time we had no way of knowing that these failures were prerequisites to her becoming a *mudang*. . . . Three times I built up a business to a point where we could live like the "best of them" only to fail mysteriously. Once, we even owned our own three-wheeled motor vehicle.

After the bakery failed, Mr. Kim formed a partnership with another man from his native province and, for a time, enjoyed tremendous prosperity in the construction business. However, he has been unemployed for the last seven years or so.

They had other difficulties as well. Namsan-mansin wanted to legalize their common-law marriage, but Mr. Kim was reluctant. Mr. Kim explains that to finalize his union with Namsan-mansin at the time was to recognize and accept the finality of his refugee status in South Korea and his permanent separation from his first wife and daughter in North Korea. It would have cost him "the eternal hope of ever returning home to see my parents before they died of old age."

Namsan-mansin tells her view of the situation:

> Sure, I knew he had a wife and a family in North Korea. Didn't I take care of his brat for him? But what about the kids we were having together? . . . Most of our fights started over our common-law marriage status. . . . He used to beat me up so that I could neither stand up nor walk. He used to have to carry me on his back to the doctor's afterwards. . . . But I had my reasons for being so persistent. . . .

As a child, Namsan-mansin had seen how concubines' children were treated. She remembers in particular the son of a relative's concubine; he was always pointedly discriminated against by everyone, especially on holidays, and his mother could not help him. Namsan-mansin says she used to get upset for him.

I had vowed that no child of mine should ever know the bitterness of that boy's lot. So, whenever one of my kids came in
crying because someone had called him or her a concubine's
brat, my blood would boil. . . . I'd start agitating about legalizing our marriage. It would go on like that for several days until
we got worked up to a real knock-down drag-out fight over it.
. . . I'd threaten to leave him whereupon he would promptly
start pummeling and kicking me . . . , but no matter how many
times he beat me up, I'd just not give up badgering him about
legalizing our marriage. No children of mine were going to be
pointed at in public as a concubine's brats.

Namsan-mansin insists that her stubbornness was not a ploy
to get Mr. Kim to marry her for her own sake.

The first time I got pregnant by my old man, I didn't tell him
about it. I quietly took some herbs and aborted it in the toilet.
But I bled so much I nearly died, and of course he found out
about it. He go so mad he nearly killed me himself. He said he
wanted more children. But the more I thought about it, the more
convinced I became that it would be kinder to give birth to
cripples than to children who'd have to bear the stigma of being
a concubine's brats. So, when I got pregnant again, I aborted
again. . . . Only this time, the fetus died inside and began to rot.
I had a hell of a time getting rid of it. It almost killed me. . . .
Well, when I got pregnant again with my oldest girl, I just
couldn't do it again. So, one after another I had four—four who
were *sojok* (a concubine's offspring) as far as the world was
concerned. I tell you, life is a joke; it's harsh.

They were ultimately married but continued to have other
difficulties. According to Namsan-masin, there were always other
women in her husband's life. If she objected, he simply beat her.
While he never set up housekeeping with any of them, Mr. Kim
apparently conducted his dalliance with women flauntingly.
Namsan-mansin estimates that there must have been about thirty
such women in her husband's life. Mr. Kim who had been listening says the number is more probably around fifty or sixty. He
corrects her with the earnestness of a man correcting errors in the
sums of money changing hands, but Namsan-mansin laughs off
his comment with, "Who should know better than the man himself!"
When she continued with the recounting of her marital life,

though, her voice grew somber. Unlike most men who "take up with other women," Mr. Kim did not form any lasting relationships. She says that he just chased after every skirt that "flapped in the wind." He was a lavish spender with women, though it was his wife's money that he generally spent. With a shrug of the shoulder, Namsan-mansin now dismisses her husband as "simply not a family man"—he has little sense of responsibility for his family. Even when there was no money for food for the family, he would "get his hair all slicked up and steal away" to chase women with whatever money he had, leaving his family to starve. She says her bitterest memory of her husband is of the time that her son, now fourteen, was about to be born.

> The old man was running the bakery then and making good money too, but his eyes were bloodshot with the smell of "flapping skirts" and he didn't give a goddamn about what happened to me even though I was pregnant. I remember he didn't bring home a single *toe* (about 1.8 liters) of rice for me to eat after I gave birth to my son in March. . . . That accursed old man would actually bring home girls to sleep with in the same house, but never once did he bring me anything to eat. . . . I don't know if it was because I was already destined to be like this (a *mudang*), but I felt no anger or jealousy over his behavior. I felt only the uttermost contempt for the dog of a man that he was. I wasn't torn up with jealousy. . . .

Namsan-mansin's youngest sister who was living with them at the time used to get so upset by the way Mr. Kim treated her sister that she would scream at Namsan-mansin, "What's the matter with you? Something is not right with you . . . no sane woman would let her husband bring in girls to screw in the same room she and her kids were sleeping in! You're crazy!"

Namsan-mansin says that her husband's philandering fluctuated with their financial state, always peaking when there was any extra money. "It never failed. We'd be as good as beggars, but as soon as we get a little money together, he'd start chasing them all over again. . . ." When their daughter who is now twelve years old was born in 1960, they were at one of these low points. Though he knew she was about to give birth, he did not stay home. She says:

> When I knew the time was close, I made a pot of *myŏkkuk* (seaweed soup usually given to postpartum mothers) before I

went to bed that night. Shortly, the labor pains began to come
. . . I gave birth to her at dawn all by myself. . . . The kids slept
right through it. By the time I finished taking care of the baby
and cleaned up after myself, I felt terribly weak. I thought I had
better eat something, but I just couldn't move. So, I tried calling
softly to my landlady: "Auntie, Auntie." I heard her sit up and
say, "*Aigumai* ("good god"), she must have had her baby." She
helped me; otherwise I have not known the luxury of postpartum care since I hitched up with this old man. I always had to go
back to my business in two weeks or less. . . .

She has many other bitter memories. By this time, however,
she had come to realize that she could not depend on her
husband—that it would be "as smart as turning over the water in
the Han River." She decided to "look out for myself and the
children from then on." As a first step, she joined a *kye* ("mutual
aid society") and obtained her first substantial capital, about
$1000. With that she ventured into a wholesale dealership in fruits
in one of the large open-air markets in Seoul. The business
proved very demanding. She had to rise at four o'clock in the
morning to meet the suppliers, or she got stuck with picked-over
supplies that were difficult to sell. If she failed to unload her stock
to the retailers, she often took it to the retailer section of the
market and sold it herself. She usually kept some back to take
home to the children and her husband, who now stayed home
and looked after the children.

She recalls with obvious pride that she was an exceedingly
competitive business woman; she usually outsold everyone
around her. She was so successful that in less than four years she
leased a proper store space on *chŏnse* (a contract to rent a house,
office, or store space with a deposit usually amounting to two-
thirds of the market price of the rented space; there is no monthly
rent and the deposit must be paid back upon termination of the
lease. In the meantime, the lessor has the use of the money.) She
has a photograph of herself surrounded by boxes of fruits of all
kinds in her store. It is among her most prized possessions today.
She keeps it carefully stored between her costumes for performing *kut*. Her children are not allowed to handle it, only to view it
while she holds it.

Shortly after she leased the store and expanded her business,
she had enough money to buy a small house near the market and

move out of their rented quarters. She felt that she had "arrived."
But once again she succumbed to her husband's persuasion and
used her working capital to buy him a partnership in a contracting
firm. She says:

> From 1960 to 1964, while I was building my wholesale business
> up, I took no holiday, I barely ate a hot meal on time, or got
> more than three or four hours of sleep. I hardly ever saw the
> children and didn't know what was really going on at home.
> Looking after the children and the house was the least the old
> man could do for his part, I figured. But of course he didn't like
> it. What man would? He kept nagging me to finance him in just
> one more venture. He wanted to go in with some fellows from
> his home town in setting up a contracting firm for various
> government construction jobs. I knew better but of course I got
> sweet-talked into it. . . . For a while they seemed to be making
> barrels of money. . . . The old man even bought a three-
> wheeled vehicle that he drove himself. Once in a while he took
> us places in that thing! But that didn't last very long. I knew
> things were pretty bad when he got rid of the three-wheeled
> vehicle. He didn't tell me about it; I just didn't see it any more.
> Then, when I found out that he was chasing women, I knew the
> business was in trouble for sure.

One day while visiting with her stepson's family, she learned
from her grandson that her husband had been seen feeding ice
cream to a woman in a theatre. Her embarrassed daughter-in-law
added obliquely that she ought to monitor her husband's spending more closely. Somehow, Namsan-mansin got the impression
that the woman was her husband's first wife, although in retrospect she thinks it almost comical that she did. Having lived in
constant dread of his first wife somehow appearing on the scene
and challenging her legitimacy, she was half-relieved that it was
only a young girl with her husband. Notwithstanding, she could
barely contain her swelling rage. She had been duped again and
could see the repetition of the old cyclic pattern beginning all over
again. Worst of all, her ninth pregnancy had gone too far to be
aborted.

She lost little time in making some serious decisions:

> It didn't take me long to know what I had to do. I knew I had
> been fooled by the accursed old man for absolutely the last time.
> I had to keep the store going somehow. I had to keep alive the
> three children I already had. It was three against one, as simple

as that. The baby arrived on March 1 (1965) . . . ; it was a girl. On March 31, I strapped her on my back and left for the house I had picked out before she came. I left her at the gate. . . . when you think about it, I'm no ordinary person . . . I'm a vicious woman . . . I carried her on my own back and left her there, just outside the gate of the house I had settled on after many weeks of scouting. . . . Adoption? What adoption? Don't you understand anything, woman? I'm telling you that I abandoned her there. That was almost eight years ago! . . . Of course, I don't know what's become of her. How should I know?

Her older children were now big enough to fend for themselves, so Namsan-mansin returned to her wholesale business, vowing "to make the big time . . . to live well just once."

As usual, Mr. Kim had not been home when his wife gave birth. Nor did he realize that the baby had been abandoned for some days afterwards. He says he nearly fainted when he learned what his wife had done. He says:

To this day, it remains a thorn in my heart that I drove her to it. This woman (his wife) doesn't know much about day-to-day caring of children, but she loves her own flesh and blood as much as anyone else. She'd not have done such a thing if she hadn't been desperate.

He speaks movingly and with much feeling. Namsan-mansin seems to find his sentimentality annoying. She shouts to him that she had abandoned her first son also. Her husband dutifully points out that there is a difference between abandoning a child in his father's home and at the gate of a stranger's house. Namsan-mansin seems almost unwilling to let her husband feel his remorse, but even she acknowledges that the incident seemed to have had a tremendous impact on her husband's behavior. He curtailed his extra-marital affairs thereafter.

Perhaps Mr. Kim's evident sincerity and desire to reform had come too late to suit Namsan-mansin. Not in the least inhibited by her husband who sat less than two feet away from her, she continued with her account of his philandering:

Woman chasing is that old man's single specialty. When the "wind gets into the man's blood," he is beside himself . . . he forgets everything, especially his family responsibilities. . . . Since I myself did not get in from the store until curfew time, I had no idea that he usually got home just before I did. . . . The

kids didn't tell me and of course he didn't tell me. All the time I
thought he was home minding the children, he was probably
out chasing women on the housekeeping money I gave him. . . .
I worked seven days a week, and when I closed up shop, I used
to walk home . . . to save the car fare. . . . By the time I washed
up a little and ate, it was usually one in the morning and I was
up again about four. . . . So, I didn't know what was going on. I
thought I was working to get the family a little ahead . . . all the
time he was out courting other women on my money. No, no
woman should have a spoiled son for a husband . . . , such a
person knows only himself. What you want is a man who's had
some suffering and experience, one who can earn a living and
provide for you.

Despite these comments, Namsan-mansin shows considerable insight into her husband's behavior.

I am sure the old man felt bothered by the way I treated him.
Why else would he chase women so? In his own way, he was
trying to find some relief from his *sanaun-p'altcha* ("harsh fate").
. . . He didn't know whatever became of his other family and
parents. . . . Besides, our roles had gotten switched around;
that's obvious. . . . Because of my business, I never knew what
it was to sit around worrying just about my husband and children. I was out hustling even on New Year's day, trying to catch
a few last minute shoppers.

When asked how he had felt about their general life style and
the reversal of roles that his wife referred to in her conversation,
Mr. Kim replied that it was a chronic condition with him, that he
was barely conscious of it any longer. He says he had never been
able to think, "Ah, I'll go home now for supper or lunch; I'm
hungry." Continuing, he says:

I have raised our kids, not my wife. Even their laundry, I did.
There is not a thing that a woman can do that I can't do just as
well or even better. . . . Take cooking, for example. You can
bring the most famous homemaker, and I will show you that I
can cook better than her. . . . Well, what else could I do? She
went out and earned the money that kept the family going,
didn't she? I had to do the things that needed to be done around
the house that she had no time for, right? Well, that's how it
was. She has always been totally insensitive to such matters as
whether or not I have had anything to eat all day. When I come
in late, she never asks me if I ate. (Namsan-mansin laughed on

hearing this.) Once in a while, the kids ask me if I have eaten.
. . . Never once in the time we have lived together has she fixed
a tray of food aside as the father's supper—a custom you will
find in all other households.[7]

Namsan-mansin fully supports his claim:

He is the one who worried about whether or not the kids ate,
where they went to play, how they behaved. . . . He was the
mother to them. I don't know anything about the children. . . .
He was their disciplinarian. . . . When the kids were very
young, he played with them and helped them with their school
work. When they got sick, he nursed them. . . . When she felt
sickly, my oldest daughter used to lie down in a corner and cry
"Dad, Dad, I hurt." She never called me . . . I don't think they
had much affection for me because they didn't grow up with
me. . . . These days, I help him now and then with cooking and
washing dishes because I am home. Also, the kids can do a lot of
things now for themselves and for me, so the old man doesn't
have much to do. Before, when I was in the wholesale business,
he used to do everything, even the laundry. . . . When I got
home at midnight from my store, he would bring me my supper
all set on a table sometimes. . . . If he found holes in his or the
children's socks, he would mend them himself—in stitches none
too neat, but that was more than I was doing. Why, if I saw any
of them walking around in socks with holes, I'd buy them new
socks when I was in the market the next day and throw out the
old ones. I had no time to sit and mend them. My husband used
to call me a *kkŏllŏng-i* ("good-for-nothing wretch").

Mr. Kim was not always so nice to their children. Once he
beat their son so badly that he fell ill.

The first six or seven years of their living together,
Namsan-mansin enjoyed good health; however, beginning in
1960 or 1961, after the birth of the second daughter, she began to
have strange dreams and behave oddly even though she was
doing well in business.

In the first of these dreams, she saw a double rainbow enter-
ing her room, bringing a *ch'onggak* ("a virgin male") and three
ch'ŏnyŏ ("virgin females"). The three maidens claimed to be *sinsŏn*
("Taoistic supernatural beings or spirits"). They and their male
companion urged her to accompany them to heaven. She balked
at the invitation, saying to them, "Why should I go up to heaven
with you when I shall only fall from it? No, I don't want to go with

you." But they insisted, becoming forceful in their behavior and speech. "Let's go," they said, "we must go up."

Unable to resist them, she accompanied them up to heaven on three flights of stairs. When she looked down, she saw a vast field of the most magnificent flowers. The sight, she recalls, was breathtakingly beautiful. She asked her hosts about the field of flowers below and was told it was Seoul. As she gazed down upon it, she recalls that she was transported into a state of absolute ecstasy. But soon she began to be worried about returning home and asked to be taken back. The young man who had escorted her up earlier was now standing guard at the gate with a spear and would not let her pass. She became frantic, but when the three maidens began to dance around her, she felt calmer. Still, she wanted to go home to her children and begged them to let her go. (As she related this part of the dream, she enacted her part of the scene by rubbing her palms together vigorously in the gesture of one supplicating and by repeatedly bowing her head.) Ignoring her, the three maidens continued their dancing. Feeling helpless, she turned once again toward the young man standing guard at the gate and pleaded with him with her eyes.

Finally, the guard, addressing her as *tang-ajumŏni* (a mistress of a shamanistic shrine where the *kut* is performed), told her that it was not up to him but to the three *sinsŏn*. She was struck that he addressed her as a *tang-ajumŏni*. She braced herself and addressed the three *sinsŏn*: "You wenches, you let me go, do you hear! I've got to get back." At this outburst from Namsan-mansin, the three *sinsŏn* stopped their encircling dance and replied, almost casually, "If you must go, you must go, but we want you to come back." Saying that, they opened the gate for Namsan-mansin, and she ran down the staris. But on the third, the last stairway, she fell and woke up. She claims that if she had not fallen and woken up, she would have been possessed and become a shaman right then.

Two or three days later, she had another dream similar to the first. This time, however, there were seven *sinsŏn*, all new; only the *ch'onggak* was the same. As before, they asked her to accompany them to heaven. This time, she followed without resistance. When they reached the top of the stairway, she saw the three maidens from her first dream waiting. They welcomed her, "Oh, Auntie, you have come." Before she realized what was happening, the three joined the seven new *sinsŏn* in an encircling dance about her. Namsan-mansin began to get worried about returning home and told them that she wanted to go home. The three *sinsŏn* from the first dream said, "No, not this time, Auntie. We let you go back once already." They motioned to the young man to stand guard at the gate with his spear. Namsan-mansin became extremely scared, got down on her knees and began to beg furiously. Finally, they opened the gate and told her to leave. But this time there was only one flight of stairway between heaven and earth. She fell off the stairway, tumbling repeatedly in the air until she hit the ground with a thud. With that fall, she woke up.

> If I hadn't fallen and woken up, they'd have had me this time. It was between these two dreams that I uttered a lot of *hŏt'ŭn-sori* ("utterances which make no rational sense"). I don't remember it myself, but others have told me so. You see, that second dream was my third call from the spirits to become a *mudang*. But I didn't want to become one, so I resisted it.[8]

This episode involving the two dreams and her nonsensical utterances was followed by three significant events in succession. First, about 1964, her six-year-old son developed the habit of wandering away from home, sometimes going as far away as two or three thousand meters. Then, also in 1964, after a short period of spectacular success, her husband's construction firm failed mysteriously. The bankruptcy occurred shortly after Namsan-mansin learned about her husband's philandering from her grandson and was in turn followed by the birth of her third daughter—the one she abandoned.

Namsan-mansin's son wandered from home so frequently that it had become a family routine to make the rounds of police boxes, stations, and centers for lost children in their neighborhood and ward. On one such occasion, the boy could not be located at any of the usual places. Despondent when he did not show up for a whole week, Namsan-mansin and her husband consulted a *mudang*.

The *mudang*, according to Mr. Kim, divined his son's mysterious disappearance as a message from his first wife in North Korea. The *mudang* said:

> Your wife died without anyone to do the proper rituals for the dead—no one to 'prepare the road' for her after her death

(*kil-takka-chul-saram-ŏpsi*). Her spirit is resentful and has lured your boy away. This time, her ghost has piggy-backed the boy away from home. . . . You must appease her wounded spirit.

Namsan-mansin and her husband held the usual *kut* for the dead for his wife. Mr. Kim says:

Well, it was the first news I had had of my first wife since I left North Korea in 1950. . . . Well, as you know, we Koreans do this for the dead, to godspeed their journey to the other world. I didn't know if my parents or daughter were still alive, or, if alive, they would be allowed to do the ritual by the goverment. It seemed the least I could do for my first wife's ghost. Anyway, we were told that my first wife's ghost would meddle in our lives until her grudges were appeased . . . and that we had little time to lose.

What could we do? What would you have done? . . . Our son was missing for over a week; no amount of searching turned him up anywhere. So, we hired the *mudang* for 20,000 *wŏn* ($50) to perform *ch'ohon-kut* (one in which spirits are invited to possess the shaman and thus be able to communicate with the living).

. . . both my wife's ghost and my daughter entered the *mudang*, but only my daughter would speak to me. She asked to sit above the threshold of our room so she would know when I came and went and be near me. I agreed to do that for her. . . . I had her name written and, along with a *pujŏk* ("talisman"), put it up over the doorway. . . . I never left the room without calling her name and telling her where I was going, what I expected to do, and so forth. Of course, whenever I returned home, I informed her that I had returned. Sure enough, the same week we had the *kut*, the boy showed up—as if he had never been gone.

. . . Later I learned that my wife and daughter both died as an indirect result of my defection to the South . . . and it was the same week that my son had disappeared. My daughter was sixteen when she was "slaughtered" for my sake.

During this period, which lasted about three weeks altogether, Namsan-mansin was very sick and was confined to her bed. They were living in a rented room at the time,[9] in a house where there were several families, each renting a room and using other facilities communally. Mr. Kim came home one day to find their fellow tenants clustered about his wife. She was sitting up in her bed and talking as if in a dream. Mr. Kim describes the episode:

I asked her, "What are you talking about? Wake up." But she kept mumbling, saying things like, "This house was built with lumber once used for an outhouse . . . the lumber was never purified. If a purification *kut* is not performed right away, someone living in this house is going to come home injured or dead". . . . Well, can you believe it? That afternoon, the son of one of the other families was brought home hurt . . . in an accident in the factory where he worked. . . . Of course, someone remembered that my wife had prophesied it earlier and now they came to her to beseech her, then to badger her to do something to save the boy. My wife wouldn't hear of it. . . . I think she was scared. She denied ever saying anything like that. . . . Finally, she begged them to consult the same *mudang* that we had used.

The shaman confirmed Namsan-mansin's story about the outhouse lumber. So, the tenants got the owner of the house and questioned him. The landlord confessed that part of the house had been built with lumber that had previously housed a toilet. He was pressured into paying for the purification *kut* of the house and the whole thing was soon forgotten.

Namsan-mansin soon recovered and returned to her wholesale fruit business which had suffered badly in her absence. In 1965, sometime after she had abandoned her daughter, Mr. Kim's dead daughter appeared to her in a dream. She declared that she was tired of being perched atop the door and demanded that her mother's ghost take her place there.

Mr. Kim immediately removed his "daughter" from the doorway and burned it. When Namsan-mansin reminded him that his first "wife" was to replace his "daughter" there, he got impatient and declared "Enough is enough." After that, however, one disharmony after another arose between them. Thinking back to this period, Mr. Kim says:

> She [Namsan-mansin] must have packed her belongings a hundred times, saying she was through with me and then unpacking again. . . . Our family life was utterly disrupted. . . . She would disappear sometimes for days at a time, leaving the children behind. No one seemed to know where she was. I went back to the *mudang* we had consulted when our son had disappeared. . . . She said that we had misinterpreted my daughter's message . . . when she asked to be replaced by her mother, she had meant that she wanted to enter my wife—to possess her. I told the *mudang* that my wife would never allow it. She scolded

70   SIX KOREAN WOMEN

me, saying that we had been obstinate enough, that we should
stop fighting the spirits and start serving them. . . .

I talked it over with my wife and we decided to invite the
spirits into our home and serve them. . . . We needed relief from
our many afflictions. After that, things really got much better.
. . . My wife did not become a *mudang*; she stayed in the
wholesale fruit business, and it thrived as never before. . . .

Toward the end of this period, they moved to a new place,
partly to avoid the growing number of people seeking her services
as a diviner, especially from the neighborhood. She nevertheless
continued to provide her cohorts in the wholesale business with
her divination services free of charge. She felt that so long as she
refused money for her services, she was not a *mudang*.

Mr. Kim interrupts his wife at this point to interject a lament,
"Ah, but whenever I tried my hands at something, the thing
would blow up in my face . . . everything I tried ended in a
disaster." In this manner, Mr. Kim continually calls attention to
his failures, especially his last grand business venture. He says
the venture seemed foolproof at the time. He freely admits that he
had talked his wife into backing him up against her wish and that
his losses were eventually responsible for destroying his wife's
wholesale fruit business as well. "She had to repay my debts; she
had no choice—the loan sharks would have beaten me to death if
she hadn't. We were back at the starting point once more. . . ."
But this time it was not as before, Namsan-mansin did not "roll
up her sleeves and jump in" to start life anew.

Sounding still incredulous, Mr. Kim recounts that his wife
refused to give up the lease on the store and collect the deposit
even though she did not have enough cash assets to operate her
wholesale business. She seemed determined to get back into her
business somehow. With what money was still left from leasing-
out the various rooms in their house on *chŏnse* base, she now
proposed to go on the road as an itinerant merchant. Mr. Kim,
being in no position to stop her, just watched. He continues:

She used to make up a huge bundle of assorted merchandise
which she carried on her head. By train, bus, and sometimes on
foot, she'd go into remote countrysides to peddle her wares,
sometimes for a week or more at a time. . . . Of course, she'd
leave me the children to look after. . . . Sometimes the kids
would wonder out loud if they were ever going to see their
mother again.

Namsan-mansin returned from one of these trips strangely determined and secretive. Without so much as a word to her husband, she subleased her store space for $500 and simply disappeared. That was in 1969. Mr. Kim tells the story:

> She didn't leave any money for me and the children. No one seemed to know where she might have gone. . . . I looked up some old friends who owed me favors. One of them offered me a job, but it was out of town. I was very, very tempted to take it, but then what would become of the children? I couldn't take them along with me to the job site; I also couldn't leave them by themselves, though maybe they were old enough. . . . I wasn't sure when I could come for them if I took the job, and only the spirits knew when their mother might show up, if ever. . . . Of course, if the children became desperate, they could have gone to my other son's place. Even though they come from different wombs, still, my son would not have cast them out on the street. Don't they share my blood after all? . . . I agonized over it but decided that there was no reason for my son to have to pay for all this also—why should he have to ruin his life, too? So, I stayed with the children. . . . Actually, I even thought of mass suicide . . . of dying together with the children. But I couldn't do it.

During this trying period, Mr. Kim had a visit from an old woman, a *mudang* from his hometown. In the course of their visit, she asked him if he had certain ancestors. When told that he did, she urged him to invite these ancestral spirits in and serve them, adding, "Worship and serve your ancestral spirits. There is domestic storm in your household because you have so long neglected them. Start right away. Serve them." After some reflection, Mr. Kim decided to follow her advice; he did not see that he had anything to lose.

Mr. Kim's ancestor, fourth generation ascending, had been a village *hunjang* ("schoolmaster"). According to family legends, this ancestor knew the entire *chuyŏk* (*The Book of Changes*, the Chinese classic in divination), as did Mr. Kim's grandfather. Both ancestors were said to have been very good diviners. Mr. Kim got a crate and set it up as an ancestral altar and carried out the proper rituals to these and other ancestors in his direct line. The very same night he had a dream of his ancestors' approval:

> It was strange, but after that dream I had such peace of mind. I still had nothing to eat, all the children, and didn't know where

my wife was; yet, I felt calm. Somehow all such worries seemed to have evaporated away from the moment I set up the altar to my ancestors. . . . After I did my obeisance to them each day, I'd say to myself: "Let the day be sufficient unto the day. Tomorrow is another day."

He also looked up another friend who owed him a favor and got a room in his house temporarily, rent-free. He subleased the room they were living in on *chŏnse*; his idea was to start a small business with that money. But he felt that he ought to find his wife and settle their accounts first. He says, "I was ready to call it quits with her if that's what she wanted. I felt sure I could find another woman to look after the children, if necessary." By the time he located her, his money was almost at an end. Of this experience he says:

The more I continued my search for my wife, the more convinced I got that this time she was really possessed. There was no other way to explain her bizarre and erratic behavior that came to my attention. . . . When I finally caught up with her, I gave her an ultimatum: "You're a possessed person, so I know you can't account for your behavior. But the children and I have to live. Even you will not deny the children. Now, give me the money, the $500 you got for subleasing the store. I don't care whether or not you come back with me. That's up to you, but I need the money to look after the children." . . . She handed the money over to me . . . she still had all of it. When I got up to leave, she too stood up. She said, "I'm coming with you." That was in January [1971].

With the lease money from the store, they recovered a room in their own house and the entire family moved in together. But to the chagrin of her husband, Namsan-mansin refused to go out to work. She sat home and did absolutely nothing but stare into space. With no income, their money soon ran out. None of Mr. Kim's various strategies for getting work materialized. He began to sell one after another of the family's possessions; still, Namsan-mansin sat home oblivious. After about six months, they had nothing more to sell; it was July 1971. It was then that Namsan-mansin openly began to entreat her husband to let her be a *mudang*. According to Namsan-mansin, they were starving to death, and it did not seem to matter whether they died from physical hunger or the shame of having a *mudang* in the family.

Mr. Kim was reluctant. Had their long struggle to avoid such a fate been in vain? He consulted the *mudang* from his hometown. She advised him to support his wife's assumption of the *mudang* role; it was her destiny. So he consented, and the very next day his wife sat among street fortune-tellers and waited for her first client. He continues:

> Even from the first, she began to read at least three or four fortunes a day . . . enough to feed us better than we had eaten in months. I was ashamed, but what could I do? The choice was between salvaging my face and letting the kids starve to death. I had to accept her earnings. My hair is already gray and I have failed in so many of my ventures. . . .

Eventually, Namsan-mansin moved her practice from the street to the room where they now live. Although he talks almost eagerly about the events that led to his wife's becoming a *mudang*, Mr. Kim is embarrassed to find himself a shaman's husband. He relates half proudly that his eldest son has forbidden his family to visit them. Through it all, however, one senses that he is secretly relieved to have his wife once again supporting the family. He says:

> As I tell my son, maybe our grandfathers [ancestors] are finally looking after us. They let her say the sorts of things to clients which keep them coming back and it gives us a living. . . . Maybe the whole thing is really fated and it's useless to fight it. Maybe in time we can return to business, but for now this is the only way open to us to keep on eating. It can't be helped. It is what the grandfathers had intended for us all along, perhaps. Surely, there will come a time when I can once again do something worthwhile—with their [ancestral ghosts'] help. For now. . . . I am resigned to it.

Namsan-mansin agrees with her husband that it is their, or more particularly, her fate to be a *mudang*. She justifies this by the following remarks:

> I have always wanted to make it really big in the business world . . . to make enough money to live in a tile-roofed house, have clothes made of different kinds of fabrics, taste different sorts of food, and see different places. . . . I invariably enjoy traveling, even on business with a huge bundle on my head that grinds my neck down into my body. . . . I feel good sitting in a train, watching things pass by . . . watching people seeing people off;

seeing them get on and off trains. . . . Several times I almost
made it big, except that that old man always sweet-talked me
into giving him the money so he could chase after "wind-filled
skirts" (women given to amorous and flirtatious dalliances with
men). Well, when I took off with the lease money from the store,
I still had that dream. I knew, though, that I had to get away
from the old man if I wanted to succeed. . . . As you know, he
found me before I had a chance to do anything. I'd have come
back when I had made a bundle, of course; as it was, I came back
with him. It must be because I was going to become like this—I
just handed him the money like it was his when he asked for it. I
have lost all such ambitions now; these days I trust and depend
only on my grandfather there [*sansilyŏng-nim*, the mountain
deity which she claims as her guardian spirit].

Namsan-mansin is convinced that they could have avoided
many of their crises if she had not so obstinately ignored the
supernatural calls she received to assume the *mudang* role. Now,
there is no longer any question of choice; she must accept it as her
fate. She seems to feel a tremendous sense of blame and personal
responsibility for the misery that her entire family experienced.
She says:

I've made my old man a beggar and we have neither our house
nor any furnishings now. So, I must do this [function as a
shaman] for a living, if for nothing else. But if I had not been so
stubborn about ignoring the spirits, my old man would not have
failed so utterly and miserably in all his business attempts. . . .
It's all my fault. Even the craziness that comes over him when he
"smells" women makes him crazy in the head so he will fail in
his business. It's traditional knowledge that the spirits are very
jealous . . . that they ruin the husbands of *mudang*-to-be as the
very first step in their "capturing" of women to become *mudang*.
. . . Because of my obstinacy, I brought a lot of shame and
suffering to my first husband's family too. I see my son from my
first marriage from time to time . . . whenever he is in Seoul, he
comes to see me, such as I am. I don't know what I feel for him,
but he is a fine young man . . . married with two or three
children. . . . He says his stepmother was not mean to him.

Namsan-mansin's sense of contriteness keeps coming
through as she continues her story:

If I had not given in last summer and gone out on the streets,
something dreadful would have happened. . . . Someone might

have died. . . . It is the spirits' way of getting their way—they ruin everything you try your hands on so you will have to come around to their ways just to eat. It's all a person's *unmyŏng* ("destiny"); one is foolish to resist one's predestination. Look at me! For twenty years I've resisted, only to succumb to the call now, after so much that might have been spared. If I had known how inevitable this fate was, I would have made no vain efforts to fight it.

There can be no argument that Namsan-mansin is, at least for the present, fully committed to her professional role as a shaman. For his part, Mr. Kim is convinced that he ought not to try anything that the possessing spirits of his wife—his ancestors and daughter—would object to. If he tries anything again in the way of business, he says it will be only with the blessings of the spirits, not otherwise. At her husband's mumblings regarding possible future business plans, Namsan-mansin interjects that her husband is "still an expert at plucking money away from me." At the same time, she speaks rather appreciatively of him:

He's very supportive of me now. If only with a word or two, he is helpful to me. Can he do less? After all, he is the master of this household. If he isn't supportive of me and tries to keep the family going, who will? . . . Anyway, my old man is a firm believer in all this [she gestures with the sweep of her hand toward the altar at one end of the room]. He is an unshakable believer of *sansin* ("mountain spirits") and *ch'ilsŏng* ("spirits of the Big Dipper responsible for fertility") and everything else associated with the doings of *mudang*. . . . As far as I know, there was no *mudang* either in his or my family; anyway, I don't believe in hereditary succession of *mudang*. If your *p'altcha* is harsh, it comes your way, that's all.

The month of June, lunar, is considered by all shamans I have met as the worst month of the year for income purposes; in fact, they refer to it as a *ssŏgŭndal* ("rotten month"). When I first met Namsan-mansin in June, 1972, lunar, she was earning an average of about $5 a day or about $150 a month, easily twice the salary of beginning elementary schoolteachers with four years of college. Out of this sum, Namsan-mansin paid $50 a month for the room at the inn, doled out $.50 to $.75 a day to her husband for carfare and other needs—about $15 to $23 a month. Her elder daughter who earned about $18 a month as an usher turned over most of it to her mother.

Although Mr. Kim does not contribute anything at all to the family income, he feels he is helping by keeping his expenses at a minimum. He says:

> My old cronies don't know about her being a *mudang* and my being reduced in circumstances to the point of being at her mercy. They still expect me to be a big spender, as was my fashion to be in the days when I used to make good money. If only I had known I was always being set up by the spirits!

According to Namsan-mansin, a major portion of her current income goes toward repaying still large sums of outstanding business debts incurred by her husband. She says, "The interests keep having offsprings which have their own offsprings. . . ." As if to underscore her husband's economic dependence on her, she adds: "I handle the money in this household now. After all, I am the one who brings it in. So shouldn't I be the one to dispense it?" Mr. Kim says nothing to this. Namsan-mansin speculates that if she were to join a *kye*, it would not take much time to pay off their debts, but she is frankly afraid to have access to a large sum of money at once. She says she simply does not trust herself to be able to resist her husband's persuasiveness in relieving her of what she calls her "bundle money," i.e., a large sum of money.

Since she became a professional *mudang*, that is, since she began to charge for her services, Namsan-mansin says her social life has become very restricted. Even her youngest sister whom she practically raised and who in turn had helped her with her children will no longer have anything to do with her because her husband objects to Namsan-mansin's being a shaman. Sighing, Namsan-mansin laments:

> I have no friends any more, nor any relatives. . . . I think my back [her will] was broken when I left my child at a stranger's place. When I got home without her, I felt all my strength draining out of me. I cannot describe to you how I felt. It's beyond words. I wanted to raise my voice to the high heavens and wail my heart out but no sound escaped through my lips. I felt such a heavy leadweight sitting in the pit of my stomach but nothing came through my lips to relieve me of its weight. What a pitiful thing to have done. She should be eight now.

As if to arouse herself from this preoccupation, Namsan-mansin tells me, with a snort, of her fleeting skirmishes with Christianity:

When I first began to make *hŏt'ŭn-sori* ["irrational utterances"] and people said I was possessed, my sister-in-law (husband's elder brother's wife) urged me to go to church with her. I went with her three times. Each time, it was such a crashing bore that I fell sound asleep during the minister's sermon. Once, my sister-in-law got a little angry with me and jabbed me so hard in the ribs that I jumped up with a scream! I still couldn't stay awake. I didn't want to go back, but my sister-in-law didn't ask me again either.

Mr. Kim, present during many of my interviews with his wife, now wants to explain more fully why he accepted his wife's *mudang* role. Had he had any inkling that she had had a history of spirit possession, he would never have "teamed up" with her in the first place, he says. Secondly, if she had been possessed by ancestral spirits of either her own lineage or her first husband's lineage, he would not have stayed with her after her possession. As it was, fate had decreed that it be his own ancestors that possess her. He insists, however, that his ancestors would *not* have "gotten themselves piggy-backed on her" if she had not been already susceptible to spirit possession. She was, in a word, compatible to their needs to possess someone in the family:

> I didn't know it, but my ancestral spirits recognized the symptoms of her *sinbyŏng* and, finding her congenial, possessed her. . . . So, of course, I don't see any way to obstruct her any more; after all, shall I evict my own ancestral spirits? Where will they go? . . . If she were possessed by any other spirits, why, I'd divorce her instantly. I don't care even about the children. . . . I just would not put up with all this. But since it is obvious that my ancestors are in her, I cannot help it. . . .
>
> My older son despises all this. Whenever he sees me, he argues with me, "Why, Father, do you hang around there? You have a house in Ch'ŏnŏ-dong; why don't you live there with the children? The children are big enough now; they won't tie you down as before. . . ."

Mr. Kim's first son thinks that he should get a housekeeping allowance from Namsan-mansin and live apart from her with the children. Mr. Kim agrees that it is a good idea but says they cannot operate two households on Namsan-mansin's current income. As he continues his explanation for accepting his wife's *mudang* role, his unexpressed reasons for so doing surface a little more clearly.

I've always dealt in big ventures. I won't fiddle-faddle with
smalltime operations. . . . Even if she could finance me right
now, say with about $750, it would do nothing. I couldn't do
anything with it. My friends would laugh at me. All my old
cronies are used to having me pick up the tab whenever we go
out. I can't tell them, "Hey, look, I'm living off my wife who is a
mudang, so how about picking up your own tab?" . . . I won't
grovel before my friends—I never have. . . . I don't want people
pointing their fingers at me and saying, he is a *mudang*'s *sŏbang*
("husband"). You know the old proverb: "Nobody likes
freeloading as much as a *kisaeng*'s brother and nobody likes
idleness as much as a *mudang*'s husband." . . .

Well, the truth is the spirits will turn anything I try my hands
at upside down. They will do anything to make me a failure so
they can possess my wife more easily. I don't even feel like
trying anything anymore, although, you understand, it would
be nothing, given my experience, to recover the wealth we lost if
I had a big enough capital to start with.

Namsan-mansin interrupts her husband, saying there is no
real need for him to work. She insists that they can manage well
enough on her income. Ignoring her completely, he continues:

Today it's nothing whether or not you are a *mudang* or *paekchŏng*
("butchers", another outcaste category). In the olden days, the
custom was that *mudang*, *paekchŏng*, and *hain* ("servants") were
not considered human beings. Today, things are different. So
long as you have money, it is nothing whatever else you are.
I've come to feel the same way. . . . My embarrassment and
shame have "washed away." At first I dreaded her becoming a
mudang. As you know, I've tried to prevent it . . . as recently as a
year ago.

Professionally, Namsan-mansin is still a novice with few or
no specialized skills in *kut*. However, being possessed by multiple
spirits, she is confident she has a wide range of versatility as a
medium. She does not seem as yet to have made cooperative
arrangements with other shamans who may refer clients to her for
particular kinds of *kut*. Nevertheless, she has full confidence in
the efficacy of her shamanistic power and delights in recounting
one case after another in which she has had good results. It is
evident that she finds the *mudang* role personally satisfying. She
says:

I am happiest these days when I am in the mountains [where she visits her guardian spirits in their shrines and performs her *kut*]. Next to that, I like staying home and seeing clients. . . . Even when I have not been feeling well and in bed, if I see a client approach, I sit up and carry on as if to say, "When was I sick?" . . . It does not matter if it's three in the morning or in the afternoon; it's all the same. Sometimes when I am like that, why, I can go on all day and night. I don't feel the tiredness while I am like that, only afterwards. . . . I feel physically at my best when I return from my visit to the mountain where I've just performed a *kut*. . . . If on some days clients are scarce, my stomach gets all funny inside. . . .

Asked if she felt any sense of conflict in being a *mudang* and also a wife and mother, she responded without hesitation that she didn't. She points out that she has not fulfilled the obligations entailed in the domestic role for most of her second marriage. She sees her role in the household primarily as a general provider and troubleshooter, a role typically expected of the male household head. While she is no longer willing to underwrite him in any big ventures, she is completely committed to keeping her husband supplied with a decent personal allowance. In her words, "What else can I do but pick up after him? . . . How else can I maintain a harmonious household?" They seem to have reached a new accord in their relationship. Namsan-mansin relates that recently she and her husband had attended a movie together for the first time, adding that it was "not hard to take." When she dozed off during the film, her husband teased her, "Ah ha, it's no fun coming here with your old man, eh?"

Her children, especially the two younger ones, quarrel a great deal, though not usually when clients are present. This disturbs Namsan-mansin somewhat, not so much it would seem from concern over possible reasons for their frequent quarrels as from feeling them a nuisance. Not infrequently, Namsan-mansin becomes vituperative toward her children, particularly if they do not do her bidding instantly. According to Mr. Kim's and the children's own accounts, life with Namsan-mansin, especially in recent years, has been difficult for the children. They quit school at least in part because of the severe social ostracism they experienced as children of a *mudang*. Namsan-mansin's own perception of herself as a mother is more favorable:

I don't think I'm particularly an indifferent mother. I'm
average—just like most mothers I know and see, anyway. Still,
I'm happiest away from home. I don't like staying home. . . . Of
course, my old man likes for me to stick around the place. . . .
Now that I am home, though, he doesn't help me with any of
the housework. So, now I have to do both jobs—earn a living
and keep the house too!

From my observation, the children are delighted to have their
mother home even though she is usually preoccupied either with
her clients or card games with her husband or neighborhood
women and has little time for them. Generally, she interacts with
them only when she needs their service or when they demand
something of her. For the most part, the children are compliant.
When I remarked that her children seem very sympathetic and
supportive of her, Namsan-mansin replied, "No, not really; but,
of course, we are a family and a family has to be mutually sympathetic." She seemed to be implying that if her husband and
children were being sympathetic and helpful, it was more out of a
sense of family obligation than out of an understanding of her
needs as a person.

Namsan-mansin's daily routine varies, depending upon the
number and kinds of clients she has and any *kut* that may have
been scheduled for the day. She helps her elder daughter prepare
breakfast and, if there are no clients to be seen, she usually goes
back to sleep or plays cards with her husband. If he is not available, she sends one of the younger children to find any willing
neighborhood women to join her. When no one is available, she
usually naps. The only occasions when I observed her actively
engaged in domestic chores were those times when she had to
prepare the ritual foods for a *kut*. Her practice is not yet lucrative
enough to hire an assistant for that function. Their noon and
evening meals are highly irregular, and their life in general is
extremely lacking in privacy by the general standards of Korea.

Namsan-mansin professes that since "going public," i.e.,
becoming a *mudang*, she has had great peace of mind. She has
lost, she says, all her competitive aggressiveness that had so
characterized her throughout her life, especially during her career
as a merchant when she got "the biggest thrills" in putting her
competitors out of business. Now, she leaves everything in the
hands of her guardian spirits. She prays to them daily and is sure

that they will watch over her so long as she does her best to serve them. Her husband concurs with these remarks, adding that her daily behavior has certainly become less bizarre since assuming the shaman role. For example, she no longer strips to her waist in the middle of winter to shampoo her hair and bathe in cold water in the courtyard as she used to, claiming the need to purify herself.

Still, Namsan-mansin finds much to be discontented about. She observes that most women her age are having the best time of their lives, going here and there in groups to have fun, whereas she is a despised shaman shunned by everyone. She blames her karma, but her husband is not entirely exempt from accusations:

> If my old man did everything expected of a husband, I'd not suffer like this. It's because he is unable to that I have to have such a fate. . . .
>
> When my daughter is ready to marry, I'd like to find a self-made man who has known hardship early in his life and has overcome it. Such a man can take what life has to dish out sometimes. The worst thing for anyone is to have grown up in the lap of luxury and then be faced with the hard knocks of life later on. . . . You can't stand up under such treatments. . . . Well, my girl has had a rough life herself. What she needs is a man who has gotten the best of his bitter life experiences. Not a man like my old man. I say this even though he is here listening, because it's the truth. That man had everything more or less his way as a child and much of his adult life until he came south as a war refugee and he can't take the hard knocks of life.

Namsan-mansin has equally definite notions about what kinds of women have a "good life" or a harsh one. She says:

> Women who are born with a generally masculine personality are doomed to a tumultuous life. Why? Why not! In our society, a woman's voice is not expected to carry farther than the inner walls of her house. You know the proverb: "If a hen cackles, the household is doomed." In other words, a woman is expected to be very gentle and docile. If a woman is born with masculine traits, she will be inclined to want to do the things which are properly the domain of the male. How can she then avoid being saddled with a harsh fate? Actually, such women can do these things well enough; but if it is a woman's destiny to sit quietly at home and be provided for, is it not a tough life for her to have to go out and hustle herself? . . . Some women are women only in

the bodies they have been born with; otherwise, they are male.
. . . It does not matter if their husbands can keep them well;
they must venture out and become involved in extra-domestic
matters. We Koreans think of such women as harshly fated
women. . . . The strange thing is that nobody can force such
women to do what they do. In one way or another, they have to
want to do it. A masculine women is a person who has exceeded
her limits. Her fate is bound to be harsh.

  Despite her views on the masculine female, Namsan-mansin
nurses a grand professional ambition for herself:

  As soon as I have saved up about $125 to $150, I want to have
  my *naerim-kut* ("initiation rite"). Soon as I've had that, I'll team
  up with someone. But of course, it can't be just anyone for me.
  It's got to be someone who knows how to "play big." I've got
  my eyes on someone right now . . . ; she comes to the same
  shrines in Samgak Mountain where I go, but I don't know yet if
  it will be she. I pray to my *momju* ("guardian spirits") to tell me
  when I shall be having my initiation. They tell me it will come in
  its own good time—that I should be patient . . . I'm confident
  that once I've had that, I shall be in popular demand . . . I'll be
  able to perform in large *kut*. . . .[10]

  Namsan-mansin is especially confident that she will become
a successful shaman because she had a vision just before she
started to practice professionally that she would have foreigners
as clients as well, and this vision has since been validated. She
was, she says, sitting idly one day when three airplanes appeared
in the sky in quick succession. To her surprise, the airplanes
headed directly toward her and entered the room in which she
was sitting. A beautiful girl with blonde hair emerged from one of
the planes, and they began to talk. She is not sure in what
language they communicated, but thinks it must have been in
Korean as they had no difficulty speaking to each other. The
blonde girl told her that she had come all the way from another
country just to consult her. Namsan-mansin got excited and
exclaimed "aigomai" ("good god") and the girl disappeared. No
one else in the room had seen the airplanes or the girl.

  At the present time, Namsan-mansin's most critical professional task is to make an astute selection of a shaman to officiate at
her initiation rite, for thereafter she will act as Namsan-mansin's
"adoptive mother" and a professional sponsor. In the meantime,

she gives her clients basically conservative advice that is supportive of traditional values in general. A theme that recurs throughout her sessions with all types of female clients is that when one
acts out of the role character of one's sex, one invites the puni-
tiveness of the supernatural. She regards the masculine female
personality the way the Greeks regarded hubris. One exceeds the
range of traditional norms, especially in filial responsibilities and
sex roles at one's own risk, for one is bound to be humiliated in
the end.

*

4

P'YŎNGYANG-MANSIN

BRIEF CHRONOLOGY OF P'YONGYANG-MANSIN'S LIFE

1925	Born, second child and first daughter
1933	Grandmother died
1935	Family immigrated to Manchuria
1938	Father died; family relocated to another town in Manchuria
1939	P'yŏngyang-mansin fell ill; symptoms diagnosed as *sinbyŏng*
1943	Graduated from commercial high school
1944	Second bout with *sinbyŏng;* hallucinatory experiences
1945	World War II ended. Repatriation to P'yŏngyang and later flight to South Korea
	Employed in a printing firm; met husband
1946	Became pregnant out of wedlock. Married and gave birth to first son
1948	Second child, a son, died in the second month of his life P'yŏngyang-mansin had her third bout with *sinbyŏng*
1950	Third child, a daughter

	Just beginning to get along with mother-in-law
	Korean War began and husband drafted
	Refugee life in South Chŏlla Province
1953	Returned to Seoul; natal family lived with her
	Fourth child, a daughter
1954	Husband discharged from the Army and returned home; unable to find employment
	Natal family moved out
1955	Fifth child, a daughter
1957	P'yŏngyang-mansin had her fourth and final *sinbyŏng*
	Evicted from mother-in-law's house
1958	Sixth child, a daughter
	Seventh pregnancy, aborted
1959	Eighth child, a daughter
1960-1964	Aborted three pregnancies
1960	Bought first house
	Mother-in-law moved in with them
1965	Ninth child, a son
1971	First son married and established in own drugstore a year later
1972	Bought the present house/shrine complex
	First grandson born
	First daughter went to Los Angeles

P'YŎNGYANG-MANSIN

P'yŏngyang-mansin takes her name from the capital of North Korea, P'yŏngyang, where she was born in 1925. At ten, she and her family moved to Manchuria, returning to Korea at the end of World War II. Upon repatriation, they went first to P'yŏngyang but ultimately settled in Seoul, where she married a native twenty-seven years ago. She now speaks the standard Seoul dialect with ease, though she retains readily identifiable linguistic features of her native region in her use of certain words. She slips comfortably into her native regional dialect when conversing with people from there. Because P'yŏngyang is also the regional center for a distinctive tradition of Korean shamanism, P'yŏngyang-mansin is at pains to explain that she follows the Seoul tradition lest she mislead her clients. Her "adoptive mother" had been a shaman of the Seoul tradition.[1]

Extraordinarily tall for a Korean woman at five feet eight, P'yŏngyang-mansin is also uncommonly good looking. She attracts special attention even among other shamans at *kut* gatherings, a true testimony for her beauty as most shamans are attractive.[2] On the streets, people turn around to look at her. She is forty-six, but most people think she is at least ten years younger. There is about her an infectious vivacity, especially when she flashes her gold-capped teeth in a broad grin and her eyes come alive. She is a good drummer and a captivating dancer, but her voice is weak, becoming strained in chants sustained over a long period.

Without being overbearing, she is formal in her speech with co-workers and clients. She does not, as a rule, take part in the merry exchange of ribald jokes that goes on at most *kut* between shamans and their male musicians. A capable stage director, she usually keeps track of the organizational details of any *kut* she participates in with other shamans and musicians. She does not seem to ever completely lend herself to the frenzy so characteristic of shamanistic rituals. Her bearing and manner communicate self-control and confidence. On two occasions, however, she wept with abandonment, both times following a frenzied dance in a *kut*. Each time, an elderly shaman whom she calls "mother" came to her and, embracing and rocking her as one might a child, urged her to cry as much as she wanted to.[3] And each time, P'yŏngyang-mansin stopped crying almost unceremoniously abruptly, apologizing. She explained that she pitied her son, referring to her second son who died in early childhood over twenty years ago.

Although her appearance belies it, she has had twelve pregnancies, four of which she terminated in induced abortions.

When I first met her in 1971, she was living with her seven surviving children, aged six to twenty-six, her husband, mother-in-law, and a niece (her brother's daughter) in a moderately sized Korean-style house on the very outer limits of Seoul. An ordinary house from the outside, it was extraordinarily well tended inside, reflecting devoted care. Plants and flowers filled the courtyard where a latticed structure shaded a Western-style children's swing set. P'yŏngyang-mansin's youngest child spent most of his time on the swing. She received her clients in the *sarang-bang*, traditionally a male room, which had been converted into an altar room. The arrangement shielded her visitors and family from one another's view.

As she took me into the inner portion of the house, P'yŏngyang-mansin called to her daughters and niece to come and meet her guest from America.[4] She also called to her husband, who was pasting labels on match boxes in another room. An old lady stuck her wrinkled face in the doorway and, having surveyed me for a moment, withdrew without a word. It was P'yŏngyang-mansin's mother-in-law. When her children had assembled, she introduced me as a married woman and a mother of two growing children, who nevertheless was attending a graduate school in Hawaii and doing her fieldwork in her mother country. Remarking that America must be a wonderful place, especially for women, she enjoined her daughters to ask me questions about America and listen carefully.

When one of the daughters served me iced coffee made of Maxwell House instant coffee, P'yŏngyang-mansin wondered aloud whether, while it was the best of what they had to offer me, it was not in fact a poor thing to serve a guest so recently arrived from America. She asked if I would not prefer a slice of cold watermelon. When her husband joined us, she ordered a glass of iced coffee for him also, and the children shuffled around to make a spot for him by the window where it was cooler. The children were obviously accustomed to treating him with deference, and he, to being so treated. Mr. Lee, the same age as his wife and only slightly taller, is a handsome man. The children having inherited their parents' good looks, they make an attractive looking family together.

A high school graduate, Mr. Lee had been an office clerk before the Korean War when he was drafted into the Army. He

served for four years before his discharge in 1954; he had liked the
Army and would have stayed in had he not been married. Since
his discharge, he has been unemployed "outside," but he does
not idle away his time as many unemployed husbands tend to do
in Korea, particularly husbands (or other male dependents) of
shamans. He is always engaged in some sort of cottage industry
at home, such as pasting labels on match boxes, or making paper
bags of old newspapers for retailers. He says apologetically that
he does what he can to earn his own pocket money, but the
children and his wife are quick to point out that his earnings had
purchased all the family luxury items such as the television, radio,
and electric fans.

Mr. Lee seems realistically resigned to not finding any "outside" occupation that he would consider suitable. He adds that
even if he were to find employment "outside," it would create as
many problems as it would solve.[5] He means, of course, that
having a shaman for a wife would be embarrassing to him in the
society of men. Besides, he reasons that someone has to stay
home to hold the family together as his wife is frequently away for
extended periods performing *kut*.

He takes care of all family affairs that require official transactions with outsiders, including attendance at PTA meetings for
his younger children. For diversion, he likes to watch historical
dramas or travelogues on T.V. with his second son, aged six. He
says he also likes to read. There is a fairly large collection of
popular historical novels in the house, as well as a few outdated
Japanese magazines for homemakers, since both he and his wife
speak and read Japanese. He is almost always at home.

P'yŏngyang-mansin feels that her husband's talents have
gone unrecognized in the "outside world" and hence wasted,
attributing this to the fact that he lacks a college education and the
concomitant social network of influential classmates so necessary
to occupational placement in Korea. Lack of formal education has
been equally a handicap in her own case, she feels. She regrets
having had to quit post-highschool vocational training to help
support her natal family. She is convinced that she could have
become anything she chose to, if she had had the necessary
educational background. She had been a bright student throughout her school career. Because of these regrets, she and her
husband have directed all their energies to providing their chil-

dren with a sound education and have achieved a high degree of
success. She laughingly refers to her chidren's diploma as their
"estate."

Their eldest son, a pharmacist, graduated with distinction
from Seoul National University, the most prestigious university
in Korea, and expects to obtain a good job with a German phar-
maceutical firm based in Korea when discharged from the Army.
The two eldest girls are scholarship students at the School of
Nursing, Ewha Woman's University, the best university for women. The remaining three daughters expect to follow their sisters'
footsteps.

Having heard that overseas job opportunities for professional
nurses are best in West Germany and the United States and that
nurses in these countries are treated with respect, P'yŏngyang-
mansin has had her daughters take both German and English as
foreign languages in high school and college. She hopes that her
youngest son will want to study medicine. She is determined that
each of her children shall have a professional occupation which is
in high demand both at home and abroad; but most particularly
that her daughters be prepared to start their adult lives abroad,
away from the social stigma of being daughters of a shaman
which might prevent them from making advantageous marriages.
She has already had one bitter experience of the stigma that
haunts the children of shamans in Korea.

Throughout his college years, her pharmacist son had been
dating a classmate, sometimes spending days together at her
home studying for examinations. When both graduated, he proposed marriage and was accepted. P'yŏngyang-mansin and her
family were overjoyed. They not only liked the girl but thought it
would be ideal to have a pharmacist daughter-in-law for their
son. To their surprise, the girl's family reacted violently. They
forced her to sever her relationship with her fiancé and renounce
him permanently. P'yŏngyang-mansin feels that the girl's family
exploited her son. He was good enough to help her study but not
good enough to be her husband. After all, being neighbors, they
had known of P'yŏngyang-mansin's shaman role and the nature
of the young people's relationship.

Apparently, both her son and his fiancée were deeply
traumatized by the incident. Her son's melancholy was beginning
to worry her when he asked her to arrange a marriage for him.

He had no further use for romance, he said; he wanted to get married as soon as possible after his discharge from the Army. P'yŏngyang-mansin was actively looking for a potential daughter-in-law in the summer of 1971 when I first met her. She was also trying to sell her house and feeling quite bitter about the harsh bargain prospective buyers drove because it was a shaman's house. Then, with a smile, she told me that ironically she herself was getting an exceptional deal because the *tang* ("shrine") she was negotiating to buy could only be sold to a shaman. It had belonged to her recently deceased "adoptive mother" shaman. It is an old building—she guesses at least seventy years old—and as there was no shaman in her family or kin group, her survivors were anxious to be rid of it.

As the shrine was within walking distance of her house, she took me to look at it. The place is an ideal one for a shaman with a family. Surrounded on three sides by vegetable fields, it is relatively isolated and combines the living quarters with a traditional *tang* on an impressive scale. The front entrance has two gates leading into a spacious courtyard measuring about thirty by forty feet with both a well and a tapwater pump in one corner of it. Midway in the court, against a stone wall, there is a traditionally built, semi-subterranean storage house with a roof deck for crocks of soy sauce and bean pastes. Six rooms, including the *maru*[6] and the kitchen, are arranged in an L-shape around the courtyard. Heavy wooden sliding doors at the far end of the *maru* separate the living quarters from the *tang*, a mirror-image of the living quarters in the arrangement of rooms; only the kitchen is missing, and the courtyard is about a third of the other in size. Each room is a complete and separate shrine, each with a different clustering of painted images of deities on the wall. The *maru* in the *tang* is crowded with antique furniture and shamanistic paraphernalia. Tossed carelessly about beneath the *maru* are dusty but genuine porcelain dishes from the Yi Dynasty. Costumes for various *kut* fill several chests and closets. It is the most elaborate private *tang* I have seen; it is second only to Kuksadang, a government designated cultural treasure of Korea!

P'yŏngyang-mansin wanted to buy this *tang* for a number of reasons. Every serious shaman dreams of building a *tang* of her own, but to buy an established *tang* with a clientele already attached to it is preferable. It is analogous to buying a good medical practice in America. She will be able to "inherit" her deceased "adoptive mother's" clients, most of whom she already knows. The *tang* would also be a good insurance against old age and diminishing energy, for she can always rent out her *tang* to shamans for a share of their *kut* performed there. In the meantime, she does not have to share the revenue from her own *kut* with any *tang-jigi* ("shrine keeper") and may be able to reduce the number of *kut* she has to perform for a given level of income. She says a *kut* is "exhausting to the body."

P'yŏngyang-mansin speculates that she could have bought the *tang* many times over with the money she has had to "kick back" to her "adoptive mother" shaman for all the *kut* she held there during the sixteen years of her practice. The place will also enable her to maintain a better spatial segregation between her domestic and professional activities. Her present home is too small for her large family and growing clientele. She also has sentimental reasons for wanting to buy the *tang*; she was initiated in this *tang*.

When I saw P'yŏngyang-mansin and her family again in 1972 they were settled in their new place and had a telephone as well. During my absence her son was married and established in a drug store of his own, and his wife was expecting their first child. P'yŏngyang-mansin's eldest daughter had graduated from Ewha Woman's University School of Nursing and was working at Seoul Municipal Hospital to comply with a condition of her scholarship. P'yŏngyang-mansin brought out a stack of photo albums for me to look over, appreciate, and be brought up to date on the many events which had taken place in their lives during my absence.

P'yŏngyang-mansin's daughter-in-law is attractive, college educated, and the only daughter of a wealthy man who owns a chain of entertainment houses in Seoul. P'yŏngyang-mansin contends that since entertainers and people in related businesses have traditionally been scorned almost as badly as shamans, it would have been difficult for her daughter-in-law to make a socially respectable marriage, her wealth and college education notwithstanding. She thinks her daughter-in-law did very well to get her son and admits that she considered her family background the most outstanding feature in making the marriage arrangement. She need not fear that her son will be constantly subject to humiliation by his wife or her family for being a shaman's son.

P'yŏngyang-mansin persuaded her daughter-in-law's father to set her son up in a drugstore of his own in a provincial capital where no one knows of their respective, socially embarrassing family backgrounds. She thinks they have a good chance at a respectable life there, especially if she herself refrains from visiting them. After all, her son is a pharmacist from Seoul National University and owns his own drugstore.

P'yŏngyang-mansin's own practice was also flourishing in 1972. On the seventh of July (lunar calendar, a day of special significance to believers of shamans), she had two assistant shamans, two hired women, all five of her daughters, her niece, and her mother-in-law working at breakneck pace to accommodate clients who filled every room but the *sarang-bang* in the house. Like modern American medical doctors who keep several examination rooms going and shuttle among them, P'yŏngyang-mansin had each of her five shrine rooms occupied by clients who were at different stages of rituals. She and an assistant shaman at the drum followed the other assistant shaman from room to room, picking up the ritual procedures where she had left off. The hired women and the younger daughters and niece worked in the kitchen under the supervision of the mother-in-law while the older daughters performed all the supportive activities necessary to keep the various groups of clients moving smoothly through their rituals. The only non-participating members of the family were the seven-year-old son and the husband. They watched T.V. in the *sarang-bang* where they invited me to join them if I got tired of the shamanistic activities.

In 1973 when I last saw her, P'yŏngyang-mansin's practice was suffering from the general, nationwide governmental suppression of all traditional activities that it deemed wasteful and obstructive to modernization. Shamanistic rituals were foremost among those forbidden activities, but she had an idea that shamanistic rites (*kut*) presented as an art form would be a popular attraction for foreign tourists in Korea and wanted official sponsorship to stage such a show. She was not optimistic about such a plan materializing and asked if I knew any influential government official who might help her.

Her other plans were unfolding according to schedule, however. She was now a grandmother and her son's pharmacy was thriving. Her eldest daughter was about to embark for

Los Angeles where she had obtained a nursing position. P'yŏngyang-mansin called her at the nurses' dormitory to instruct her to come home with her passport and visa to show me and to receive orientation from me about working and living in America. Her second daughter, to graduate in another year, and her third daughter who had just begun her first year at Ewha Woman's University School of Nursing expected to follow their eldest sister to America when they too had repaid their scholarships.

P'yŏngyang-mansin was the second child and the first daughter born to her merchant parents. Her birth was accepted as a matter of course by her parents; her brother had been born three years earlier.

Her father sold dry goods in one of the city's open markets where he was assisted by his wife, who divided her time between home and the market. Though not wealthy, they lived in their own small but tile-roofed house with her father's mother. Unlike her father, a native of P'yŏngyang, her mother had been a peasant's daughter, moving to the city only upon marriage. Apparently, she quickly learned the intricacies of city life as well as features peculiar to the life style of marketplace merchants. P'yŏngyang-mansin remembers her grandmother praising her mother for her energy and quick wit.

P'yŏngyang-mansin's mother recalls[7] that some members of her family and kin group disapproved of her marriage, considering it humiliating for a farmer, a *yangmin* ("the good people"), to marry his daughter to a merchant, a member of the inferior *sangmin* ("common people") class.[8] Others, especially young women in the family and the village, reassured her that she was lucky to marry into a city family. They said any life was bound to be easier than that of a farmer's wife. She was too young, she says, to worry about marrying up or down in social status. She was just exicted about going to the city which she had visited only once before, and hoped for a kindly mother-in-law.

Once married, she found she liked her husband well enough, though he was nearly ten years her senior. Her mother-in-law turned out to be a kindly person who was continuously impressed with her energy and hard work and did not refrain from openly praising her. Not being constitutionally strong themselves, her husband and mother-in-law appreciated her robust health and untiring strength. The early years of her marriage, she recalls, were without any outstanding difficulties. When P'yŏngyang-mansin was born, she strapped her on her back, as she had done with her son, and resumed her activities both at home and at the marketplace as soon as the traditional postpartum convalescence period of twenty-one days was over. When P'yŏngyang-mansin was old enough not to require frequent breast-feeding, she left her in the grandmother's care, along with her brother, while she assisted her husband. She says her children had a smooth childhood during their early years. P'yŏngyang-mansin was a happy and a healthy infant, already quite large for her age and cheerful in disposition. Apparently, she did not have much time to "enjoy" her children in the sense that modern American mothers are told to or claim to do.

P'yŏngyang-mansin has no particular recollection of her early childhood, but has fond memories of her grandmother as a kindly and warm person. Her father, typically, did not concern himself personally with her daily care.

As she grew, P'yŏngyang-mansin was left increasingly in the care of her grandmother. During this period, her brother was almost her only playmate, for her grandmother was fearful of letting them play outside the house. According to her mother, P'yŏngyang-mansin and her brother got along well and were not troublesome to their grandmother. Nevertheless, she tried to relieve her mother-in-law whenever feasible by taking P'yŏngyang-mansin to the marketplace where she played quietly or watched her mother conduct business. By then, her mother enjoyed the full confidence of her father and dealt with both retail customers and the wholesale dealers who supplied them.

At home, P'yŏngyang-mansin's mother did all the heavy household chores while her grandmother cooked the evening meals. Her mother routinely went to the marketplace to help her father pack up the merchandise for the night and transport it home. During meals, her father had a separate table but generally ate in the same room with the family, who sat around a common table. P'yŏngyang-mansin's mother recalls that her mother-in-law used to urge her to try this and eat more of that, saying: "You must be hungry after your day in the marketplace." For her part, she showed her gratitude by declining while urging her mother-in-law to eat. At the same time, both women picked out and fed choice morsels to the children. P'yŏng-mansin herself recalls that her father frequently left uneaten the major portion of some dish or other that she and her brother were fond of (but which was served only to him), saying, "Here, Mother, I can't finish it. Please taste some." Her grandmother would protest that he should have eaten more, but would take the food and feed it to her and her brother.

P'yŏngyang-mansin's mother explains that because her mother-in-law was a city woman, she was much more sparing and gentle in her treatment of people than farm folks were, and continued to be kind to her throughout her life. She says she and her mother-in-law got along like a mother and a daughter.

Her husband was not given to small talk or complaints; if he had something to say about their business or the family, he discussed it with her, her mother-in-law, or both, as was appropriate. He was content with his children but did not fuss over them.

P'yŏngyang-mansin's childhood continued uneventfully until, at age eight in 1933, when she lost her grandmother. She feels that she and her mother were the most deeply affected by her grandmother's death, which heralded far more serious changes in their lives than just the loss of her familiar presence.

About this time, the Japanese colonial regime was tightening its reins on the Koreans and exploiting them far more systematically and harshly than before. For example, their program of deculturating Koreans and assimilating them into Japanese culture and society was already quietly but deliberately being implemented in urban centers (Cf. R. Kim 1970). As a merchant family, P'yŏngyang-mansin's family did not suffer quite so severely as the peasants whose dependence on the market exchange economy, which they neither understood nor could influence meaningfully, grew alarmingly each year. They were, in addition, the most heavily taxed of all groups.

For some time before his mother's death, P'yŏngyang-mansin's father had been feeling discouraged about their future prospects and had talked of moving to Manchuria where, according to rumor, the Japanese treatment of Koreans was less restrictive and where economic opportunities for Koreans were better. When his mother died, P'yŏngyang-mansin's father decided to move and two years later, when P'yŏngyang-mansin was ten, the family emigrated to Manchuria, settling in a small town just south of Harbin. The year was 1935.

P'yŏngyang-mansin remembers the long train journey across the border as having been exciting in a "spooky sort of way." She was enthralled by the strange scenery, language, clothes, and people. She was shocked to discover that some people dressed in Chinese clothes were actually Koreans. She did not see any place, however, that she thought she would like better than her hometown of P'yŏngyang.

With her grandmother no longer available, P'yŏngyang-mansin had to assume most of the household chores that used to be performed by her. Her mother's time was required almost totally in helping her father manage a small general store they had opened. P'yŏngyang-mansin does not think she minded the nearly complete responsibility she had of running the household at age ten, for she had been helping her grandmother all along and could manage most of the tasks fairly well. Besides, she says, her older brother was always very helpful.

In Manchuria, she and her brother resumed their schooling which had been interrupted for over a year because of their relocation. As there were not enough Koreans in their town to justify a segregated school for them, Korean children were enrolled in the local Japanese school. According to P'yŏngyang-mansin, she and her brother were the only Koreans in their respective classes. Although she had wanted desperately to return to school, she felt terrified each morning at the thought of actually going to the Japanese school. Her Japanese was very poor, she was older than anyone in her class, and she was a head taller than almost everyone in the class, including the boys. What was more, her breasts were conspicuously large by comparison.

Her Japanese classmates were perfunctorily polite and friendly in the way that is "characteristic of the crafty and fawning Japanese," but no one really befriended her. She kept mostly to herself, applying herself diligently to her studies. Her mother counseled her that she was going to school for education, not to make Japanese friends. Education, her mother said repeatedly, was the key to gaining a measure of personal freedom and independence for herself. Her mother was convinced that education was the chief difference between their situation and that of the people whose life styles she envied. She was determined that both of her children should get as much education as possible.

In 1938, three years after they had moved to Manchuria, where their life was now fairly well settled, P'yŏngyang-mansin's father died unexpectedly of acute pneumonia. P'yŏngyang-mansin was thirteen, and her brother almost seventeen. Her mother did not feel that she could manage the store alone as a widow, not because of the work involved—she had always worked with her husband—but because she felt too vulnerable as a widow with no one to rely upon on matters of business. She felt her son was as yet too young to be considered a reckoning factor by her counterparts in business. She therefore sold the store and moved the family farther south to a Manchurian border town. It was close enough to P'yŏngyang for easy travel by train (and possible on foot during the winter when the Yalu River froze over).

There, her mother rented a room with a kitchen in the house of a Korean family and, having enrolled her children in school, started her career as an itinerant peddler. In 1938, train transportation between Manchuria and Korea was still a matter of purchasing a ticket, although subsequently during World War II travel across the border became highly restrictive for Koreans. Her mother went back to P'yŏngyang to old business associates to purchase goods in demand by Koreans living in Manchuria and peddled these items from house to house to support the family. She was gone from home a week at a time. During her mother's absences, P'yŏngyang-mansin kept house and cooked for herself and her brother, who was always protective and helpful. He did most of the heavy chores.

When she was fourteen and nearly ready to graduate from elementary school, she began to feel unwell but without any well-defined symptoms. She suffered from a general condition of malaise. Every doctor her mother consulted said there was nothing the matter with her physically. In desperation, her mother consulted a *mudang* who diagnosed P'yŏngyang-mansin's illness as *sinbyŏng*. She prophesied that P'yŏngyang-mansin would become a *mudang*. Alarmed, her mother kept the information secret. (P'yŏngyang-mansin first learned of this when she was twenty-three years old and suffering from her third bout with *sinbyŏng*.)

She cajoled and encouraged her daughter to eat and get well for the sake of her mother, suggesting when P'yŏngyang-mansin got well, she could go to the local Japanese Commercial High School and learn to be a typist. As it was a newly emergent occupation and considered a highly skilled one for females, she told her daughter that if she became a competent typist she might be able to help support the family and perhaps send her brother to college. With a college education, her brother would surely be able to help improve their lot in life.

P'yŏngyang-mansin's mother also realized that her long and frequent absences had been very difficult for her daughter, although she had never complained about them. P'yŏngyang-mansin had no close friends of her own age, only the children of the landlord, and this concerned her mother. She decided to give up her itinerant peddling and find something near home. When she told her daughter that the increasingly stricter border patrol by the Japanese made her trips to Korea too risky to continue and that she decided to find work near home, her daughter seemed to rally noticeably from her illness. P'yŏngyang-mansin recovered from her mysterious illness shortly after her mother stoped traveling, but attributes it to her mother's devoted nursing. When she graduated from the elementary school, she enrolled in the local Japanese Commercial High School as had been planned.

In the meantime, the fear that her daughter might indeed be destined to become a shaman rooted itself firmly in P'yŏngyang-mansin's mother's heart, for the elderly shaman she had consulted persisted in wanting to adopt her daughter. Although she flatly refused the request, she became sufficiently alarmed by the implication that she continued with the daily devotional rite prescribed by the shaman during her daughter's illness, long after recovery. She thus hoped to keep the spirits appeased and distracted from her daughter.

At eighteen, P'yŏngyang-mansin graduated from the Commercial High School with a successful record and obtained a position as a typist with a Japanese printing firm, where, with one exception, she served satisfactorily until the end of World War II two years later. When she was nineteen she began to feel vaguely unwell again. As before, her mother offered daily devotional ritual to shamanistic spirits, and P'yŏngyang-mansin recovered in the course of several weeks. She was able to work most of the time but suffered from an inner terror bordering on panic. Unlike before, she was hearing voices, and her hallucinatory experiences were so frightening that she was afraid to confide even in her mother. Now, reviewing the experience retrospectively, she says it was her second call to the role of *mudang*. Her mother echoes

her. She says she knew at the time that it was another supernatural call for her daughter to assume the shaman role, although
she said nothing of it to her daughter. She was all but resigned to
her daughter's becoming a *mudang* by this time but still hoped
that she might marry first.

Asked if there had been any extraordinary, stressful conditions in their lives at the time, neither P'yŏngyang-mansin nor her
mother can recall any. However, the onset of P'yŏngyang-
mansin's second bout with *sinbyŏng* in 1944 coincided with highly
charged rumors in the Korean community there that Japan would
lose the war. While such rumors nearly always ended in happy
speculations of an independent Korea and the expatriates' return,
they also presaged a future of great uncertainty for them. It was
generally an anxious period for Koreans in Manchuria. When the
Japanese surrendered the next year on 15 August 1945, the consequences for Korea as a nation and Korean expatriates in Manchuria proved devastatingly different from what had been specu-
lated and hoped.

There was no question in their minds but what they should
return to Korea, and P'yŏngyang-mansin's family were among
the first to return. However, they had no sooner settled down in
their hometown of P'yŏngyang than they sensed the development of a political climate frighteningly reminiscent of the
Japanese colonial rule. In October 1945, they fled to Seoul in
South Korea where they knew no one. P'yŏngyang-mansin was
twenty at the time. Fortunately, she soon found a job as a typist in
a printing firm and became the mainstay of her family's support.
Her mother supplemented their income by selling used household items in the marketplace, and they managed to avoid starvation, although her brother could not find work that winter.

It was at the printing firm that P'yŏngyang-mansin met her
husband, then a minor clerk in the firm. She says he was young,
handsome, and touchingly kind to her. Though she was embarrassed to speak with her strong P'yŏngyang accent, he found
excuses to engage her in conversation, to take her to supper after
work, and to court her ardently in general. She fell in love with
him and began to see him regularly after work in prearranged
places. Three months later, she found herself pregnant. When her
partner learned of it, he offered marriage which she gratefully
accepted. But they kept it a secret until the physical evidence of

her pregnancy was no longer concealable. When her mother learned about it, she was somewhat disturbed but not excessively so. She liked her son-in-law but could not invite him to live with them as she and her two adult children were sharing a single room at the time. Since both P'yŏngyang-mansin and her husband were contributing to the support of their respective families, they could not set up independent housekeeping. Unable to think of any other options, he simply took her over to his own family one day and announced that she was his wife.

During the post-World War II period of their courtship, the entire Korean society was in a state of chaos. Many once inviolate cultural norms were being circumvented under the unusual conditions. Even so, unchaperoned courtship without parental consent was clearly viewed as wrong. Certainly, contracting their own marriage in secrecy was an act of defiance against both family and society. P'yŏngyang-mansin says she knew she was misbehaving in seeing her future husband secretly but adds that she felt unable to help herself about it. He was almost her only source of solace during this period, but she also remembers feeling heady with excitement and fear, mostly fear, in carrying on her clandestine romance with him. As it turned out, her love affair and resulting pregnancy and marriage were secretly welcomed by her mother, who saw in the events the possibility that her daughter might escape her destiny to become a shaman; but her husband's family was enraged.

They felt violated in one of their most sacred privileges, that of selecting a daughter-in-law, and balked at having to accept P'yŏngyang-mansin. Although they ultimately took her in—after all, she was carrying a member, potentially male, of their lineage—they were at pains to keep her constantly reminded of the resentment and hostility they felt toward her. They made the necessary adjustment in living space to give P'yŏngyang-mansin and her husband a room of their own, but the house, though above average in size, was already overcrowded with about twenty people living in it. Among them were her husband's married sister and her several children who were living there temporarily because of some circumstances in her husband's business affairs.

Although pregnant, P'yŏngyang-mansin was asked to continue her job as a typist, as the family needed her income if it was to feed and house her. She accepted this demand and contributed her earnings to the household purse, controlled by her mother-in-law and sister-in-law. She did not feel that she had an alternative. Not only that, she was so grateful to them for taking her in that she was, she says, willing to do almost anything to repay them. But the atmosphere of hostile tension between her and her in-laws, especially her mother-in-law and her sister-in-law, continued unabated. She had anticipated strain in her domestic role even before she went to live with her in-laws, but the actual conflicts which emerged immediately exceeded any of her expectations. She says of the first year of her marriage:

> . . . My sister-in-law proved to be the most difficult one for me. If I lay down—I was always fatigued because I worked all day and was pregnant too—she called me lazy and other choice names; if I ate anything, she said I ate like a bull . . . that I was a North Korean clod. If anything went wrong, whether it was burnt rice or a serious mishap in her husband's business, she said it was my fault—it was all because a stranger had intruded into their household. . . . My mother-in-law's temper was quick and her tongue, razor sharp, too. . . . She and my sister-in-law used to watch every spoonful of food that went into my mouth. . . . My mother-in-law would tell others in my hearing that I ate like a bull and slept like a hibernating bear. They continuously insinuated that I did not work enough, but I was working at my job all day and turning over all my pay. . . . They never said a kind word about that.

She continued with her job even after her son was born. She had hoped to stay home but no one suggested that she quit, and she knew that the money was tight. She remembers hurrying home from work with painfully gorged breasts and being too tired to do anything but lie down with her son as he nursed greedily. It had been agreed that her sister-in-law would do the cooking for supper and she would clean up afterwards, but the arrangement did not seem to please her sister-in-law.

> The very sight of me with my son cradled in my arms seemed to rankle my sister-in-law. . . . She'd bang things around in the kitchen and say to no one in particular but always loud enough for me to hear: "Look at that! Her luck is bursting. She lies about and waits for her elder sister-in-law to cook for her so she can eat like a bull."

It galled her so much to have the in-laws begrudge her the food she helped them buy that she often went without food, feigning illness. Sometimes the family finished eating before she got home from work, but no one greeted her with "You must be hungry. Here, we have saved your food."

> I'd look around in the kitchen but there would be no evidence of food being kept for me anywhere. . . . I just didn't feel comfortable enough to go scrounging in the kitchen to see if there was something I could eat. I often went hungry that first year.

P'yŏngyang-mansin concedes that her in-laws had some good reasons for being upset with her at times. For example, having grown up in a simple household, she did not know how to fit smoothly into the patterns of a large extended household. Also, there was considerable regional variance in the way cooking and other domestic chores were done between Seoul and P'yŏngyang. Her North Korean ways constantly irritated her mother-in-law and sister-in-law. Since she worked six days a week and had an infant son to care for when she got home, she says she actually did little housework.

> I guess they just took a dislike to me because of the way I came into their household. . . . It seemed at times that they were determined not to like a North Korean daughter-in-law . . . they found the way I did anything at all a source of aggravation. I think the very sight of me was a thorn in their eyes. Certainly, I heard all that I ever care to hear about being a North Korean clod from them in the early years of my marriage. . . . One thing to be said in their favor is that they never complained about having to look after my son while I was at work.

Even more vexing than her mother-in-law and sister-in-law during the first year of her marriage was her deteriorating health, she says. She felt sickly throughout her pregnancy and, as she had to return to her job right away, she never really recovered fully from her childbirth. She says the first year of her marriage was more hellish than living through the Korean War with small children.

Of her husband during the first year of her marriage, she says:

> He never stood up against his mother or sister when they abused me verbally or in any way take my side against them in

their presence. But he always tried to comfort me and console me when we were alone at night . . . he used to apologize for his mother and sister. . . . I could not have endured the first year of our marriage without his comforting reassurances. He wanted so much for me to be able to quit work so I could stay home. . . . He thought it would ease a lot of the tension. . . .

All her husband's soothing reassurances notwithstanding, P'yŏngyang-mansin remained entrapped in a dilemma as long as she continued to work outside the household. The only way she could have satisfied her mother-in-law's and sister-in-law's demands that she perform all the domestic duties incumbent upon a daughter-in-law was to quit her job, but they also insisted that she keep her job. In addition, they made the situation even more intolerable by attacking her on personal attributes which were beyond her help. Though she tried not to take their criticisms personally, she found it almost impossible. She felt shredded by conflicts. She yearned for their acceptance and approval but felt helpless to earn it, for they attacked her mostly for being a Northerner. To deny their accusations, she would have had to disprove their accusations for every person of her regional origin. She felt that her only defense was withdrawal and concealment of her feelings from her in-laws.

While she was still struggling to evolve more effective ways of coping with these difficulties, she realized that she was pregnant again. Her first child was barely a year old. As her pregnancy advanced, she could no longer keep up with the demands of the family and her job, so she quit her job without first seeking permission from her mother-in-law. But even after she quit her job, she was unable to contribute significantly more to her domestic role as her health was poor. Her mother-in-law and sister-in-law became furious with her and accused her of malingering.

P'yŏngyang-mansin recalls that she became so sensitive to their accusations that she did not feel free to eat until her hunger was satisfied or even to eat every meal. She suffered from poor health and malnutrition throughout her second pregnancy as a consequence, though she sometimes managed to escape to her mother's place nearby for the comfort and food that she craved. However, since her brother still had no steady work, she could not impose on them too frequently, either. They still lived in a single rented room.

Her second child was also a son. He screamed almost inces-
santly from hunger, as, unlike with her first child, P'yŏngyang-
mansin's breasts were nearly dry. Her mother braved the inhospi-
tality of her in-laws to come over daily to help her and assist her
in-laws in household chores to assure her the traditional twenty-
one day postpartum recovery period, but P'yŏngyang-mansin
remained in a weakened condition for months afterwards. Her
son died when he was two months old. It was during the months
following his death that she had her third bout with *sinbyŏng*; she
was twenty-three at the time.

By now she had little difficulty in recognizing the symptoms
of her possession sickness. This time her symptoms were more
sharply defined and more severe as well. She was not only hearing things but seeing things as well. Her ears rang a lot, and she
could hear voices whispering in them; and, when she yielded to
the urge to talk, she uttered prophetic statements. Neighbors and
relatives began to speculate that she had been "caught by the
spirits," and was possessed. She suffered from terrible palpitations of the heart, indigestion, and dizzy spells, sometimes alternately and sometimes in combinations. She was constantly afraid
of being caught hallucinating by her husband or his family. She
was determined to overcome these symptoms and began to read a
lot of novels as a way of fighting off the hallucinations. Her
in-laws, however, pointed to her engrossed reading as additional
proof of her laziness and were severely irritated.

Her mother alone knew what P'yŏngyang-mansin was undergoing. Heartbroken by her daughter's suffering, she urged
P'yŏngyang-mansin to receive the spirits and end her misery. She
was convinced that her grandchild had been taken by the spirits
to "break the back" of P'yŏngyang-mansin's resistance to their
call. She was sure that worse things were yet to come, that
P'yŏngyang-mansin's own death would follow. She declared that
she preferred a live *mudang* for a daughter than a dead one,
arguing that it was an unavoidable fate and that such fate had
befallen others.

P'yŏngyang-mansin was pained to see her husband's bewilderment over her illness and behavior. Her in-laws, who believed
in shamans, were becoming frightened. They eased their relentless attacks on her and brought in the prescribed Chinese herbal
medicine to nurse her back to health. Though slowly, she reco-

vered and had another child in 1950, the year the Korean War
broke out. In the meantime, with the departure of the spiteful
sister-in-law and her brood of children from the household,
P'yŏngyang-mansin and her mother-in-law developed a more
tolerable relationship with each other. Together they managed a
frugal household on her husband's meager salary, which was
supplemented by income from rooms which they rented out.

The still precariously balanced harmony in the household
was just at the threshold of becoming a pattern when shifting
events in the Korean War forced them to evacuate from Seoul
with the retreating ROK Army and the United Nations forces.
P'yŏngyang-mansin's mother and brother, who had married in
the meantime, joined them with his family. They left Seoul the
last week in December 1950, not knowing where to go except to
head south. Eventually, they set up temporary housekeeping in
Chŏlla Namdo (South Chŏlla Province) and began their life as war
refugees for the next three years. In the meantime, her husband
and one of his brothers had been drafted by the Army. Left alone
with her mother-in-law to look after the entire household,
P'yŏngyang-mansin depended heavily on her mother for
psychological support. Materially, however, it was she who
needed to help her mother and brother out periodically. As her
husband's Army salary barely paid for his own personal needs
and his occasional visits home, P'yŏngyang-mansin enlisted the
help of her mother and mother-in-law to set up a business, selling
hot meals on the streets, thus eking out a survival existence for
both households.

When Seoul was reclaimed by South Korea following the
cease-fire of 1953, they were among the first to return. Fortunately, their house had escaped destruction, but they had neither
income nor food. Though they were facing starvation,
P'yŏngyang-mansin herself could do little to alleviate it. Shortly
after their return, she gave birth to her fourth child, another girl.
Discharged from the Army in the winter of 1954, her husband
joined them at home. Though he went out daily looking for work,
he found none. Taking advantage of the critical housing shortage,
they again rented out every spare room in the house and thus
staved off starvation. Although her mother and brother's family
had come to live with them by her mother-in-law's invitation, it
soon became apparent that she resented them living there rent

free. P'yŏngyang-mansin's husband did not complain, but the general tension reached such a point that she felt it best to move her natal family out to a nearby shack made of cardboard and flattened American beer and soda cans soon after their return to Seoul.

In 1955, P'yŏngyang-mansin gave birth to yet another daughter, but her postpartum recovery was slow and problematic. She hemorrhaged intermittently, often fainting at the slightest exertion. Her husband became despondent and gave up all pretenses of hope for finding a respectable job. He went to his mother-in-law and brother-in-law for help in getting the kinds of piece work they had been doing for a living. He mobilized everyone old enough to paste pieces of newspaper into cone-shaped bags or to put matchboxes together. The work was backbreakingly tedious and paid miserably. The adults no longer ate three meals a day.

It was during this period that P'yŏngyang-mansin felt the call of the supernatural once again. She was thirty-two at the time. Despite her weakness from the prolonged postpartum hemorrhaging, she would awaken abruptly from sleep sometimes and rush out of the house, heading toward a Buddhist temple. At other times, she would just go into the mountains. Or, sometimes, she would start jumping up and down vigorously, stopping only when someone in the family restrained her. If her family questioned her as to her whereabouts, she would answer, "Oh, to see *sinjang-nim* ("a shamanistic general of exceptional ability")." Speaking from her experiences of this period, P'yŏngyang-mansin says that no one would "go in for 'shamanizing' " if the symptoms of spirit were not so extraordinary.

> It's because you get so sick, faint so many times, and such that you finally invite the spirits in and become a *mudang*. . . . At a certain point, it's simply the lesser evil. . . .

P'yŏngyang-mansin likens the course of possession sickness to the fluctuating behavior patterns of an insane person. "They [the spirits] come to you in spasms. At the peak, the symptoms intensify for a few days and then let up." Strange dreams which are vividly recollected are also a part of the process, she says. She herself dreamed a lot during this period. ". . . Soon as I woke from them [dreams], I knew their meaning. I tried to suppress my own understanding of them because I was scared."

In one dream, still vivid in her memory, she went to a Buddhist temple said to be Japanese; in front there was a woman, who looked Japanese and was dressed in a *kimono*. Her long hair hung loosely about her hips, and there was a halo about her head. P'yŏngyang-mansin saw many people going up to her and bowing. She did likewise. At this point, the lady in the *kimono* singled her out from the crowd and, calling her by name, motioned her to come nearer. When P'yŏngyang-mansin approached her, she asked:

> "Why do you bow to me?" I told her I was in pain but couldn't describe it to her. Hearing this, she took a golden cup and, filling it with crystal clear water, handed it to me, saying: "Drink." As I drained the cup, an old woman who had been bowing next to me asked me why I had come there. When I told her I had come because I was sick, she pulled out a Buddhist rosary and put it over my head. I got a strong feeling that if I used a rosary that had been used in a temple, I would get better. And while thinking this, I woke up.

In another dream, P'yŏngyang-mansin was again at some Buddhist temple where all the gates were bolted. When she pushed a door, however, it opened. Inside, there were banner-carrying generalissimos of olden days riding away with fierce looking, wide-open eyes. Scared, she closed her eyes and tried another door. She saw the same scene. But when she opened a third door, there was a lady who looked as though she might have had her *hwan'gap* ("sixtieth birthday"). A handsome woman, she was sitting on a divan and turned around toward P'yŏngyang-mansin. Very casually and as if she had been expecting her, the old lady said, "Oh, you have come." And as she said this, she pulled out her *pinyŏ* (a hair pin which is a straight rod made of silver, gold, or jade, measuring sometimes sixteen inches or more) and handed it to P'yŏngyang-mansin. She noticed that it was slightly curved from wear but shone with a brilliant luster. As she took the pin from the old lady, the latter said, "I've been waiting for you here because I wanted to give that to you."[9] Holding the pin in her hand, she was taking detailed notice of the old lady's face and body and thinking, "What a handsome woman!" when she woke from her dream.

P'yŏngyang-mansin continues:

> The dream had been so vivid that I couldn't forget it, but I had

not thought of it much for some time when I went to attend a
chaesu-kut ("a rite invoking good fortune") that my mother was
holding for my brother. The instant I entered my mother's place,
I recognized the handsome woman of my dream. She was the
chief officiating shaman at my mother's *kut*. There was no mistake. That happened about three months after the dream. I
recognized her right away; I wondered how a person I had met
in a dream could have come to do a *kut* for Mother. I was
shocked, so I told her of meeting her in my dream. . . . The old
shaman said: "We must have been fated to tie our knots together by the spirits. You must become a daughter to me. . . ."

It was at this *kut* that P'yŏngyang-mansin invited the spirits
to possess her. At one stage in a full-scale *kut*, having twelve
distinct stages, patrons are invited by shamans to don their costumes and dance.[10] P'yŏngyang-mansin was dancing during this
stage when suddenly she began to clap her hands and talk.[11] She
says:

My *malmun* ("gate of speech") was loosened by the spirits.
People exclaimed that I was "caught by the spirits." . . . I had
finally become fully possessed. . . . On that day, the old
mudang and I agreed to become adoptive mother and daughter.
. . . We worked together ever since, she teaching me whatever I
needed to know and I, assisting her and learning by doing and
watching. . . . She officiated my *naerim-kut* ("initiation rite").
. . . When she died, I "inherited" her clientele. . . .

It was this old shaman's house/shrine complex that
P'yŏngyang-mansin was negotiating to buy when I first met her
in 1971. In any case, the old shaman identified the spirits which
possessed P'yŏngyang-mansin during the latter's subsequent
naerim-kut. As far as P'yŏngyang-mansin knew, there had been
no *mudang* either on her side or on her husband's side. But she
had a grand-aunt, her grandfather's sister, who died while possessed without ever becoming a shaman. According to
P'yŏngyang-mansin:

When my grand-aunt's in-laws discovered that she was possessed by the spirits, they subjected her to moxabustion and had
Buddhist prayers read over her to rid her of the spirits. When
these measures didn't work, they tied her up and locked her
away in a room. Still, the spirits would not leave her. She finally
died, while still chained in her room. It is her ghost which
possessed me. . . . It has taken her three generations to find a

lodging place. There was also a Buddhist nun in my family, some generations back. Her ghost had been homeless all these generations too, and now she too possesses me. . . .

P'yŏngyang-mansin says that until this, the fourth call from the spirits, she had not been able to imagine becoming a *mudang*, only the horror of becoming one. In fact, she had even attended a Christian church for a while hoping that the Christian God would get the spirits "off my back." She had also considered suicide to avoid becoming a *mudang*. But the fourth time, she reassessed her feelings about the prospects of becoming a *mudang*. She says:

> I looked over my situation and decided that, since our life was so poor, I might as well accept my calling and see if I could use my calling to give the children a full belly and a good education. . . .
>
> Just numerically, I figured that by sacrificing myself, just one person, I could possibly make life better for many more, especially the children. So, I decided to give myself up for my children and become a *mudang*.[12] It was my destiny, anyway.

It is a Korean folk belief, particularly strong among followers of shamans, that the newly possessed *mudang* is at the peak of her potency as a medium. Consequently, clients travel far in search of such a *mudang*. The word of P'yŏngyang-mansin's "clapping of hands" spread fast, and she was immediately in demand. She began receiving clients in her mother's place the very next day. She saw forty to fifty clients in a single day in the beginning, making more money in one day than she had ever had for a month of housekeeping even when she and her husband were both working.

Her professional popularity posed several immediate and serious problems, however. First, she was absent from her husband's household for the major part of the day every day without adequate explanations for her absence. In her absence, her children's care fell on others, mostly her mother-in-law, and her neglected children became an irritable source of conflict between them. Third, she had no way of sensibly explaining the source of money that she used "greedily to buy some decent food for the family," unless she divulged her secret occupation. Fourth, it also created a problem for her natal family, as they had no privacy. Initially, she was unaware of these problems, so ecstatic was she with her new power.

She describes her feelings in the initial weeks following her possession as "intoxicating," as being "afloat on a cloud," and as being totally unconcerned with the mundane affairs of routine living. However, as she withdrew almost completely from her domestic role and moved more fully into her professional role, the problems already cited and other conflicts became magnified and forced themselves on her, demanding attention.

Her mother had anticipated these problems and suggested that she let her husband and mother-in-law know of her possession state and seek their support in having her initiation *kut*. Her mother reasoned that since people had been saying she acted like a possessed person, her mother-in-law would understand that it had finally come to pass.

Besides, she argued, they were believers in *mudang* and would certainly realize the inevitability of her becoming a *mudang*. P'yŏngyang-mansin did not share her mother's optimism.

Before she could resolve the matter in her own mind, however, they learned of her practice as a *mudang*. Clients calling early at her mother's place and not finding her there found their way to her husband's place. Her in-laws' reactions were swift and drastic, confirming her worst fears. They denounced her hysterically, bemoaning the shame that she brought upon their *kamun* ("reputation of the family"). Her mother-in-law demanded that she take her belongings and leave at once, never to "cast my shadow on their doorway." Her husband did not join his family in denouncing her but was dazed with bewilderment.

P'yŏngyang-mansin says she was herself in a terrible state of excitement and conflict, wanting to see her clients and yet being afraid to leave her husband's house lest she not be permitted to return. After a few days, she could not restrain herself; she began to see her clients again at her mother's place. She says that it is in the nature of *sinbyŏng* that one becomes indifferent to concerns that had normally had priority. Gradually, she grew indifferent to her mother-in-law's "ranting and raving" and even her children's sobbing. She sometimes completely forgot about her youngest daughter who still nursed, until the pain from her engorged breasts brought her sharply back to realization.

In terms of psychological pain—*kasŭm-ap'ŭgi* ("the hurting of the heart") she says her two eldest children suffered the most. She usually took the youngest with her when she went over to her mother's place to see clients. Someone, generally her mother-in-law, looked after the four-year-old girl left behind, but the two older ones ran loose in the neighborhood or hung about her mother's place. If she did not return home until late in the evening, her eldest son, eleven years old, waited outside the house, out of his grandmother's sight. He knew his grandmother would not bolt the gate against his mother so long as he was not yet home himself.

The tension generated in her husand's household by her *mudang* role reached a breaking point when her mother-in-law began to insist publicly that her husband do his filial duty by divorcing her. He finally told his mother that he could not throw out a woman he had never been able to treat properly as his wife and who had suffered such abuses from his own people all the years of their married life. He declared that he would sooner die that divorce his wife. He pleaded with his mother to consider her grandchildren—did she want them motherless children? His mother was not to be appeased. She said she would not suffer any further humiliation caused by "that Northerner," and persisted in demanding P'yŏngyang-mansin's return to her *ch'injŏng* ("natal household of married woman"). Her husband was equally adamant; for the first time, he stood up against his mother in open support of his wife. As a result, they moved out into a small rented house of their own in 1957, during the second month of her shaman career.

Her professional popularity continued unabated both for *chŏm* ("divination") and *kut* so that they could afford a house where she could receive clients and yet remain accessible to her children. Whenever possible her mother came to help with the cooking and other housekeeping chores that P'yŏngyang-mansin could not attend to. Her husband began to stay home almost all the time, partly out of shame, and he too looked after the children and other general household matters. If the baby needed to nurse, he called discreetly from the inner section of the house, and her clients, accustomed to male priority in daily life, deferred to his claim upon her and waited for her while she tended to the baby or fed the family. This also gave her a chance to take a much needed break from her clients and take some nourishment as well. If she had to go away overnight for a *kut*, then he was home to care for the children and deal with clients who called in her absence.

Although she assumed the role of household mistress when she and her husband moved out on their own, the functions normally entailed were actually carried out mostly by her mother and her husband. With P'yŏngyang-mansin pre-empted by the *mudang* role, there occurred a reversal of roles between her and her husband. She functioned as the main provider while he oversaw the internal management of the household and performed tasks normally carried out by women. P'yŏngyang-mansin describes the process of role reversal and the effect it had on the household.

Between ourselves, my husband and I have always gotten along just fine. . . . We don't even quarrel. My becoming a *mudang* hasn't changed the way we get along; in fact, in some ways, it has gotten better. . . .

Since I became a *mudang*, I haven't concerned myself with the management of the household much. I just bring in the money; my husband does the rest. You might say that my husband helps me immensely with work usually considered the duties of a wife and a mother . . . he does all the maintenance repair work around the house and manages the household money. . . .

I'm very open with him. I report to him every penny I earn and turn it over to him. How else am I going to uphold his authority and prestige before the chldren? And if he is belittled by me before the children, how can he manage them? From their pocket money to their school tuition, the children have to go before their father and ask for it. I never interfere with his decisions in front of the children. . . . Sometimes I try to influence his decisions, but never in front of the children.

If I were to lord it over my husband because I am the bread-winner in this household, would the children have any respect for me, his wife? The way I see it, the only way I can hope to accrue the respect due me as their mother and the wife of their father is by upholding his authority and prestige before the children while they are growing up. . . . Maybe not so much while they're young, but when their "heads have grown big," if they find they cannot respect their father because I have belittled him before them, they would have still greater contempt for me for having given them a father they could not respect. So, I have always kept my husband on a pedestal for the sake of everyone, including myself.

On ritually important occasions, I accompany my husband to

the homes of relatives or help him receive guests; otherwise, he does all the major purchasing for the household. My mother-in-law and/or daughters do the daily marketing. . . . As for official business, like paying taxes or registering a new child on the family genealogy, my husband again takes care of everything. He even goes to all the PTA meetings, although of late the older children have gone in his stead for their younger siblings. . . .

We generally discipline the children together, but because my husband is home more than I am, he ends up helping the children with homework and such more than I do. It's their father that the children go to to ask permission for going somewhere or to report back. . . .

Other difficulties which arose from P'yŏngyang-mansin's dual roles were not so easily resolved, however. She sometimes saw her first client at five in the morning, receiving sometimes forty to fifty clients in the course of a single day. She often worked through mealtime, stopping only when the threat of curfew sent clients hurrying home at about nine in the evening. Although her husband called her in periodically to nurse the baby, eat, and rest, clients left her completely exhausted. She suffered from a constant headache that grew worse as the smoke from the cigarettes and incense became thicker. When the last client had gone and the baby was nursed for the night, all she wanted was to lie down and rest. Sometimes she was too tired to fall asleep. At such times, she fantasized about going to a Buddhist temple in some isolated mountain and devoting herself completely to preparing for her professional role.

She became troubled when she realized that, despite his sympathy and support, she felt repelled by her husband sexually. Contrary to the impression her many pregnancies might give, her husband had shown little interest in sex, even during their courtship. Usually, he approached her about once a month, but her repulsion grew stronger as she continued in the *mudang* role. Although she had been told that this was an expected and natural phenomenon with *mudang*, she could not help feeling surprised and disturbed by it, especially as she had been the one always dissatisfied with their inactive sex life prior to her possession.

P'yŏngyang-mansin claims that she is by nature much more introverted than anyone is likely to suspect and that she found performing in *kut* excruciatingly embarrassing at first. It mortified

her to dance before male clients, especially when she was pregnant, a condition she repeated seven times after she became a
mudang.

> Imagine how I felt, not to mention how I must have looked,
> jumping up and down in a *kut* with my stomach bulging like a
> mound with a child! What I found even more humiliating were
> the whispered comments among the audience: "Tsk, tsk, what
> shame for so young and handsome a matron to be a *mudang*."

In any case, she was usually overcome by a shortness of
breath before her sense of shame could overwhelm her. Her
colleagues usually excused her from the most rigorous routines
involving dancing, but it made her feel guilty.

Her frequent pregnancies caused not only embarrassment
and difficulties for her in her *mudang* role, but they also presented
practical management difficulties and hazards to her health. Except for her first pregnancy (which she calls a "thief's baby"
because he was conceived in secrecy), she experienced difficulties
with all of them, suffering more after each illegally obtained
abortion. She had four in all, beginning in 1958 when she had just
had her sixth child, a girl, and could not afford another baby so
soon again.

Most of the difficulties she had with her pregnancies seem to
have resulted from poor prenatal care. She says:

> Between the commotion created by an endless stream of clients
> coming and going at all hours of the day and the normal noises
> of a bunch of growing children, I had very little peace and quiet
> during the day. . . . In addition, I often had to work at times
> several nights and days in succession. Nightwork in big *kut* took
> a terrible toll on my body, although of course that's where the
> money was. . . . Once, I stayed up more or less without sleep
> for fourteen nights straight. . . . It was the biggest *kut* I ever took
> part in. . . .

Even when she weathered the difficulties of the pregnancies,
she did not make good postpartum recovery. She had a tendency
to hemorrhage heavily after each delivery so that she suffered
chronically from anemia. She receives weekly injections now for
this condition.

When she became pregnant with her seventh child, she decided to carry it to term, for she had suffered drastically from her

abortion a year previously. Needing money, however, she returned to work immediately after giving birth. Since both pow-
dered milk and nursing bottles were available then, she decided
to bottle-feed this baby, but it refused to drink it. As a result, she
had to hire a person to carry the baby and accompany her when
she had to travel far or for several days in order to participate in
kut. She says of this period:

> What painful and miserable years they were. My breasts were
> always painfully swollen and constantly overflowing . . . some-
> times I'd feel a gush of hot milk spurting out of my nipples while
> I was in the middle of a frenzied dance. . . . At times I had to beg
> off from my co-shamans and come home before the *kut* was
> over. . . . It always made me feel guilty and obligated to the
> other shamans to do that, and when I hurried home, the child
> seemed just as hungry as when I came home after finishing the
> *kut*. . . . The child suffered so much from being left home with-
> out my milk, because I couldn't always find or afford to hire
> someone to tag along with the baby. The child was almost
> always crying when I got home and would pull at the nipples so
> greedily. The tears used to stream down my cheeks as I nursed
> her but only half the tears were from the pain of relief as the milk
> drained. I suffered a lot, too.
>
> After that experience, I couldn't carry the next pregnancy to
> term; I aborted. . . . Between 1958 and 1965, I aborted four
> times. . . . With my last abortion, I got infected down there. . . .
> I had lots of pain and a high fever that persisted. I was told I
> needed to be hospitalized, but who can afford hospitals? . . . I
> just took some medication, but soon as I worked in a *kut*, I began
> to hemorrhage again. One doctor I saw told me that the best
> cure for me was to become pregnant again and carry it to term.
> So I did, and sure enough, it stopped and I got this "prize" [her
> youngest son].

She was just finishing an all night *kut* in the last month of
pregnancy with her youngest son when she began to have labor
pains. She was so exhausted from the *kut* that midway through
her labor she could no longer exert herself and had to be taken to
a hospital for a Caesarian section, which put them hopelessly into
debt.

She found it extremely taxing mentally, physically, and
economically to look after so many children even with her husband's generous help. Intermittently, she tried using hired help

to do some of the domestic tasks that her husband was unwilling to do, such as cooking and laundry, but she found them indifferent to her children and her belongings. She felt that the mental anguish they caused her was simply not adequately compensated by the services they rendered. For example, if one of the children came in crying—as all of them did from time to time, because they had been teased or left out of games for being a shaman's children—the servants did not comfort the child. Her husband who normally did so was embarrassed to do it before hired help. Frustrated, P'yŏngyang-mansin sometimes rushed out of the house and screamed at her children's friends, but it only compounded the difficulties for her children the next time they went out to play. This problem was finally resolved somewhat by her mother-in-law who gradually began to spend more time with them and finally moved in with them. She took over the motherly functions that her son was either unwilling or inadequate to undertake. She kept the children busy with chores or had them playing with one another at home. She was there if any came in from outside and needed comfort.

Such social problems for the children were not limited to the neighborhood alone. P'yŏngyang-mansin says:

> I noticed that by the time the children reached the third or fourth grade, they no longer wanted to go outside to play with friends. . . . They were beginning to understand what their friends' teasing was about. They stayed inside and played with one another. In school, too, they did not mix well with other children. . . . They'd tell me that they didn't like to hear other kids say, "Hey, you, your mom is a *mudang*, eh?"
> . . . when they went to the middle and high school, they could conceal my occupation more effectively from their classmates because these schools were not in the neighborhood. Anyway, my children were usually the only ones from their classes to make it into the top schools, so they didn't have to worry about their old classmates telling the new ones about me. . . . Of course, they never brought friends home, but we lived so far out of the city that no one probably questioned them.[13]

When they first moved out on their own, P'yŏngyang-mansin's mother-in-law was scandalized and enraged. Instead of finally being rid of a daughter-in-law she had never accepted, she now lost her son and grandchildren. P'yŏngyang-mansin's husband seemed to suffer no less, although he never complained about their estrangement from his mother. She felt it her duty to mend their damaged relationship. Since she was making an excellent income, she bought groceries —some eggs, a couple of chickens, a slab of pork or beef, or some bean cakes—and sent these with her children to her mother-in-law's house, instructing them to hang about the place until their grandmother asked them to eat. Eventually, her mother-in-law acquiesced enough to send the children back for their father as well as for meals. She was sure her son was not eating properly at his own house.

As her mother-in-law thus showed signs of reconciliation, P'yŏngyang-mansin bought a supply of rice periodically and, according to the season, raw material for winter *kimch'i* or soy sauce and hot bean paste for her mother-in-law's household. She also supplied her mother-in-law faithfully with cloth for new clothes whenever the season changed. (Today, her mother-in-law's birthday is the most elaborately celebrated one of all family occasions.) Despite these efforts, her mother-in-law was not so easily won over. Although she received the gifts which she surely knew had come from her daughter-in-law, she would not come to their house for visits. P'yŏngyang-mansin and her mother-in-law did not interact directly with each other for over a year.

Their estrangement ended unexpectedly one day when P'yŏngyang-mansin's mother-in-law brought home one of the children. She had found her crying in the playground because other children had teased her about being a *mudang*'s daughter. She was so incensed by the sight of her sobbing grandchild that she picked up a piece of firewood and chased after the teasing children all over the neighborhood, calling out invective descriptions of their own parents. Following this episode, the relationship between the two women and their households became more normalized. Her mother-in-law began to come over more frequently and stay longer, helping with the children and assisting in the preparation of ritual foods for P'yŏngyang-mansin's *kut*.

For her part, P'yŏngyang-mansin gradually assumed the responsibility for supporting her mother-in-law's entire household. As her mother-in-law grew more dependent on her, she became less hostile and critical of her. (Today, P'yŏngyang-mansin's behavior toward her mother-in-law is elaborately deferential in form, while the mother-in-law in fact performs all the duties that normally should have been her daughter-in-law's. She goes about her activities in the house with an air of deprived proprietorship so typical of first daughters-in-law still waiting to inherit the household mistressship from their mothers-in-law. Anyone observing her without background knowledge might mistake her as an old and faithful servant of the household.) She moved in with them permanently three years after P'yŏngyang-mansin became a *mudang* when she bought a house of their own in 1960.

P'yŏngyang-mansin feels that her personality has changed as a result of being a shaman. Never very socially gregarious, she thinks that she has become even less outgoing. Beyond exchanging cursory greetings, she has little to do with her neighbors and has no personal friends though she works closely with half a dozen other shamans. The ramifications of her *mudang* role pervade the other aspects of her life so completely that she says she cannot have a normal relationship outside of her profession. She admits she is hypersensitive about being a *mudang*; she can almost hear people whispering, "She's a *mudang*," the minute she turns her back to them whether in fact they say it or not.

> I understand why my children avoid going out to play when they are old enough to figure things out for themselves. When everything is going just fine, O.K., but soon as there is conflict or trouble, everyone turns on my children and says it's the fault of the *mudang*'s kids. . . .

P'yŏngyang-mansin feels grateful for the way her children have turned out and are turning out to be. She thinks her children are more self-confident and self-sufficient than the average child and attributes this to the fact that she had not been a constant and hovering presence in their lives, and also to their early and lifelong experience with discrimination. Under her husband's supportive relationship with her, she feels her children have learned to care for one another. "Of course, some of them have a way to go yet," she comments, "but so far none has shown signs of 'derailing'."

Her children are indeed very exceptional. Their professional and academic achievements are outstanding. They are hardworking and cheerful; all are also outstandingly good-looking. When they are together there is easy and frequent laughter among them. According to P'yŏngyang-mansin, they pity her and are compassionate with her for having had to become a *mudang*.

Her relationships with her children are, to all appearances, ideal, though they have had to overcome many obstacles to reach such a state.

> Now there is hardly any conflict within the household itself because of my being a *mudang*. As you have seen, even my mother-in-law helps me now. . . . As the children matured, they grew more solicitous of me: "Mother, rest. You must be tired. We can do that ourselves," they tell me. . . . Of course, I don't sit back and have them wait on me always. When I am feeling well, I pitch in and help with whatever work needs doing about the house while the girls are in school. . . . If I want and expect them to continue their good will toward me and help me, I have to show them that I am also willing, you know. Things like that work both ways. . . .

I have talked with P'yŏngyang-mansin's older daughters alone on several occasions. In their independently expressed feelings about their mother, they were uniformly grateful to her for all that they feel she has done for them. They are equally awed by their mother's intelligence. If their mother had had the opportunities which she was making available to them, they think she would have been a sensational success as a career woman. The least they can do to show their affection and respect is to excel in whatever they have to do, whether at home, school, or work; they must be a credit to her, they say. They are all anxious to succeed as registered professional nurses and are completely in agreement with their mother's plans to send them abroad when they complete their training and obligatory services for the scholarships that all three have received.

The daughters concur with their mother that, although they tried to minimize the hurt they felt by the discriminatory treatment they received from neighbors and peers, it was often difficult not to feel resentful toward them. P'yŏngyang-mansin tells of some particularly bitter episodes:

> Once, before the neighborhood got hooked up with the city water supply, we had a community well. If the well dried up because of drought, the neighbors used to say loud enough for all of us to hear that the water level had gone down because I, the *mudang*, took all the water for my *kut*. It was true that I had more children than most of my neighbors, but really!
> We also had a community garbage dump which the city

cleaned up at irregular intervals. If the dump overflowed, that too was because the *mudang*'s family lived in the neighborhood. No one stopped to analyze the situation or the problem. . . . There we were, the built-in scapegoats for anything you please. . . . Naturally, I don't feel like being neighborly with my neighbors. . . .

P'yŏngyang-mansin refuses to see any of her neighbors as clients, although some have sought her professional services. She does not want to compound her already existing tensions with her neighbors by superimposing a professional relationship with them. She generally feigns illness or fatigue and puts them off when they call on her.

Inasmuch as I'm not a spirit but only a medium, I'm bound to make mistakes. My neighbors aren't going to thank me for the nine times I was right but very likely to broadcast the one time I was wrong. So, why should I set myself up for them to abuse? . . .

Of course, I'm sometimes lonely and hanker for normal womanly sociability. But as I have a large family I don't feel that way very often. The main thing is to strive hard not to obligate ourselves to others or feel beholden to anyone.

In general, P'yŏngyang-mansin has tried to keep a low profile in the neighborhood, lest she antagonize her neighbors needlessly. She has held most of her *kut* in her adoptive mother's shrine, not only because the latter had better accommodations for it but also to avoid disturbing her neighbors with the noise of *kut*.

There were other, more personal, conflicts that emerged because she was a shaman. For example, it was only through a conscious struggle that she maintained an interest in her family and carried out her responsibilities toward them. Such conflicts were sharpest, she says, when she had been away for several days for *kut*.

I noticed subtle changes occurring in my mental and nervous attitudes and energies with regard to the internal affairs and management of the household. . . . I became unconcerned about them . . . to the point that my domestic role seemed unreal to me at times. . . .

There are times when I am so tempted to go to parties or other pastime activities with the other *mudang* that I work with, especially when I have been working with them outside the

house. . . . So far, I've not succumbed. I just don't want to hear,
"Well, another *mudang* whooping it up!" Neither do I want to
hear, "I went to such and such recreational place and there was
this *mudang* that . . ." I guess I am obsessed with anxiety about
being called a *mudang* by strangers. I really strain my nerves too
much for that. . . . So, even though I see hundreds of people,
you may say that I have less personal interactions with others
than even housewives. . . .

The two things that I have resented the most about being a
mudang have been being pointed out as a *mudang* in public places
and having my children stigmatized as *mudang*'s kids. . . . My
husband has also slowly given up all his friends and doesn't
even see his relatives except for necessary occasions. He is all
too aware of how the world regards a man who is the husband
of a *mudang*. . . . Of course, the positive aspect of such discrimination has been that it has kept me unceasingly motivated to
give my children the best education that my money can buy. I
want all of them to turn out better than the children of those that
have pointed their fingers at me and mine.

P'yŏngyang-mansin attributes her success in retaining her
household intact while working as a shaman to the following: (1)
she endeavored always to keep her domestic role the primary one
in her mind even though she spent more time and energy in her
professional role, and (2) her husband was faithfully loyal and
supportive of her. For her part, she proudly declares, she has not
deviated one iota from the narrow path of a wife, mother, and
daughter-in-law, beyond that of becoming a shaman—an act she
did not choose. She points out that her mother-in-law, who
probably caused her the greatest amount of grief when she was
first married, now treats her with respect.

P'yŏngyang-mansin confides that she is sometimes bone-
weary of her *mudang* role. She began to feel bored with her
professional role about the twelfth year of her practice; she found
it increasingly difficult to get into a trance state.

At first, you are so possessed and filled with spirits that you are
unaware of your own efforts. You're moved by forces and sustained by strength that come from the spirits. Then, gradually,
after a few years, you realize that shamanizing is a job just like
any other job and you get tired of it. But you keep at it because
you have to make a living somehow. So, you grit your teeth and
go on. You lose your enthusiasm and that naturally makes the
role more onerous.

At first it bothered me a lot that I was growing bored with being a shaman. But now, the role is a routine, and I'm not so concerned with my *kibun* ("mood") as I'm with making a living. . . . Let me explain. . . .

Take these modern doctors. . . . Those who have been at it for a while look at the patients that come in *not* as human beings needing relief from pain, but as carriers of diseases. . . . They treat their patients quite mechanically. It's the same with us *mudang*. You get that way when every client that comes to you has the same problems, more or less. . . . Most of my clients are women, and almost without exception, they have heartbreaking problems or situations having to do with mean mothers-in-law, philandering husbands, sick children, and so forth. When you deal all day with people like that, you end up feeling just like one of the jaded M.D.'s. I make a real effort not to be mechanical, but it's tiring—it's hard not to. . . .

When I receive unhappy women who are faced with unwanted divorces or other women in their husband's lives, their problems do not seem like strangers' problems anymore. I have so many daughters myself that I cannot help wondering, "What if the same thing should happen to my daughters?" . . .

Then, I have clients who suffer from chronic poor health; I know what they are going through and feel genuinely moved to do what I can, but sometimes I feel very helpless to help them. . . .

Despite boredom and frustration with her professional role, P'yŏngyang-mansin readily admits that her greatest personal satisfaction comes from knowing that she can earn a good living through it and at the same time give helpful counsel to her clients occasionally. If she had not become a shaman, there is no doubt, she says, that her family would have starved to death. Certainly, they could not otherwise have given their children the kind of education they have been receiving. Still, she worries endlessly about her daughters' marriages, especially after the painful experience of her son.

It is because of this fear about her daughters' marriages that she wants to send them abroad. She would like to divorce them completely from their social background short of severing ties with them. She says:

I want them to have a professional capacity that will always be in demand in any society. . . . I want them to go abroad and succeed professionally. . . . There, they won't have to conceal their mother's occupation; no one need know. They can find husbands of their own liking. . . . I realize I'm taking a risk of their marrying foreigners, but I'm willing to take the chance. I'd much rather they marry Koreans, but the first and the most important condition is that my daughters' husbands respect them and not humiliate them for being daughters of a *mudang*. . . . Maybe because I have heard so much about being a North Korean clod from my in-laws, I am leary of their marrying foreigners—they may say my daughters are inferior because they are Koreans.

As for her own future, P'yŏngyang-mansin sees another fifteen to twenty years of active practice as the most probable course of development. Her youngest child, a son, is now eight (1973), and she is already moulding him for a career in medicine. She delights in envisioning the possibility that her children may one day jointly establish a modern medical clinic. After all, one son is a certified pharmacist, three daughters are in nursing, and two more are prepared to follow suit; all that is lacking is an M.D. When asked what he wants to become when he growsup, P'yŏngyang-mansin's youngest son answers without hesitation, "A doctor."

In more modest moments, P'yŏngyang-mansin would just like to work until all her children are married and on their own and she has a little money saved. She is sure one of her children would be glad to look after her husband in his old age. She herself would like to build a small Buddhist temple in the mountains and retire there with a servant to look after her needs in old age. She wishes above all else for solitude in her declining years.

At the same time, she feels a strong sense of mission about correcting the distorted views that Koreans have about shamans. The Korean government does a disservice to the people, she contends, by its misrepresentation and persecution of shamans and their activities. In fact, she has been willing to help me, she says, because she hopes that through studies such as this, the government will come to realize the richness of the shamanistic heritage in Korea. If they had such knowledge, she thinks that they would not only proudly permit some shamans like herself to present *kut* as an art form to foreign tourists but also would stop the present governmental persecution of shamans and their followers. She is firmly convinced that *mudang* make a real contribution to the welfare of the society, though this is not recognized by the public.

Speaking of her own experiences with clients, she says:

> People come to us when they're in trouble. . . . Some even address me as *sŏnsaeng-nim* ("honored teacher"). But as soon as they are over their difficulties, they point their "holier than thou" finger at me behind my back and call me a *mudang* in the most denigrating manner. The exceptions are my regular clients who have stayed with me through the years and trust me completely. They know that I've their welfare at heart. With some of them, I've a relationship that's more characteristic of two close siblings than of a shaman and her client. . . . We consult with each other and help each other get through. . . .
>
> . . . *mudang* have been socially abused for hundreds of years, but today, the media are responsible for representing the *mudang* as evil. . . . Television and movies are great for portraying us [shamans] as sorcerers who work black magic in palace intrigues in historical dramas. . . . I object to such biased portrayal of *mudang*. . . .

There is, P'yŏngyang-mansin points out, a real and deliberate attempt by the government to project to the general public an image of the *mudang* as a deceptive, exploitative, superstitious, harmful, and evil person. These are certainly the adjectives one hears most often in official descriptions of shamans in newscasts and public service messages over the radio and television. There is also an undercurrent of folk belief that shamans make a living "selling their words" and that all they want is "money from the oppressed and the sick." P'yŏngyang-mansin complains:

> I'm sold with the rest of the *mudang*, both good and bad, so when I'm out in the society and treated by the public with contempt, I have to accept their perception of me as a *mudang*. . . . A person can come to despise herself because everyone else does, you know.

According to P'yŏngyang-mansin, many households in Korea are now divided between the older and the younger generation over the issue of *mudang*. The older folks living with their married children still want to cling to tradition and feel a *kut* is mandatory for certain occasions. The younger generation does not believe in such practices but will consent to having a *kut* out of a sense of filial duty.

But if we happen to be still at it [*kut*] when the sons return home, they're not above muttering aloud, "What! Can these *mudang* still be jumping around here?" . . . Even people like that . . . filial to their parents, don't see us as human beings.

P'yŏngyang-mansin gets visibly excited when she talks about the general persecution of shamans. She says there have been many historically recorded incidences of *mudang* doing good work. "They [*mudang*] traditionally took care of the insane, including those so crazy that they were like untamed horses!" She continues:

> If the well-born and well-placed of the society would give it some thought . . . they'd see that there are a lot of good purposes and uses to which *mudang* can be put for the good of the society. . . . Not only do *mudang* patch up broken hearts and shore up sagging hopes of the many who need succor, today's *mudang* are probably the only and the best source of knowledge if anyone wants to study old Korean tradition now becoming obsolete. . . . The young people today do not know. . . . People my age who studied under the Japanese don't know any better than today's children how ancient Korean was spoken; *mudang* are a valuable repository of traditional Korean culture.

In terms of physical facilities, P'yŏngyang-mansin has an ideal situation for taking in apprentice shamans, i.e., "adoptive daughters." Even a small number of adoptive daughters would enlarge her network of referral system and thus increase her income considerably. Therefore, I was surprised to realize that she had no adoptive daughters. When asked about it, she explains:

> Now, most *mudang* will deny it, but there are certain steps that you have to take to "qualify" as a *mudang* after you're possessed by the spirits. . . . First, you must find a "teacher" . . . she is the one you call "mother" and refer to as your adoptive mother. It is usually the *mudang* that officiated at your *naerim-kut*. . . .
> The reason that I don't have any adoptive daughters is that not everyone you initiate becomes a successful *mudang*. You're lucky if three out of ten *mudang* you initiate can hew their role. You can't be a *mudang* just because you've been possessed and initiated. . . . Even a modern doctor who can hang out his shingle with the government's approval cannot really function as a doctor until someone presents himself as a patient to him.

The same way, a *mudang* can be a working one only if she is
called to act as one by clients. . . . Some who are initiated as
mudang are bright; others, dumb. The bright ones get called . . .
the dumb ones don't get called or called back, anyway. When
that happens, the unsuccessful *mudang* blame their adoptive
mother rather than realize it is their own ineptitude as mediums.
I don't want to be blamed by nitwits, so I don't do *naerim-kut*.
Besides, I really don't feel qualified to undertake such responsibilities. Also, I don't want my children enmeshed in a network
of *mudang* beyond my own life. When I die, I don't want my
children to have any ties with any *mudang* who say they have a
claim on me as their adoptive mother. . . . I've already instructed my children to give away all my shamanistic paraphernalia on my death to any *mudang* who wants it, or to donate it to
a shrine. I don't want a designated successor to me, if I can help
it.

P'yŏngyang-mansin never once mentioned the possibility
that one of her daughters may become a *mudang*; yet, I was certain
she was aware of the common folk belief that a shaman's possessing spirits will, upon the shaman's death, possess either her
daughter or daughter-in-law more commonly than others. So, I
brought up the subject and asked her how she thought she might
feel if one of her daughters were to become a *mudang*. It was
apparent from her answer that she had given the possibility much
thought and has taken steps that she feels will prevent such an
event.

If any of my daughters were to be possessed by spirits, I'd
oppose her from accepting them and becoming a shaman. You
usually can guess who will be selected by the spirits from an
early age. . . . A person destined to be a *mudang* is somehow a
little different from the others even in childhood. Their health
and personality give some indication of the likelihood that they
will become *mudang*. . . . I don't think any of my daughters is
predisposed to become a *mudang*. . . .
But of course one can never be sure. So when they were
younger, I forbade them from watching me perform in *kut*, or
any of the other activities whenever possible. I was afraid they
might be noticed by the spirits and singled out. . . . One reason
that I've worked so hard to make sure I could give them the best
education possible is that if a person has a good education, has a
good job, and is solidly established socially, spirits tend to shun

such a person for possession. You see, when displeased ancestral ghosts or spirits of the house-site want to make their displeasure known to the living, they usually attack the most vulnerable of the descendants or the weakest organ of the chosen victim
for attack. . . . So, you may say that I have worked all my life to
prevent the possibility of any of my children becoming possessed. . . .

Although she herself was thirty-two when she finally succumbed to the supernatural call to become a *mudang*,
P'yŏngyang-mansin curiously insists that if a girl reaches her
thirtieth birthday safely, she is unlikely to be possessed thereafter.

Her older children, especially her pharmacist son and nurse
daughter now working in Los Angeles, are ambitious in their
careers. They want to succeed in order that they may "retire"
their mother as soon as possible from her shaman role. They are
willing to contribute to the support of their parents and younger
siblings. They would like to see her terminate all shamanistic
activities if she wants to. If not, they would like her to hold only
the established, seasonal rituals for her old clients and rent out
the *tang*.

5

TTONGKKOL-MANSIN

BRIEF CHRONOLOGY OF TTONGKKOL-MANSIN'S LIFE

1921	Born
1930	Father died
1932-1933	Was given away in *minmyŏnuri* marriage
1939	Was officially married
1940	First child, a daughter
1943	Second child, a son
1948	Third child, a son
1950	The Korean War. Fled home and became refugees in South Korea
1951	Moved into the city of Seoul and began selling noodles on the street
	Fell gravely ill late in the fall; retrospective interpretation — first bout with *sinbyŏng*
1951-1952	Survived by begging in the streets
1951-1954	Refused to have sexual intercourse with husband
1952	Regained relatively good health. Began door-to-door peddling of groceries with stepdaughter

	Set up street-vending of small P.X. merchandise for the eleven- and eight-year-old to keep them from begging and roaming the streets
1955	Fourth child, a son
	Became seriously ill again in the winter; went into coma but recovered
	Had first hallucinatory experiences. Second bout with *sinbyŏng*, but the first time it was recognized publicly
1955-1956	Went on a "vision quest" to receive her possessing spirits
	Neighbors and relatives have her initiated as a *mudang*
1956	Fifth child, a son
	Acquired some adjacent shacks and rented them out for income
1957-1958	Husband moved out
1959	Built the present house. Married out first stepdaughter. Hired a live-in housekeeper
	Husband had a baby girl by concubine
1961	Husband moved back in with daughter by concubine
1962	Sixth child, a son
1963	Seventh child, a son
1964	Own first daughter married
1967	First son married
1971	Suffered a stroke but recovered
	Hallucinatory experiences

TTONGKKOL-MANSIN

Out of Seoul in a westerly direction, beyond where the Western Gate of the City used to be during the Yi Dynasty, are three prominent universities, all of them Christian. Within walking distance of one another, they form a triangle, with a compact neighborhood of modest dwellings on a knoll at the center. These dwellings do not follow any architectural patterns but seem to reflect the raw materials that were available at the time of their construction. Here and there summer squash and pumpkin vines relieve the dust-gray monotony of the exterior of the houses. The neighborhood is an anachronism; it is an urban village. The residents are mostly North Korean refugees or rural South Koreans, displaced by the Korean War and subsequently by industrialization. Whatever their origin, they share the remembered experiences of peasant life in rural Korea. Among the residents themselves and people in adjacent areas, the neighborhood is known as *Ttongkkol-ch'on* ("village of shit alleys").

It is an improbable name even in Korea where place names tend to be descriptive of some feature of the place. Ttongkkol-mansin, who takes her professional name from it, would not have it changed even if she could. For her, the name is a constant and symbolic reminder of the phoenix-like transformation both she and the place have undergone since she first set foot upon it twenty years ago. When some of her more modern and educated clients address her as *sŏnsaeng-nim* ("honored teacher"), she snorts like a horse and loudly demands that she be called Ttongkkol-mansin. If prospective clients making telephone queries hesitate to use her geononym, she shouts into the phone, "This is Ttongkkol-mansin. Whom are you looking for?" According to her, when she and her family first sought shelter here in the winter of 1951, the place was so crowded with refugees that there were garbage and feces everywhere. The nickname, "shit alley village," evolved in those days and has stuck stubbornly to the present.

A homely looking woman of portly build, Ttongkkol-mansin appears at home in the neighborhood. She lives in one of the larger houses with her husband and five of their nine children. There is also a live-in housekeeper. With tile roof and L-shaped arrangement of rooms, the house is properly traditional in style. A closer look reveals an interesting modification, however. The *sarang-bang*, the male room which typically faces outward and is the first room accessible to the exterior of the house, is, in this case, the innermost room. Its door and windows open into the side and backyard from which there is no direct exit to the street. Ttongkkol-mansin conducts all her shamanistic activities in the remaining rooms, and this structural modification affords her husband and the other members of the family a measure of privacy. The largest room in the house is set up like a miniature *tang* ("shrine"). It is in this room that Ttongkkol-mansin receives clients and conducts small scale *kut*. The *maru* and the second room connected to it serve as extensions of the small *tang* during her practice. At night, these rooms double as sleeping quarters. Usually, Ttongkkol-mansin sleeps alone in the *tang* while her housekeeper and stepdaughter sleep in the second room connected by the *maru*. Her husband and sons sleep in the *sarang-bang*, where they also take their meals.

The courtyard is small but neatly kept. It is crowded with colorful flower beds that vie for space with crocks of soy sauce and bean paste. Ttongkkol-mansin also keeps several portable chicken coops there, for she often uses chickens in her *kut*.

Ttongkkol-mansin's husband is in his sixties and appears to be in good health, but he does nothing resembling work about the house. He is always immaculately dressed in traditional white garments and rarely stirs out of his room except when he leaves the house. On such occasions, he pokes his head into the *tang* and asks Ttongkkol-mansin for tobacco and bus money. She mechanically reaches into a pocket sewn on her underwear and hands him one or two hundred *wŏn* ($.50 or $1). Once, I observed him protest that the amount was not enough, but Ttongkkol-mansin simply ignored him. But her husband's stubborn refusal to withdraw his outstretched hand made me think that he sometimes gets more by protesting. He occasionally asks her, in an incidental fashion, if he may do some shopping or other errands for her, but she invariably refuses his offer, saying that her hired man can do it.

In addition to the live-in housekeeper, Ttongkkol-mansin has a hired handyman, about fifty, who does all the odds and ends left untended by others, including marketing for *kut*. During peak periods in her practice, Ttongkkol-mansin also employs one or two additional female helpers. They assist her at the drum or help her housekeeper prepare the ritual foods. The handyman's gender seems to be totally eclipsed in this environment, for the women go about practically in their underwear in his presence. When he is not busy, he squats down in their midst and helps with food preparation, joining with ease in their conversation and exchange of jokes. In contrast, the women make a gesture of modesty when the shaman's husband approaches.

The oldest child still living at home is her third son, now seventeen and attending a post-high school vocational training school to become an auto mechanic. He spends most of his time at school. When he returns home, he goes directly to the *sarang-bang* with neither a word nor a look to anyone in the front rooms of the house. Of all the children living at home, only the youngest, aged eight, tries to hang about Ttongkkol-mansin, although he gets little nurturing from his mother. What is more, he gets ridiculed for his behavior by his ten-year-old brother. Ttongkkol-mansin's fourth son, aged fifteen, keeps a low profile about the house, spending most of his time at home in the *sarang-bang* during school vacation. When he leaves home, he tells either his younger brothers or the housekeeper of his whereabouts.

Ttongkkol-mansin has a twelve-year-old stepdaughter, one that her husband brought in from his liaison with a concubine. She spends most of her time doing small chores for the housekeeper or reading unobtrusively in a corner of the second room. Ttongkkol-mansin has another stepdaughter, aged thirty-seven, married, and from her husband's first wife. The two, having nearly grown up together, are quite close, and the stepdaughter comes home for periodic visits. Neither she nor Ttongkkol-mansin's own daughter, aged thirty and also married, is permitted to bring their children on visits home. The same prohibition applies to her eldest son and his wife. Ttongkkol-mansin refuses to let her grandchildren see her in her shaman role. She says she has swallowed enough bitter tears with her own children who had to and still bear the brunt of the social ostracism customarily directed against shamans and their families.

Her two oldest sons, aged twenty-eight and twenty-three, are both in South Viet Nam with the Korean Army. They regularly send home their earnings for Ttongkkol-mansin to hold for them until their return. The eldest son wants to go into some kind of wholesale business for himself when he returns. The second son, who has a B.A. in political science from Chungang University, hopes to find a civil service job with the government. I was struck by the very different kinds of education her sons had had or were receiving. As if she had anticipated my peplexity, she explained that the discrepancy in their educational background

was due in part to fate and in part to their own individual ability
and inclinations. Depending on her financial state at the time, she
sets the ceiling limit to which any child may aspire in education
with her help. She insists, however, that whether a given child
elects to maximize the opportunity or not has been, and is, strictly
his or her own decision. She points out that her third son chose to
go to a vocational school, although she had offered to send him to
college.

Ttongkkol-mansin is determined that her children should
have at least a high school education; she considers it as mandatory for social and occupational competence in urban Seoul. At
the same time, she is equally vociferous that she is not going to
waste her hard-earned money forcibly educating an unwilling
child beyond high school. Her view that enforced education
beyond the high school level is useless is somewhat unusual. The
prevalent tendency among Korean parents, especially among
mothers, is to make uncritical and extreme self-sacrifices to provide a college education for their children. Ttongkkol-mansin
herself is completely illiterate.

Ttongkkol-mansin is not positive of her age, but she thinks it
is fifty (in 1971). If she is right, then she looks at least ten years
older than her age. Her face is generally swollen and mildly
jaundiced. She does not always bother to comb her hair which is
nearly all white. She claims that since her stroke earlier in the
year, it is difficult to do her own hair which she wears in the
traditional *tchok*.[1] Her housekeeper has to double as her
hairdresser when she has time or when the occasion demands it.
Ttongkkol-mansin wears an old-fashioned *chŏgori-ch'ima*,[2] reminiscent of the peasant style thirty or forty years ago in her native
province of Hwanghae-do in North Korea. She speaks well but in
coarse uncultured Hwanghae-do dialect. She has a strong pen-
chant for vocabulary which is more appropriate to peddlers in
marketplaces than to a farmer's wife such as she had been before
the Korean War.

The high point of Ttongkkol-mansin's anachronistic presen-
tation of self is the traditional bamboo pipe which she smokes
between appointments of clients, perhaps to give herself a break.
The stem of the pipe is so long that it requires a second person to
light it. As she puffs on the long bamboo stem, she notes that
bamboo pipe smoking is almost obsolete today even in rural

Korea: "Everyone has 'drunk modern water' and prefers cigarettes these days." With a sigh of regret tinged with disapproval Ttongkkol-mansin observes further that it is impossible to buy the right kind of tobacco for the bamboo pipe in Seoul. She has to order it from a particular supplier in the province. When asked why she sticks with such a troublesome old custom,[3] she replies that she is an old-fashioned person. But her careless old-fashionedness has an air of theatrical staging; the old-fashioned, Hwanghae-do style brass ash tray and a wooden tobacco box had to have been searched out in antique shops.

Ttongkkol-mansin is a popular shaman. No matter when one visits her, she is seldom without clients. Even when she is temporarily free of clients, she is hardly ever without an appreciative audience, for most of her callers are either clients or persons dependent on her for occasional employment. I once waited seven continuous hours for a chance to interview her. Though she rewarded my persistence by inviting me to join her at her special lunch table, she was otherwise simply not free from clients who kept coming all day. Clients sometimes have to lean against the wall or squat in the courtyard to await their turn. On a good day, she grosses as much as $50, but her operating expenses are also quite high. She must supply almost all the ritual food involved in *kut* and pay her hired help.

Ttongkkol-mansin evidently finds great personal satisfaction in her earning capacity, for she constantly compares it with that of "able-bodied men who sell their labor." Yet, she does not seem greedy. She frequently returns part of the money offerings, the payment for her services, to clients who are obviously poor. She explains that her "grandfather" does not want her to take it all.[4] Asked about such generosity, she cites some unnamed sages and scholars of old: "Wise men and scholars of ancient times have said that for the relief and rescue of the poor and the oppressed, there is nothing save charity and fortune-tellers."[5] She expresses an abiding sense of identity with the very poor and the downtrodden who seek her. She angrily explains: "Well, how can I think of easy money, eh? I've been there; I know where they are at now. . . . So far, I've managed to keep these many lives [gesturing to her family] together without bleeding the already bled." She unquestionably sees herself as an undiscriminating champion of all who need succor. She proudly lists the various places throughout

South Korea to which she has travelled for *kut*. She has gone even
to the DMZ (demilitarized zone) along the thirty-eighth parallel
where her clients were Korean soldiers about to go on risky
assignments.

At home, her clients are predominantly female, with a smat-
tering of male customers. Some are Christians. Ttongkkol-mansin
has an undisguised contempt for Christians who seek her services. She sees them as capricious opportunists lacking in loyalty
to their own God and determined to maximize their chances with
all kinds of spirits. When she suspects that her clients are Christian, she forces a confession of the fact through her preliminary
interviewing and then ridicules them, saying: "Anyone who
claims such an exclusive God ought to be ashamed to go sneaking
to other spirits through the back door." She does not refuse them,
however. She feels it would be presumptuous to withhold her
help from anyone if the problem is within her range of competence.

If she sees the problem as a medical one, particularly requiring surgical intervention, she advises her clients to see doctors
trained in modern medicine, or, if too poor to afford them, then
those trained in Chinese medicine. She explains to her clients that
her efficacy in such cases is limited. As the mouthpiece of spirits,
a spiritual medium, she is limited to opening up the spiritual
channels in patients to facilitate and enhance their benefit from
medical treatment. She cites her own quick recovery from a stroke
as evidence of the wisdom of combining modern medical treatment with shamanistic ritual interventions. She says she is not
like some dumb shamans who take on anything for the immediate
money. "When 'Grandfather' there says 'hands off,' I send my
clients away."

Ttongkkol-mansin is not always so self-confident. She confesses that when she sees a client returning too soon after a visit,
she has a sinking feeling inside.

> I think, "What has gone wrong?" . . . I tell you, the one thing
> no one in the world should be called upon to do is "shamaniz-
> ing."[6] Sometimes, I do believe I'm the charlatan that people
> accuse us *mudang* of being. I wonder: "Am I a peddler of make-
> believe? Do I believe anything I say?" . . . At times like that, I
> curse having been born a woman. Why couldn't I have been
> born a man? I'd have aspired to the office of the district magis-

trate, at the very least. Instead, I was born a woman and had to
become a shaman! . . .

When a client has done everything sincerely as I bid her do,
and the problem persists, I get fighting mad at "Grandfather"
and all the other spirits there [at the altar]. . . . I go up there and
have a fist-banging, shouting match with them [the spirits at the
altar]. I don't like their recalcitrance. It's not as though I was
shamanizing strictly for a living. . . . If I can't help anyone,
what's the point of my shamanizing? Oh, I let 'em know what I
think of them [spirits]. . . . I tell them that so long as I'm their
slave and medium, the least they can do is back me up. . . .
Sometimes I think they are playing tricks on me, but if I retaliate
by neglecting them [by not performing certain periodic rites for
them], they nearly "kill me" [she falls gravely ill]. . . . They let
me make a living but they take their share all right. . . . Still, I
try to fulfill my clients' every wish; it's not for nothing they call
shamanizing a wish-fulfilling job.

I feel the saddest when I have just stepped down from
dancing on the glinting, razor-sharp blades of fodder choppers.
. . . No one should have to do that . . . I really wish I had been
born a man.

Her self-doubt and remorse sometimes make her a generous
employer. "Why shouldn't I pay the people who do the real work
while I peddle lies from these spirits?" Ttongkkol-mansin's hired
hands are generally very willing and hard workers.

Ttongkkol-mansin states that the one uncompromising guide
in her conduct as a shaman has been that none of her children
should one day have cause to say, "I've come to grief because of
my mother's deceptions and greed."

She thinks ahead in other ways too. Ttongkkol-mansin
would like to buy out some of her immediately adjacent neighbors
and build a modest tang named after herself. She predicts that
Korea will remain in a state of uncertainty for a long time to come
and that shamanism will gain in popularity and strength, not
decrease. She thinks that with her own tang, her future will be
fairly secure. Her poor health worries her; she would like to live
long enough to see the youngest, now eight, married with a good
living before she dies. She also worries that her husband may
outlive her in spite of his fifteen-year seniority. "From the olden
days," Ttongkkol-mansin confides, "people have said: 'He who
likes to be idle and fool around is a shaman's husband and he

who likes free things is a *kisaeng*'s brother.' Who of my children should be saddled with him after I die?"

Ttongkkol-mansin was born the fifth of seven daughters, all homely, she says, of a comfortable farmer. Her birth place is near Haeju, Hwanghae-do, a province on the northwest coast of the peninsula in what is today North Korea. By the time she was born, her parents had branched out from their *k'ŭndaek* ("the main household of the lineage"). Their lineage was one of the largest landholding ones in the village, and their *k'ŭndaek* supported a number of tenant farmers. Her father, the youngest among his brothers, needed to hire no more than a few laborers during peak periods to work the farm himself, but he kept his family well-fed and warmly clothed during the winter.

Her father was an exceptionally gentle person. He was without greed or malice but others tended to see him as a weakling. He rarely came home drunk from the marketplace or smoked very much. He had few demands and was easily satisfied, but his elder brothers were impatient with him. They accused him of being unambitious and unfilial because he refused to acquire a concubine to get a son. He quietly pointed out to his brothers that they had enough sons to insure the safe continuity of the lineage. Ttongkkol-mansin thinks her father was reluctant to take a concubine not so much because of his scruples or special attachment to her mother but rather because he was a simple man who did not want a complicated life.

Ttongkkol-mansin says her mother was a homely woman who passed on her looks to all of her daughters. She was thoroughly embarrassed about having borne so many daughters that at one time she too urged her husband to take a concubine. She was always grateful that her husband was silent whenever she presented him with yet another daughter.

As far as Ttongkkol-mansin knows, her infancy was uneventful and without any serious childhood diseases. Her eldest sister was already married when she was born so that she was cared for by her second and third elder sisters when not directly under her mother's care.

Ttongkkol-mansin grew impatient at having to talk about her childhood. She insists there was nothing noteworthy in her early childhood. An older sister, also a *mudang*, concurs; there was nothing unusual about their childhood, individually speaking.

The whole household suffered mildly from the pity (and some-times contempt) of neighbors and relatives for having so many daughters and no sons, but they made no complaints to anyone, keeping a low profile, especially with regard to the *k'ŭndaek*. Otherwise, neither their unbringing nor their daily life differed much from the typical life of the villagers.

As the fifth of seven daughters, Ttongkkol-mansin received no particular attention or neglect. Of her many sisters, she has memories only of the ones immediately above and below her. She met one elder sister, twelve years her senior and also a *mudang*, by accident in Seoul where both had taken refuge from the North during the Korean War. The two have few common memories of life in their natal household, for their tenure did not overlap by much. But the older sister remembers that Ttongkkol-mansin was a good-natured, easy-going and healthy child.

Ttongkkol-mansin's clearest memories of her family are of her mother and a younger sister she looked after and played with as a young girl. She has no distinct memories of her father, although her elder sister remembers him clearly.

Ttongkkol-mansin has fond memories of the fun she used to have about this time with her village agemates and sisters. She says that children in those days had no toys, books, or any other forms of amusement, but as they did not know what they were missing, they had a "grand time just the same." She also recalls that her mother was constantly worried about her daughters being tomboyish.

More specifically, she says of herself during this period:

> No one wasted many words on my good looks but everyone praised me for being a hard and a fast worker. . . . I've never lagged behind anyone in any group work. . . . Even now, I prefer to work alone if possible. It's frustrating and a waste of time to work with a bunch of lazy talkative shamans. I prefer to "solo" and do it at home, unless the nature of the *kut* demands teamwork for its proper execution. Then I get one of the rooms at Kuksadang [a nationally famous shrine] and call in two or three of the shamans I work with regularly. But I have to be in charge, and they understand that very clearly.

As a child, Ttongkkol-mansin had to learn the full range of domestic skills and acquire other attributes of her sex and age role. Like all the other girls in the village at the time, Ttongkkol-mansin received no formal education. When she speaks of her lack of education, she seems to take a sense of pride in having gotten along as well as she has without it. She frequently prefaces her comments with: "I'm an ignorant old woman who can look at a sickle all day and not recognize the letter, *kiyŏk*.[7]

Ttongkkol-mansin's relatively carefree and happy childhood came to an abrupt end when her father died. She says:

> When my father died, there was no man in the house to do the farm work. . . . There wasn't enough land to make it worthwhile to lease it to a tenant farmer, especially after my eldest uncle took away most of the best land. . . . It is truly sad for a woman to have no son. Our situation got worse with each passing year, and my mother had to give me in *minmyŏnuri*-marriage[8] when I was not quite twelve years old.

Talking about her "marriage," Ttongkkol-mansin's voice grows impatient and thick as she continues:

> I remember my aunts [her father's brothers' wives] coming over and talking things over with my mother, who had taken to crying a lot in the kitchen when she was cooking. . . . It wasn't my mother's habit to explain things to her children, and although I heard snatches of conversation about "this good place" and "that good place," I had no idea that my future was being decided. . . . Of course, my marriage was arranged for me. In those days, nothing else was thinkable. I had no say in it, not so much as whether or not I liked the idea, much less the man. Actually, I didn't know I was being married off when I was sent away. I was just told that on such-and-such a day I would be taken to my future husband's house. . . . So, I went, and have lived in marriage ever since. I was so very young . . . I didn't know enough to be even scared. So, carrying the *katsangja* [a hat box for the traditional hat worn by married men], I followed my elder uncle to my husband's house. . . .

Barely on the threshold of her pubescence, Ttongkkol-mansin arrived in her future husband's household and found it very different from her own. It was an active household with a lot of people coming and going, with the male presence very evident. The core of the household consisted of her parents-in-law-to-be, a man she vaguely understood to be her future husband, his two younger brothers, and their respective wives and children. She was introduced formally only to her parents-in-law-to-be by making deep bows to them. The relationships of others were simply ascertained in the course of time. Among the children she originally assumed belonged to one or the other of her two sisters-in-law, there was a two-year-old girl whom they told her specifically to look after. She learned later that this was her stepdaughter-to-be.

Her husband and his brothers were the fifth generation of Yi's to live in the village as self-cultivating farmers. They were not rich, but comfortable, and had enough land to keep all three adult sons and the still active father busy.

Ttongkkol-mansin found her mother-in-law and two sisters-in-law very tolerant and easy-going. They made few demands on her in the way of household tasks, asking only that she look after her stepdaughter. As she grew more accustomed to her new environment, Ttongkkol-mansin began to help with chores as needed and in ways she was capable of without being asked. She says that she learned most of the dmestic skills required of a farm woman from her mother-in-law and two sisters-in-law.

Of the very early phase of her life in her husband's household, Ttongkkol-mansin says:

> I was scared but I didn't cry. . . . I came to realize I couldn't go home *ever*. . . . My mother had told me that I had to be liked by my in-laws. . . . I hated so much having to eat *nunch'i-pab* [meals eaten under the watchful eyes of people who are gauging the quantity one consumes] at first, but they [her mother-in-law and sisters-in-law] always urged me to eat more. . . . I did whatever they asked me . . . and never said a word to any of the menfolk, including my husband. . . . He didn't speak to me either.

For the next six years, Ttongkkol-mansin was treated and socialized much like a prenuptial daughter, and her life proceeded uneventfully in the routine of rural life. The quid pro quo arrangement implicit in her relationshp with her husband's household as a *minmyŏnuri* worked out agreeably, in spite of the fact that she made a much stigmatized form of marriage. Ttongkkol-mansin attributes the relatively painless life she had as a *minmyŏnuri* to the fact that all her female in-laws were supportive of her and willing to provide her with guidance as necessary.

There were, however, some aspects of her life in her husband's household that puzzled her, but she did not push for explicit resolution of these questions and doubts. In fact, she does not think she ever initiated a conversation with anyone herself. No one, for example, ever told her who the two-year-old girl was that she was charged to look after, and she did not ask. In time, she was able to infer that the little girl was her stepdaughter. It is not clear if Ttongkkol-mansin was able to cope with such ambiguities because she was insufficiently curious and had a high level of tolerance for uncertainties, or because she preferred ambiguities to explicit but potentially unpalatable knowlege, or because of a combination of both. In any case, Ttongkkol-mansin seems to have tolerated many ambiguities about her role in her husband's household in the initial period, and this seems to have worked as a strategy for managing her anxieties. When asked explicitly why she did not question anyone for clarification, she looked at me with an expression of incredulity and said: "In those days, children were afraid of their ŏrŭn ("elders") . . . you didn't go around popping questions to them!"

Ttongkkol-mansin remembers feeling uncomfortable about one ambiguous situation, though. Her sisters-in-law, who were much older than she and who kindly taught her the many things that she needed to learn, were potentially her "younger" sisters-in-law, since wives are ranked in terms of their husbands' birth order. They had at first let her relate to them as though they were her elder sisters; however, as she got older they not only discouraged that but began to behave deferentially toward her both in speech and manner.

Ttongkkol-mansin's relationship with the males in the household was governed strictly by the rule of sexual segregation and patterns of avoidance behavior.

The year that Ttongkkol-mansin became eighteen, she was married in a brief ceremony held in the house. In describing her marriage, Ttongkkol-mansin says:

> My mother-in-law and sisters-in-law prepared a small feast and invited some relatives and neighbors. They then put my hair up in a tchok, dressed me in the finest silk I had ever worn, and made me bow to my husband. I was married.

After the brief ceremony, life went on much as before for Ttongkkol-mansin. She still shared a room with her stepdaughter, although for quite a while after the ceremony they had taken the girl away to sleep elsewhere. Instead, her husband had

shared her room at night every night for a while and then intermittently afterward.

> I was still very ignorant in those days . . . I didn't know any-
> thing about relations with men [sexual intercourse]. . . . But it
> happened, and I managed. . . . After they put my hair up, my
> husband began to come to me in my room in the night to do
> what he liked. When he was finished, he got up and left as
> quietly as he had come in and went to the men's quarters to
> sleep. I soon became pregnant. . . . Before the ceremony, my
> husband had completely ignored me . . . maybe because I was
> such a tiny "bride."

Her mother-in-law and sisters-in-law treated her differently
too. Her mother-in-law now referred to her as *k'ŭn-myŏnuri* ("eldest daughter-in-law") and insisted that Ttongkkol-mansin's
stepdaughter address her as mother now. Her sisters-in-law deferred to her even more ceremoniously, and she was now expected to serve her father-in-law's meals in place of the older of
her two sisters-in-law. Ttongkkol-mansin remembers feeling
keenly awkward about such sudden changes in the household,
but says characteristically that she "managed."

The first nine years of marriage went smoothly for
Ttongkkol-mansin. A year after her marriage ceremony, she gave
birth to her first child, a girl. Her mother-in-law delivered the
child and her sisters-in-law assisted in caring for her during the
traditional twenty-one day postpartum period. There followed,
after the birth, unspoken but unmistakable further changes in the
way her mother-in-law and sisters-in-law related to her. It was
she whom her mother-in-law consulted or assigned tasks to be
done by all three daughters-in-law. Her two sisters-in-law deferred to her in all daily routine matters, though generally it was
merely a matter of form.

The transition in their relationships had been taking place
now for some time, but Ttongkkol-mansin found the many role
reversals extremely uncomfortable, especially with her sisters-in-
law. They too apparently found it sometimes spurious and at
other times clumsy to adjust to the changes in their relationships.
Ttongkkol-mansin describes it as follows:

> I was neither gruel nor rice. Though I was their elder sister-in-
> law, I couldn't act like one . . . for one thing, I was a lot younger
> than both. But then, I couldn't act like the child that I still was in

many ways in their eyes. . . . After all, they had practically brought me up.

Despite her ambivalence about being the youngest "eldest" daughter-in-law, life amidst her husband's extended family household progressed more or less normally. Having grown up in the household for six years prior to the wedding, she did not have the problem common to brides of having to familiarize herself with the lifestyles and individual peculiarities of her husband's household.

As for her relationship with her husband, there was little change except for his occasional nocturnal visits which continued. His visits did not become any less perfunctory with the passage of time; they did not provide Ttongkkol-mansin with opportunities for personalizing her relationship with her husband. On the other hand, he made no specifically personal demands on her either. So, life continued uneventfully, punctuated every other year or so by the birth of a new child until the advent of the Korean War in 1950. She was twenty-seven and her husband, forty-two at the time.

Reminiscing about her life to that point, she says:

> World War II came and went in those years, but none of our menfolk was taken away. . . . Then the Soviets came, but we didn't see any in our village. . . . We didn't like some of the things the new government [headed by Kim Il Sung] did to farm folks, but we weren't rich, so we didn't lose any land. . . .

Their experience with the Korean War was not to be so innocuous. Ttongkkol-mansin draws a contrasting picture:

> When the War came, I hadn't carried so much as a *mal* [a unit of measure approximating 18 liters] of rice to the marketplace to sell. I'd been a real homebody, doing what I needed to do as a farmer's wife and tending to my parents-in-law and children. . . . There was always enough to eat and warm clothes and firewood for winter months. I had no complaints. My parents-in-law were devout believers in *Milyŏk* Buddha [a variant pronunciation of *Mirŭk*, i.e., Maitreya]. The family observed a number of Buddhist rituals throughout the year. I didn't understand them but I didn't think it right to question them. When they [her in-laws] said do this or do that during the rituals, I did.

If she had initially followed her parents-in-law's Buddhist

ways out of dutiful obedience, she came to acquire a personal conviction in the power of the Buddha during the Korean War, she says. The most immediate problem when the war came was concealing their men safely from both the air raids and the North Korean government agents:

> . . . They were capturing every man old enough to be weaned of their mothers' breasts and young enough to walk without canes. . . . In a village, there just aren't that many places to hide which aren't obvious to anyone with two eyes. We prayed to Maitreya Buddha day and night to spare our men and nothing happened to them or to our village.

When Communist China entered the War, they helped turn the tide swiftly. With their help, the North Korean soldiers forced a hasty retreat on the ROK and the United Nations forces. Ttongkkol-mansin's husband and brothers decided to escape south with the retreating soldiers. They were afraid there would be no escape from conscription this time if the North Korean soldiers reached their village. The brothers left their aged parents to guard their farmland and house against the day when they would be able to return. Then each brother took his own family and left the village where they had lived for five previous generations and headed south on foot. The winter was bitter in 1950, and they suffered from exposure, though each had on as many layers of clothing as possible for walking.

Even so, on their first day of walking, Ttongkkol-mansin and her husband, with their four children—ranging in age from two to sixteen—travelled farther than any of them had before. It was also the first time that each of the brothers had acted independently of each other with regard to their respective nuclear families. They were catapulted on a course of experience totally unanticipated and for which they were unprepared. The three families tried desperately to stay together, but in the confusion of thousands upon thousands of refugees swarming on the road, Ttongkkol-mansin's family lost track of the others. They barely managed to keep their family of seven together. Ttongkkol-mansin says she prayed constantly to Maitreya Buddha and, trusting her husband, brought up the rear of the family procession.

Ttongkkol-mansin's husband had six years of education at a country school, but, having lived all his life in the village and worked his father's land under him with his younger brothers, he had very little experience with the outside world which now came rushing at him. He felt lost and fretted about having lost track of his younger brothers and their families. Some days later, they caught up with one of the brothers and his family by accident, but it proved of no value to the immediate survival of the group. Her husband grumbled that he wanted to turn back, but his younger brother wanted to continue on their southward journey. Ttongkkol-mansin sided with her brother-in-law; how would they explain to the North Korean authorities their having left the village? Very reluctantly, her husband acquiesced.

It did not take many more days on the road for Ttongkkol-mansin to realize that her husband could not take care of them. He was in a dazed state and did not seem to have a thought of his own as to how to keep his young family alive. She was utterly frightened. Now and then, they encountered people heading back north, but the greatest majority of the refugees shuffled on, doggedly headed southward as though under some command. Ttongkkol-mansin and her family were among these.

Ttonkkol-mansin and her brother-in-law steered their families through the country roads, stopping in villages for food and shelter. They started to avoid the highways, feeling unaccountably lost and afraid in the densely packed throng of people and the neverending convoy of retreating army trucks and jeeps. They thought they would have a better chance of survival among their own kinds of people. However, most villages had already been badly plundered by streams of refugees, and they were poorly received. When neither food nor shelter could be begged, they rudely moved in on helpless farmers with other refugees or starved and froze in the open. Occasionally, they found abandoned farmhouses. They moved in and stayed for a few days, recuperating and hoping that the tide of war would turn so that they might return home. They survived the winter of 1950-51 in this manner; throughout, they were sustained by an undying hope of returning to their own farm in North Korea by spring to plant their crop.

Their hopes ran high when General MacArthur's command recrossed the thirty-eighth parallel in March 1951, but forces beyond their comprehension and control were already operating to foil their plans for spring planting. When the best planting time had come and gone, they were still living in a subterranean hovel just outside Seoul.

A shaman before her altar at home.

A shaman before her altar at home.

Sacrificial food before an altar.

A table of sacrificial food prepared for a small scale *kut* at the home of a shaman.

A shaman chanting before she enters into a possession state, necessary for divination.

A modest altar dedicated to the mountain spirit.

A shaman before her secret altar in a mountain before starting her midnight *kut*.

A shaman chanting.

A shaman before her altar to the mountain spirit.

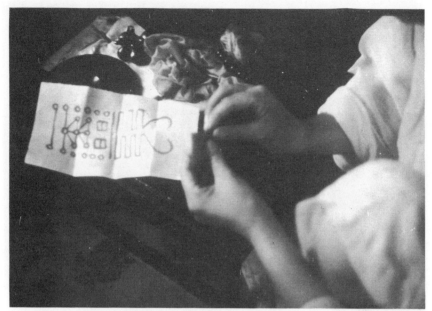

A shaman preparing a *pujŏk* (a talisman) for a client.

Clients in a state of half-undress for relief from the summer heat listen raptly to a shaman's opening incantation.

Clients at a divination session.

Clients at the conclusion of a divination session. The client on the left examines a *pujŏk* (a talisman) she received from the shaman.

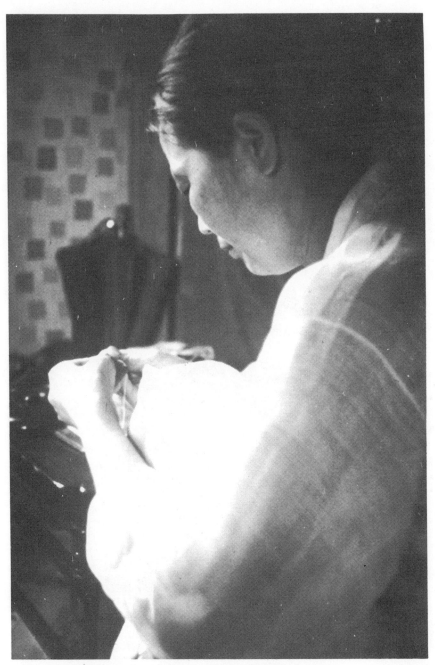

A shaman sewing a talisman into a red pouch for a client.

At the shaman's behest, a client bows before an altar of sacrificial food at a *kut*.

A shaman at the altar, with a client in attendance.

A shaman with fortune-divining flags at a *kut*.

A shaman with clients at a *kut* held on a boat on Han River.

A shaman addressing an assembly of clients in the name of the male spirit whose costume she is wearing.

Cymbals and drums play a prominent role in the ritual dances of shamans.

A shaman addressing the dragon spirit of the river for whom some of the sacrificial food had been thrown into the river moments before.

A shaman with her improvised family of widowed aunts, niece, daughter, and adopted son.

A shaman with her family.

Ttongkkol-mansin kept her family alive on wild edible roots that she and her children collected in the countryside. She picked through garbage bins outside American military camps for edibles and usable tin cans. In the meantime, she acquired an A-frame backpack and sent her husband out to work as a porter.

Neighbors and relatives alike had always praised her husband for being hardworking and kind-hearted. She had never suffered from his cruelty. But these qualities seemed to work against him now and therefore against their survival. He was simply not aggressive enough for the changed circumstances of their lives. Of course, there were more porters than people who had need of them; still, her husband seemed simply incapable of hustling for himself. He just hung back, waiting to be asked. Occasionally, women customers who feared that the more aggressive porters might run off with their cargo would choose him deliberately, but such occurrences were rare. Also, after a long winter of malnutrition, he was not strong enough for some jobs. What frustrated Ttongkkol-mansin the most about her husband was his inability to haggle for a good price. No matter how little people paid, he would make no more than a grunt for protest. Customers who were used to more abusive demands simply walked away. She realized anew that she had to think of ways to support the family herself. Ttongkkol-mansin says that the decision to take matters into her own hands was the most difficult one she had had to face till then.

She needed to know how the war was going in order to make any long-range decisions regarding the family's future. Since she could not read, the best she could do was to linger within earshot of men discussing current events for secondhand news. It appeared that General MacArthur had been called back to his country, and the new general was talking of ceasefire along the current battle lines. If such talk were true, she knew they could never return home, for they were fighting then a long way south of their home village. And if they were going to have to live in *t'ahyang* ("alien soil") for an undetermined length of time, they must somehow find a more permanent place to live, she thought. There were not many things she could do well, but she was certain she could make almost anything edible. She chose to go into the business of selling noodles in Seoul. When she presented her idea to her husband, he did not resist it. He had no other solutions to offer.

Counting on the relative warmth of late spring to keep them from freezing in the open at night, the family set out on foot for Seoul and reached their present location by nightfall. They had enquired en route for a place that people like themselves might find to live in Seoul and had been told of this place. It was swarming with refugees who, to judge from their accents and dialects, came from all parts of North Korea. The place was clamorously noisy. They found a patch of level ground big enough to spread out their mats and unload the cooking utensils they had been lugging about from their home in the North. That night, they slept under the still cold night, packing their bodies close together between the mats for warmth. The cotton stuffing in their quilts had lumped so badly that they were scarcely worth the bother to carry about. The next morning, when the sun rose, they were sickened by the sight that greeted them. Ttongkkol-mansin comments:

> A den of beggars could not have been sorrier looking. The place was worse than any nightmare a person might have. . . . The entire mountain was covered with makeshift tents and sheds, with people cooking and relieving themselves all over the place. . . . I spent my first day in the famous city of Seoul looking for straw sacks, burlap sacks, anything that I could use to put up a lean-to or a tent in that "hell on earth."

A few days later, she started her venture as a curbside vendor of homemade noodle soup. She left the younger children with her husband and stepdaughter to care for and, rising at the crack of dawn to catch breakfast customers, she hawked her soup, mostly to day laborers and other women vendors. Seoul was still largely deserted, and customers were not so numerous as she had expected. She also felt more self-conscious than she had expected; she could hardly bring herself to shout her wares to attract customers. Still, she sold surprisingly well and was encouraged by her tiny profit to overcome her sense of shame and embarrassment in her new role. She says that the smell of her soup was sometimes unbearably tempting to her empty stomach, but she did not take her own bowl of soup until she had sold several bowls to justify it. By midafternoon when she was not likely to catch even a late lunch customer, she took what was left home to feed her family. There was always enough broth left in the pot to boil up a fresh batch of coarse noodles or to heat up leftover noodles when business had not been very good.

Bit by bit, with her meager profits, she improved and enlarged their shack until it became a respectable *hako-bang* ("cardboard shack," originally a Japanese term). She used flattened American tin cans for the roof and walls. In the meanwhile, her husband sat staring into space with no effort at job hunting. Neither did he help her in her business. He insisted that he was a farmer and did not know any other work and could not learn any now. He did, however, do all the work in improving their shack. Otherwise, he slept most of the time. It began to irritate her, Ttongkkol-mansin says, to have to pick her steps so gingerly to avoid piles of "shit" everywhere while balancing her heavy cooking gear on her head and come home to a house full of screaming kids and a sleeping husband. He always lay with his face to the wall. If she nagged him, he turned more resolutely to the wall and slept, waking unfailingly at meal times and expecting to be served first and most.

By July 1951, full-scale truce talks were in progress at Kaesŏng, and Ttongkkol-mansin surmised that they would have to spend another winter at the very least away from their home in North Korea. It panicked her to think of another winter without proper housing or income. Each passing day brought more and more refugees back to Seoul, but it did not increase her business. Frequently, she had to round up her older children and take them scavenging in the marketplace for wilted vegetables and half-rotten fruits to supplement their diet of leftover noodles. Late that fall, around the time when some people were fortunate enough to be making winter *kimch'i* ("pickled cabbage and turnips"), Ttongkkol-mansin fell ill. At first she thought she had a cold. She felt exhausted; there was not a part of her body that did not ache. She thought a few days of good rest would see her on her feet again, but the illness lingered on. With no one earning money, they began to starve.

Her husband went out to see what he could do but usually came back empty-handed. In desperation, she began to scream at them all to go out and beg. The children cowered and huddled together in a far corner of the shack, afraid of her but unable to go out and beg. Her husband lamented loudly about having left their home in North Korea. He kept repeating, "At least we'd have died in the home of our ancestors instead of this god-forsaken rats' nest." She began to have dizzy spells and her stomach would not keep down even the little gruel that she managed to put together now and then. Also, her extremities began to swell. She feared that she was going to die soon. Thinking back to this time, Ttongkkol-mansin says:

> I was sure I was dying, but I was too scared to die. What would happen to the children and the old man if I died? . . . Medicine was out of the question. We were starving. . . . One day, I staggered out of the house with the children. . . . I stationed the older ones around a rotary and told them to beg or I'd kill them. In those days there were so many beggars you could hardly walk on the streets. I told them to stay put and keep an eye on one another until I got back to fetch them. Taking the smaller ones, I started out on my begging career. I was too dizzy to walk, so I found myself a spot where the traffic was heavy and sat down with the children. They were cold and hungry and kept whimpering the whole time except when they dozed off from exhaustion.
>
> Still, at the end of the day we had enough money among us to make a meal with some body to it.

The older children soon learned to beg for food and roam the streets, looking for the best spots for begging. Ttongkkol-mansin still cannot believe that she had actually forced her children to beg. She says she was constantly worried that begging would become a permanent way of life for them—that begging would "seep into their bone marrows." To maintain some control over their behavior, she made her children come by her spot of begging a few times a day and forbade them to steal. At worst, she counseled them, beggars are chased away with threats of beating but kids caught stealing are practically put to death. She recalls:

> I was worried all the time, especially about the girls. . . . Some days I was too sick to go out with them. . . . No matter what anyone says, human beings have to eat somehow. And you get used to almost anything. That winter, begging was the focus of our lives. We never told the old man what we were doing, and he never asked us. But he knew and we knew he knew. Still, at night, in that rat hole, he wanted me, like a dog. . . . I wouldn't have anything to do with him. It nauseated me. We already had as many children as lice. Besides, I was always feeling sick. . . . You wouldn't believe it now, looking at me so fat, but you

could've picked up my skin and draped it around my bones twice. For the next four years, I didn't let him come next to me. . . . It might have been partly because I already had the illness of one-to-become-a-*mudang*, though of course I didn't know it then.

They survived the second winter of their refugee life through begging. With spring, her health improved enough to make her think of earning their keep once more. With her stepdaughter to help her carry the products, she started to sell grocery items door-to-door. As before, she felt that food products possessed the least risk for her. They could always eat picked-over or unsold perishables at the end of the day. She teamed up her eleven-year-old daughter and eight-year-old son to sell American P.X. goods on the streets near home. It was the best thing she could think of to keep them occupied and steer them away from begging which had become an accepted way of life with them. She left the two youngest, aged six and four, at home in her husband's care. In this manner she kept the family going from one year to the next, meanwhile establishing squatter's rights to the land where their house now sits. They never again resorted to begging to stay alive, but her health remained poor and posed a serious problem, especially during the winter months.

In 1955, as the approaching winter began to show its first signs, Ttongkkol-mansin fell ill again. After several days of raging fever and delirium, she fell into a coma. Unable to afford even patent medicine, the family hovered about her in helpless despair. When Ttongkkol-mansin failed to come out of her coma for several days, the family notified the few relatives they had. Some neighbors were already coming over with rice and firewood in anticipation of funeral rites, but Ttongkkol-mansin recovered spontaneously from her coma. She apparently frightened them more than she relieved them. They regarded her as a person returned from the dead.

Ttongkkol-mansin remembers the whole eipsode quite differently. For her, it was a long, deep slumber during which she had a strange dream. She remembers the date and the hour exactly, she says. It was 14 October by the lunar calendar and the hour was that of *sul* ("the sign of the dog," i.e., the eleventh of the twelve branches which corresponds to the period between seven and nine p.m. [Martin *et al*. 1968]).

I was like a crazy woman . . . a woman whose soul had been
wandering. I remember falling desperately sick. The chronic
peritonitis [self-diagnosis] I'd been suffering from for four years
had flared up badly. I was throwing up pus. But now, I felt fine
[when she woke from her sleep]. My body was clean, as if it had
never been diseased. People were making a commotion, shouting: "A dead woman is walking. She has come back from the
netherworld," and such. At first, I couldn't fathom their behavior. . . . All I had done was step out of the room and into the
courtyard because my mother who had died when I was nineteen called me to come out. When I went out, my mother was
nowhere; only the spirits were there—the first and the last time
I've seen any of my ancestral ghosts with my own eyes.
    . . . They were two gentlemen. One was dressed like a
groom on his wedding day, like an official of the olden days.
The other was formally dressed with *top'o* and *kat* [formal daily
wear for ordinary citizens of the Yi Dynasty]. They handed me
the *ch'ŏnja-ch'aek* [the first Chinese primer with one thousand
basic ideographs]. It was uncommonly small, the size of my
palm. There were altogether seven pages to the book, but they
turned only the first five pages for me, saying: "If we should
turn all seven pages, you'd gain passage through the universe.
We'll be back in fifteen full years to turn the rest." That would be
this year [1971] . . . anyway, after they said that, the two gentlemen disappeared. The next thing is that I am in the middle of a
ring of family members, relatives, and neighbors. . . . They
looked witless with fright. They took me back inside and into
bed.

I was incredulous, but Ttongkkol-mansin continued:

So, when 1971 came around, I had a huge *kut* for myself at
Kuksadang and brought home a couple of *ch'ŏnja-ch'aek* and left
them open on the altar like that.

I followed her motioning chin with my eyes. There were
indeed two such books spread open on a tiny wooden table on the
altar. She insists that she has died three times and been called
back as many times during 1971. Furthermore, she claims that she
returned from one of these journeys to the netherworld completely paralyzed on one side of her body. The paralysis remained
with her for twenty-one days, until she performed another *kut* at
Kuksadang. When I asked her why she did not turn all the pages
in the Chinese primers, she grew impatient with my ignorance

and snapped that if all the pages were turned, she would die this year (1971).

Going back to her 1955 episode of coma, she agrees with her family that she behaved strangely even after her recovery. As she and her family describe it, she was like a person whose soul had left her to wander. She muttered all sorts of things which she herself does not recall. Though she made what seemed like irrational statements, people, so Ttongkkol-mansin has been told, began to recognize that they were prophetic. Ttongkkol-mansin was a "fiend" at finding lost items. Some neighbors and relatives recognized her behavior as indicative of spirit possession and called in a *mudang* and paid her to officiate at Ttongkkol-mansin's *naerim-kut*. Accordingly, Ttongkkol-mansin says, she was *"made a mudang* by the consensus of others who insisted that I was possessed and acted on that belief." These people proclaimed Ttongkkol-mansin a miraculous diviner.

Asked about the time lapse between her first encounter with the spirits in her "sleep" and her *naerim-kut*, she talks about the journey she made in quest of her possessing spirits.

> I went looking for my spirits one day about two months after my mother called me out of death. . . . No, I wasn't hallucinating, but I was, I think, in a state of possession. I had my eyes closed and was muttering something when, vaguely at first and then more clearly, an old woman appeared before me. She said: "Oh, I'm so-and-so, I'm seventy-four years old and my birthday is August 2. I became a *mudang* when I was nineteen. I've three sons. Come see me."
>
> I told her I didn't know where she lived, but she would not answer me. She just left. But I saw the very spot where she lived very clearly in my mind and the way to the place. . . . I'd have to take the train first, then the bus, then cross over rice paddies and over seven mountain peaks in the deep country. Even now you have to have an official pass to get into that country—it's near the DMZ. . . . There I'd have to inquire, but everyone would know of her. I could see that there would be two identical houses, but the house with the mulberry trees would be the one with the spirits.
>
> It seemed absolutely urgent that I go and see the old woman. So, I set out right away. I took the five o'clock train. It was December, lunar calendar. So it was already very dark at that hour. When I reached Chongun-ni [a place near the DMZ along

the thirty-eighth parallel] military checkpoint, it was snowing hard. . . . I didn't have many clothes on . . . I must have looked like a crazy woman to the sentries. You can imagine. . . . They might have thought me a crazy beggar—I was practically naked.

The two sentries at the checkpoint were talking. One said, "Shall we make her eat a bean? [shoot her]". . . . I told them I didn't want to eat any roasted beans. . . . Would they just show me where there are some houses nearby. Instead, they dragged me bodily some distance away and abandoned me with curses. . . . I remained quiet for some time there, trying to see in my mind. I felt I heard a voice say, "Go this way."

I set out in that direction and kept walking. As I came down the second hill, I found at its foothill an adobe hut. I asked to sleep there for the night but was refused. . . . But I got so cold I just went into their *sarang-bang* anyway. . . . At daybreak, I went to the well and disrobed myself in that cold. Laying down my clothes very carefully on the snowbank, I bathed with ice cold water to purify myself. I say ice cold now but I don't remember it really. After the bath, I went straight to the house with mulberry trees as if it were the most natural thing to do. I walked in and without preamble asked the old lady for her spirits. She refused, saying: "I've served them fifty-five years since I was nineteen. I'll not give them away lightly. You go home and have your *naerim-kut* first. Then come back. You've come to the right place, but I can't just let you take my spirits." I was angry. It wasn't as if I had come to cook rice for them [i.e., as a housekeeper]. She told me to come, and now she refused me what I had come for. So I wheeled around and started back to Seoul without so much as a by your leave. . . .

There weren't many buses running in those days. When I got back to the bus depot, the last of the two daily buses was still there, though it should have left some time ago. It had lost its front tire so that it had been delayed. . . . The doings of spirits are very strange sometimes. I had no bus money or train tickets. I rode free. I think everyone considered me deranged and didn't bother trying to collect fare from me. When I arrived home, my old man was fit to be tied. He ranted and raved and gave me a terrible scolding. They had all given me up for dead. They were sure I had frozen to death on some street.

It was shortly after this episode that Ttongkkol-mansin had her initiation *kut* and began to receive paying clients. Her first two clients were her neighbors. They wanted to conceive boys. About her feelings at the time, Ttongkkol-mansin says:

I felt no shame in those days, only exhilaration. . . . I felt like the only human being in the world . . . on top of the world . . . I felt absolutely superior. Now, that's surely a sign that I was already not in my own mind. . . . Even though the old lady at T'anyŏn-myŏn had refused me her spirits, the spirits had come home with me anyway. She had been retired for three years, and her spirits were anxious for a "home." So, I claimed them. She died soon after without ever having a chance to teach me any-thing. . . .

At first, her husband and children were merely grateful for her recovered health. As she became more solidly established professionally, with all that it entailed, the family began to feel ashamed and resentful of her for being a *mudang*. Her sister-in-law, her husband's older sister who had been listening to our conversation, interrupted Ttongkkol-mansin to interject her own comment.

We all felt that she was bringing disgrace on our *chiban* ("house-hold"). . . . You see, in these confused times, it's nobody's business if you are a *mudang*, but in the olden days people say you could kill a Buddhist monk or a *mudang* and no one thought to call you a murderer. . . . It did not matter how high your *kamun* was; if you were possessed, you were kicked out. Why, sometimes, parents killed you rather than face the disgrace. It's a despised outcaste occupation. At first, I was so ashamed of her, I wouldn't come here. But later, I changed my mind. . . . She couldn't help it. . . .

It appears that during the first two or three years after she became a shaman, Ttongkkol-mansin was relatively oblivious to the haunting sense of chagrin and shame that plagued her family. She was preoccupied with her *mudang* role, feeling "intoxicated" with her power and the money she brought in. Her family was ashamed to go outside, but they could not stay home either. When the clients came, there was no place in the one-room shack for them. Her husband left the shack before the first client arrived and stayed away until supper time. The children hung around outside, in the neighborhood, darting in and out of the kitchen to snatch a bite of food whenever they were hungry. Sometimes they fought bitterly among themselves. It fell upon her step-daughter, now in her early twenties, to hold the domestic scene together. She supervised the younger children, washed and cooked for the family, and did her stepmother's errands. She also had to raise her one-year-old and three-year-old half-siblings who were born after Ttongkkol-mansin became a *mudang*.

Ttongkkol-mansin was finally forced to recognize that her family was suffering when her husband moved out. Although she had been willing to resume her sexual relationship with her husband following her initiation, he was finding his life with her humiliating. To get him out of the house each morning, she would fling three or four thousand *hwan* (the currency before reform to *wŏn*; 4,000 *hwan* equals $1) to him and tell him to go drink some wine. In the course of time, he entered into an extra-marital relationship with the quite young mistress of the wine house. One day about three years after she had become a *mudang*, Ttongkkol-mansin had a bitter quarrel with her husband and he moved out. As he left, he told her that he preferred a winehouse keeper to a *mudang*. Ttongkkol-mansin stoutly denies that it bothered her. Yet, she says:

> I just saw him as a hateful and a treacherous soul. A man who violated his faith. A son of a bitch who had no human sense of obligation or appreciation. I said nothing to his hateful parting words. I just thought to myself, "Let's wait and see. I'm going to see you come crawling back and beg for your life!"

Her professional practice continued to boom after her husband moved out, and she was able to save enough money to acquire several of the adjoining shacks and rent them out until she had enough money to tear them all down and build the house where they live now. It has a tile roof, a feature that not even her parents-in-law had over their house in North Korea. Ttongkkol-mansin says it was a singularly triumphant feeling to be able to build the house with her own earnings on the very site where they had led the miserable life of beggars. She designed it so that at least in one room the children could be shielded from all her "shamanistic shenanigans."

As soon as they were settled into their newly built house, Ttongkkol-mansin began to worry about her stepdaughter. She was long past marriageable age.

> I began seriously to look around for a suitable match now that we lived in a regular house. It's true I never made her do anything I did not do first and more of, but there is no denying

that she has had a rough life. I didn't want her to hang around my business much longer. I wanted her married and settled in a normal life before the die was cast too permanently. My being a *mudang* was a real drawback in finding her a husband, but since she was a stepdaughter, it wasn't so bad. I found her a hard-working young man with no parents. With no *chiban-ŏrŭn* ("household elders") to influence him against her, she has a fair chance of having an ordinary life so long as she does right by him as a wife. . . . Now, they live in Yongsan and have three children. But the children aren't allowed to come here. Why should I contaminate their lives? My children visit them, and my stepdaughter and her husband visit me here on special occasions. But my grandchildren, no. I do it for them that they may not suffer from association with me. I even held her wedding at her aunt's place for the same reason.

After her stepdaughter's marriage, Ttongkkol-mansin hired a live-in housekeeper and managed to hold the household together while practicing full-time as a *mudang*. In 1959, Ttongkkol-mansin heard that her husband had had a baby girl by his concubine. Shortly afterward, her husband began to come home frequently for visits. Then one day in 1961 he showed up with the little girl. Ttongkkol-mansin fed them both and gave him his usual tobacco and wine money but he made no move to leave. When she reminded him that it was long past time for the little girl to go home and sleep, he replied sheepishly they were not going back. When Ttongkkol-mansin demanded to know what he meant by it, her husband replied, avoiding her eyes: "If I say we aren't going back, you should understand that we aren't going to leave. Why do you nag me so much?" He then turned to his little daughter and told her to find herself a place to sleep among her half-siblings. He had come "crawling back," as she had predicted, but not alone. Ttongkkol-mansin laments:

> In that manner, he came back one day . . . and has remained idle and useless since. The girl he brought in is that one over there. . . .You know I must still be suffering, for, as you can see, the old man is still alive. . . .

Subsequent to her husband's return, Ttongkkol-mansin learned that her husband's concubine grew tired of supporting him and threw him out. Not wanting to be hindered in her business by a small child, she told him to take their daughter with him. Ttongkkol-mansin is surprised that their relationship lasted as long as it did. She chortles: "Well, he certainly can't talk big anymore about what he prefers to a *mudang* for his woman."

Asked why she too did not reject him and his daughter, Ttongkkol-mansin looked at me incredulously. She was utterly dismayed by my question. She shouted at me, "Look here, where is there a law that says one can kick out one's husband? Anyway, what good is there in divorcing an already old and broken man? Besides, he is also the father of my children."

Ttongkkol-mansin has given birth to two more sons since her husband's return, the last one when she was forty-two.

In addition to her first stepdaughter, two of her own children are now married. Like her stepdaughter, neither her married son nor her married daughter is allowed to bring their children to visit Ttongkkol-mansin. When her son married, she set him up in a separate household. When he was sent to Viet Nam, she sent her daughter-in-law and grandchildren to her natal household. She sends them support money. She feels it is better for them socially to stay there until her son's return rather than move near her. Ttongkkol-mansin is continually concerned about the socially adverse effects her professional role has on her children and grandchildren.

At present, life in Ttongkkol-mansin's household is nearly mundane by comparison with earlier periods. Her husband and children live almost a separate life in the *sarang-bang*, and her younger stepdaughter fits in where she can. She is an avid reader and always keeps a book handy even when she is busy. She jealously makes time for reading between chores. The housekeeper and other hired hands are good to the younger children and attentive to the older ones. No one seems to take particular notice of Ttongkkol-mansin's husband—beyond a perfunctory courtesy—when he comes shuffling into his wife's quarters to beg for money. I found the sight pathetic, however; certainly, it is not something witnessed in a normal household, at least by outsiders.

Whether it be in daily routines or in the observations of seasonally recurring rituals, Ttongkkol-mansin's life (and that of her household) revolves predominantly around her shaman role. Among other things, it means a highly irregular and unpredictably fluctuating income which must be adjusted to meet the rather consistently recurring expenditures. Unlike those housewives who can rely on a regular and predictable amount of income for household expenses on a monthly basis, Ttongkkol-mansin must budget for a whole year at a time. She finds school tuitions for her many children her biggest financial worry. She says:

> No money, no school—simple as that. Schools are like tax collectors; all semester long, they demand money from the children for one thing and then another. . . . If I don't give them money, the kids say the teachers shame them and they don't want to go to school. I don't want them to bear the double burden of being called a *mudang*'s bastards as well as a pauper's bastards. . . .

Ttongkkol-mansin's peak seasons for income are spring and fall. Summer months are the worst, with winter not far behind. She carefully selects several *kye* ("mutual savings or aid societies") to join during the peak seasons and arranges to have her turns for the *kye* money when bulk sums of money are needed for tuition and other seasonal expenses. Next to tuitions, her major expenses are seasonally occurring shamanistic ceremonies to which regular clients are invited. They are expected to come with gifts, usually money, to offset the cost of the rituals and leave some surplus for the shaman. If for any reason the expected number of clients does not attend the rituals, then the shaman's investment in ritual foods and other paraphernalia is lost. Ttongkkol-mansin says she has tried to be frugal about these preparations but gave that up. Her spirits, she claims, became humiliated and retaliated, so that in the long run she suffered more heavily from financial losses. Ttongkkol-mansin does not want to pressure her clients into attending these rituals; nevertheless, she is a little resentful towards clients who do not come.

> I don't want anyone's money that's not given willingly. I will not be a beggar! Most people have short memories. When they are desperate, they will find the money somewhere somehow and come to see me, but if the times are hard or if they are getting by all right, they don't remember you when you need them yourself. . . .

On the subject of "adoptive mothers" and "adoptive daughters" among shamans, Ttongkkol-mansin is uncharacteristically defensive and secretive. She contends that she has never had an "adoptive mother." When I asked her about the shaman who initiated her, she merely repeated that she never had an "adoptive mother." She insists that in everything she does professionally, she is guided by her spirits during a trance. When I pointed out that she currently had a male *mudang* in apprenticeship under her, she snapped that not all *mudang* are the same. Some are guided strictly by their possessing spirits, and she is one of these. It seems that she cannot tolerate the possibility that she might have acquired her *mudang* role the way a craftsman acquires his skills in the craft. It seems crucial to her to maintain that her assumption of the shaman role was entirely involuntary.

> When I sit facing a client across the *chŏm* ("divination") table, words tumble out of my mouth of their own accord. I have no notion of what I am going to say, but words just well up from the depths of my belly, from my guts. . . . Sometimes, my mind is a complete blank, so I begin to recite chants. . . . And before I know it, I've things to say. It's as though I suddenly remembered everything that I had temporarily forgotten. But as soon as I leave the divination table, that's it. I'm as ordinary as you.

Ttongkkol-mansin feels that since her life experiences have encompassed both comfort and unspeakable humiliation and deprivation, she can help others. She says: "In life, difficult times lead into good times, and good times aren't faithful. So, I try to meet everyone's need inasmuch as I serve these spirits for others. I do nothing unreasonable to others."

Unlike some shamans I have observed, Ttongkkol-mansin does not intimidate clients who put down only a token offering to the spirits, these offerings being in fact payments to her. She has no minimum rate, and some of her clients put down as little as 50 *wŏn* (US $.25). Ttongkkol-mansin explains that for some of her clients 50 *wŏn* is more precious than 500 *wŏn* to others. "Imagine," she exclaims, "how desperate they must feel to lose face like that in front of strangers! How can I think of easy money, eh?" She claims she does not slight such clients in the services she provides. It is obvious from watching her interact with her clients that she derives a great personal satisfaction from her shaman role, but she says "shamanizing" is an exhausting job. One feels constantly responsible for one's clients. Ttongkkol-mansin's clients come from all levels of the society and from a widely dispersed geographical area. She is quite willing to travel far to perform *kut*.

Most of Ttongkkol-mansin's clients come to her by word of mouth. She says she sees about twenty clients a week during the summer, but I think it is an exceedingly modest estimate. I have seen her receive seventeen clients in less than seven hours one June day as I sat waiting for a chance to interview her. She says she welcomes such periodic swells in the number of clients who call but contends that one-time clients are insignificant as far as her income is concerned. She derives the major portion of her income from a core of regular clients who stay with her from year to year, as some families do with a medical doctor. She makes every effort to keep her regular clients satisfied, but some leave her after a long patronage anyway. They desert her generally to transfer to a newly initiated *mudang*. A small number also leave her because she will not do what they want her to do. She is philosophical about fickle clients.

> You lose a few and pick up a few. That's how it goes. If I could fulfill everyone's desire, why would I have need to touch the soil of this earth with the soles of my feet? No, I should go flying through the sky, if that were so, wouldn't I?

There are other causes for concern. A constant source of professional anxiety for Ttongkkol-mansin lies in having to make accurate estimates of the profit margin in any *kut* she agrees to perform. From a *kut* for which she charges $100, she usually nets about $25 to $35, but it cannot be relied upon as a constant factor. The price of a *kut* is never explicitly set ahead of time. When an agreement is made regarding a given kind of *kut*, the *mudang* has the option of asking the client to supply all the needed items or of asking for a sum of money necessary for their purchase. Shamans generally prefer the latter arrangement, and no client expects the shaman to return the unspent portion. Since the cost of various items is fairly standardized, there cannot be too much padding. During the *kut*, the *mudang* can point out the appropriate moments when her clients should make additional cash offerings to the spirits, but she cannot dictate or always predict how much the clients will give. Ttongkkol-mansin says she always reciprocates her clients who have been generous with cash offerings with the ritual food from the *kut*.

> When the *kut* is over, it is customary to serve the clients a good meal from the foods used in the *kut*. . . . I always make sure that

generous clients take back at least half the cakes and fruits and other portable foods from the *kut*. But sometimes there is hardly enough cash to pay wages to hired helpers. I always pay them well even if I have to dip into my own purse. . . . Why shouldn't I pay people who do real work while I peddle lies from these spirits?

Asked if she then concurred with the popular public opinion in Korea that all *mudang* are deceiving women, she answered in the affirmative without hesitation. Her spirits sometimes lie to her so that she is deceived along with her clients, she says. Ignoring my question as to the possible motive of her spirits to dupe her, she explains further her motive for paying her helpers generously and on time.

What I sell is not honest labor like digging ditches or making cakes. I sell the labor of my mouth—words which I receive from the spirits. I try to do right by them [helpers] and my clients. I maintain a large household on a standard of living barely achieved by most working men. When I realize that, I feel grateful to the spirits.

Just as one might begin to get the impression that Ttongkkol-mansin considers all her supernatural activities a huge farce, a "put-on," she contradicts such an impression. For example, she explains her 1971 stroke as a partially fulfilled prophesy made fifteen years previously when she was suffering from her *sinbyŏng*. What her family describes as a stroke, she interprets as a visit to the netherworld from which she returned once again. She describes her experience of the stroke as a "dream-like" vision. The same ancestral gentlemen who had appeared dressed in the Yi Dynasty fashion in the earlier "dream" appeared this time as two generals. They were accompanied by five other generals, all just returning from a battlefield. Both men and beasts were out of breath and sweating from their journey. She bid her household to fetch them water and feed them. When she woke from her "dream," she discovered she had become paralyzed on one side.

Ttongkkol-mansin was sure the dream was a message from the supernatural world, but she was not sure what the message was. She sent emissaries to a few well-known *mudang* as well as a couple of newly initiated *mudang* for their interpretations of her dream. The general consensus that emerged was that she had been released from death once more and that if she did not do proper obeisance to the spirits which possessed her, she would suffer another long illness. She understood. She was about to engage the newly initiated shamans that she had consulted to perform a *kut* on her behalf to show her gratitude to the spirits, when it occurred to her that she ought to do it herself. She cast for an auspicious day which turned out to be 17 February. (She had her stroke on 23 January of the same year, she says.) She could barely walk and needed help to make it up the steep path all the way to Kuksadang, which is at a mountain peak.

As soon as the *kut* was underway, though, she felt the intrusion of her spirits; and once possessed, she had no difficulty holding up and wielding those heavy swords and spears that shamans use during their ritual. She soon dismissed to the side the assisting *mudang* and completed the *kut* herself. Her physical transformation was sensational and struck her audience dumb with awe. (The mistress of Kuksadang had related this incident to me before I ever met Ttongkkol-mansin. In fact, it was one of her main reasons for suggesting Ttongkkol-mansin as an informant.)

Ttongkkol-mansin rules her household not only as its mistress but also as its de facto head. She does not perform a single taks of domestic nature though. In fact, she is the epitome of a self-assured Korean male household head in her behavior. She even uses the masculine speech style. When guests are asked to stay for meals, she and her guests are served before her husband. Of an evening when there is a lull in her professional activities, she saunters out to the *sarang-bang* to join the rest of the family for a television show or two, the way a Korean man may visit the inner rooms to join his family in their activities. Usually, she prefers to lie down in the altar room and enjoy her pipe tobacco.

When the younger children come into the altar room where she sleeps, dragging their bedding, she yells at them to go elsewhere. Ignoring her, the youngest one (who was ten in 1973) generally makes his bed behind his mother's back wherever it happens to be, and this she tolerates. She says he still reaches for her empty breasts at night. But even he must vacate the altar room if there is a night *kut* there. If there are no early clients, the younger children are allowed to eat breakfast with their mother in the altar room; otherwise, they are shunted into the *sarang-bang* with the rest.

Every morning, Ttongkkol-mansin gives specific instructions

to her housekeeper regarding what needs to be done during the day both for the family and herself. Some of her older children, feeling awkward about giving orders directly to the housekeeper, bring their requests to her before they leave the house for the day. These, Ttongkkol-mansin delegates to her housekeeper who in turn usually has one or two hired helpers to assist her. When the boys need something immediately, they often press their half-sister into service, whether ironing or mending something for them. Ttongkkol-mansin does not feel she should be concerned with such trivia. Besides, she views hiring out her domestic chores as an act of benevolence. Does it not provide work for those who need it?

In contrast to other shamans I have observed, Ttongkkol-mansin has a congenial relationship with her neighbors. She feels very grateful to them for not complaining to the police about the noise from her *kut*. She tries to show her gratitude by donating generously to weddings, births, funerals, and victims of fires in the neighborhood. She also helps support several poor families in the neighborhood by rotating the jobs she hires out among the women who need the work. But her refusal to do domestic work is not merely a matter of time or of providing work for the needy. She feels, and says so explicitly, that she does more than her share in bringing in the family's income without also having to be the family drudge as most housewives in Korea are. In addition, she is frequently gone overnight or several nights at a time on her job and needs to have a dependable and mature woman to supervise the household in her absence. She says: "I have absolutely no qualms, no bad feelings or worries when I am gone from the house because I know there is someone here to look after everyone and everything. Not like before when I had to leave the children by themselves or, just as bad, with my old man."

Ttongkkol-mansin feels that being a *mudang* is far from being the worst thing that can happen to a woman. She would rather see a daughter a *mudang* than a prostitute, or a physically deformed freak, or starving to death. She herself seems to enjoy her *mudang* role. There is no question that she completely de-emphasizes her role as a mother and wife. She performs them in a cursory fashion. When her husband gets hungry, he comes to the general vicinity of the kitchen and indirectly inquires of the housekeeper, "Is the meal almost ready?" by addressing the words to the air about him. One day her youngest boy came in crying; after a sidelong glance to see if his mother was in the mood for it, he went instead into the kitchen to the housekeeper for comfort. Actually, the entire household moves gingerly around Ttongkkol-mansin, ever alert to her disposition at the time. This *nunch'i* ("savoir faire") behavior is not in itself unusual in a Korean household, but it is almost always displayed toward the father or grandfather.

Ttongkkol-mansin is aware of some of these anomalies. She speaks openly and unsolicited of her sense of estrangement from both her husband and children.

It's natural for the husband-wife relationship to suffer when a woman becomes a *mudang*. And it happens that there is no help for it. I didn't want to know my husband after possession by the spirits, even though I bore children till age forty-two. When you are too close to your husband or come together with him too often, the gods punish you by afflicting you with severe illnesses. Naturally, you grow distant. . . . It's the same with the children. I dislike them. I have but myself. I know no one but myself. As a parent, I feel attached to them; after all, did they not issue from me? So, I feed them, clothe them, shelter them, and otherwise look after them and rear them but that's all. Strange! And it must be a sure sign that I'm possessed by spirits. That's not how a mother feels about her children. How did I come to be so "far" from my children? I have no personal affection for either my husband or children. I feel very distant from them all. They seem unreal to me at times. . . . What worries me is that something bad might happen to my husband or children while I am a *mudang*. People will say: "After that woman became a *mudang*, her husband died, or her children died." So, I take good care of my family. Now, don't you think that's another sure sign of my possession? I can't be in my own mind. No doubt about it but what I am possessed by jealous spirits.

At the same time, Ttongkkol-mansin feels genuinely sympathetic towards her husband for having to be her husband. She says:

The old man isn't a bad person. His only sin is that he is an incompetent and a weakling. But he doesn't harm anyone. All in all, it's the old man who has suffered and been abused the most as a consequence of my becoming a shaman. It's not even likely that he'll ever again see his home [in North Korea] before his days draw to a close. My old man endures a lot. No matter what, I'm grateful to him for his understanding. But it wouldn't really do any good if he complained, anyway.

She has a similarly sympathetic understanding of what it has been like for her children:

They feel it's something I couldn't help. After all, I did not choose it; fate chose me for the role. . . . I feel it was worth the struggle because my children are educated; they understand so much. The educated are after all different from the illiterate. . . .

My children say to me now, "Mother, whatever you do, what is important now is that we repay you for your sacrifice by succeeding in the world ourselves." How different it was when they were young! They'd come in crying sometimes . . . they had got into a fight because some kids called them a *mudang*'s bastards. At times like that they'd cry all the harder—harder than when they got cut up in a scuffle. They felt so unfairly victimized; yet, there was no defense against that. With their fists, they were a fair match, but against *that*, they had no defense. The other kids' fathers might be just day laborers barely keeping "the spider from weaving his webs in the mouths of their families" but their mothers weren't *mudang*. . . . At times like that, we cried, mother and children, locked into each others' arms, until we were exhausted and our guts felt sore. I wanted to just die. Many times I thought of taking my life, but always I felt it would be selfish of me to save myself the agony of living and leave the children and the old man behind. Their father was getting on in years and could not support them anyway. How many times I wished I could give up the whole business! How can you explain being a *mudang* to your own kids? I'd just say to them, between sobs, "It's so, it's so. Your mother is a *mudang*." They are only now beginning to understand why I became a *mudang*. . . .

Her eloquence as an apologist for her professional role notwithstanding, Ttongkkol-mansin experiences genuine regret over her *mudang* role, at least periodically. She says the quirks of fate that selected her for the *mudang* role out of so many equally probable candidates gnaw at her if she thinks about it at all. She would have been content to have been able to eke out a living as a merchant woman, as she had begun to do in the early days of her refugee life. She resents her responsibility of "giving life to the dying, of lengthening short lives, and of making the childless fertile." She finds these responsibilities agonizing. She is careful to evade certain clients:

> When my divination reveals doom for my clients, I won't have anything to do with them . . . other than perform the *tarit-kut* [the *kut* performed for the dead within forty-nine days of death]. . . . Why should I hang myself on an impossible task for a few lousy *wŏns?*

Intermittently and seriously, she has considered diversifying the base of her income by going into business with one of her sons, but she says she has never had enough money saved to start such a venture. If she were willing to go into debt or to operate on credit, she might be able to maneuver it; however, she is fiercely adamant that the household operate on a "cash-and-carry" principle. As a result, it has not been possible for her to accumulate sufficient capital to start a business. Ttongkkol-mansin thinks that nothing is more ridiculous than the Korean custom of being generous, whether to one's children or to guests, on borrowed resources. She refuses to go into debt.

Ttongkkol-mansin is chronically plagued by the nagging thought that one of her daughters or granddaughters may eventually become a *mudang*. She finds a glint of comfort in the fact that the spirits which possess her are *not* her ancestral ghosts; they are, therefore, as likely to look for her successor among non-kinsmen as among her daughters or granddaughters. Still, the possibility of one of her female descendants succeeding her to the *mudang* role is too big a worry to be left to chance. Her current strategy for averting such a fate is to build a *tang* on their house site when the youngest of her children is married.

> If I were to build a shrine here, spring and fall people from all over, especially my regular clients, would come to visit it. I don't think this religion [shamanism] is going to disappear all that soon. . . . I may be wrong; the world may be turned upside down. Still, I don't think this religion will go into oblivion. . . .
>
> I would put up a signboard that will inform the visitors that Ttongkkol-mansin who built this shrine was born in such-and-such place. She came to this spot on such-and-such date as a refugee and received the spirits on 14 October 1955. She worked as a *mudang* on this spot for x number of years until her death on

such-and-such date. I will go down in history that way. When I visit Buddhist temples that are several hundred years old, I envision building a shrine that will survive me the way they have. It isn't really to have something to give to my children as inheritance that I dream such dreams. I think that if my possessing spirits have a permanent home where they are worshipped, they are less likely to bother or possess any of my descendants.

Of the many dramatic changes which have marked their lives since she assumed the *mudang* role, Ttongkkol-mansin feels that the most positive one has been the improvement of her health, followed by their relative affluence today. As she describes it, "Where there was just one spoon before, now two spoons dance [i.e., more food for spoons to partake of]." On the negative side, she lists uppermost the changes which have characterized her human relationships. The changes have been mostly sad. She feels that the only pre-shaman personality traits she has retained are her abiding sense of generosity and duty, although she finds it difficult to express even these the way she would prefer to, were she not a *mudang*.

When she is invited to birthday or wedding celebrations by neighbors or relatives, she declines, though she dutifully sends gifts with one of the children or with her husband. She is afraid that people may blame her for any untoward thing that may happen to them afterwards. She is also afraid that her hosts may suffer in social prestige for associating with a *mudang*. Even when she merely sends a gift with a member of the household, she worries that the recipients may say that she caused them *tongt'i* ("arousing the wrath of subterranean gods by disturbing the earth, referring generally to trouble brought upon self gratuitously") if anything were to happen to them.

> The truth is that I am afraid I am a liability to all whom I associate with socially. These negative tendencies make one's personality bad. There is an old saying that even distant households become closer by frequent visits and even relatives become distant if they don't see [you] often. Well, my antisocial personality traits have developed largely because of my self-imposed restrictions on social interactions. I have not been proud to go among relatives and friends "wearing my *mudang*'s garb." . . . In fact, I plan to retire to a Buddhist nunnery if all goes well when my *maknae* ("the last born") is in the eighth grade. If I can provide ahead for his high school education, I will

leave him with his eldest brother and his wife and go into a nunnery. There, even these spirits will not bother me, for I shall not be useful to them there. . . . My old man? He's already sixty-four; will he live forever? Besides, I have given him six sons. Surely, he will not want for a place to stay.

Ttongkkol-mansin tends to see herself as an alienated person, a person standing alone, apart, perhaps with only her spirits; and even they are fickle. Frequently, she speculates out loud that they are not faithful to their commitment to her. In an allegorical attempt to impart to me her assessment of human nature, she says:

There is an old saying that goes like this: "When the *taegam's* ("His Excellency's") dog died, there was a throng of mourners vying to express their condolences but when the *taegam* himself died, not a single mourner cast his shadow at his gate." The crucial things you see throughout life are, first, bitter experiences and, secondly, *insim* ("human-heartedness"). You cannot hope to fathom the minds of others. Don't you know the proverb that you can give birth to the body of a child but not to his soul? You may know gold from iron, but you cannot distinguish among human beings. But it's also true, as the saying goes, that if you grab a handful of weeds, you may find in it a lovely flower or two as well. . . . Who knows? I may learn life is otherwise; one is never too old to learn. Don't we have a saying that the eighty-year-old grandmother dies after learning her last lesson in life from her three-year-old grandchild?

*

6

SUWŎN-MANSIN

BRIEF CHRONOLOGY OF SUWON-MANSIN'S LIFE

1937	Born fourth child, first daughter. Two immediately older brothers died in infancy
1944	Enrolled in school in Seoul
1944-1945	Oldest brother died mysteriously
1950	The Korean War began just after she entered high school
1954	Parents retired; left Suwon-mansin with an old servant in Seoul to finish school
1956	Graduated from high school and entered college in Seoul
1957	Met future husband and became sexually involved with him
1959	Future husband conscripted into the army
1960	Became pregnant just before graduation
	Graduated from college and got married
	Moved to husband's main household in the province to live with husband's family in his absence
	Pregnancy spontaneously aborted

1961	Second pregnancy
	Prolonged visit to natal household with husband; did not wish to return to husband's household but forced to do so
	First child, son, born at natal household
1962	Husband discharged from the Army and obtained a job in Seoul
	Suwŏn-mansin, pregnant again, and son moved to Seoul with husband and started nuclear household living
1963	Began to become agitated about extraneous household members
1964	Third child, son
1966	Fourth child, son
	Baptised into the Catholic Church
	Hospitalized for appendectomy and recurring post-operative complications
	First experience of hallucination
	Shoulders dislocated by a "giant"
	First experience with sinbyŏng
1967	Unable to manage own household; sent back to live with sister-in-law again
	Neighbors suggested she might be suffering from sinbyŏng
	Went on a pilgrimage
1967-1968	Her natal family officially requested to take her back by her husband's family
	She "clapped" her hands at natal home, signaling spirit possession and returned to husband's home town
	Made a public prophesy regarding a police station which came true; people imputed to her supernatural power by asking for divination service
	Husband confused: Was his wife insane or was she possessed?
	Tied to a post to be sent back to her natal home
1968	At natal home, brother suggested suicide to her

Left natal home and went to Seoul and assumed the role of *mudang*

Had her prophetic power tested and started serious study of shamanism

Had ideas for organizing a utopian community for Buddhists and shamanistic believers.

Became discouraged with *mudang* role and tried to get into an entrepreneur's role; fainted en route to contract signing

Renewed commitment to shaman role

1968-1969　　In-laws relocated to Seoul and invited her to return provided she kept her *mudang* role segregated; interrupts Suwŏn-mansin's plans for initiation ceremony

1969　　Husband left for America in secrecy

1969-1970　　Husband sent for the three sons from Hawaii

Suwŏn-mansin fled from in-laws' with daughter; her in-laws kidnapped her back

1971　　Renewed her commitment to the *mudang* role; had her initiation rite

Adopted a son

1972-1973　　Husband returned from Hawaii with their three sons and invited her to join in the reunion

Daughter was finally allowed to come and live with her

SUWŎN-MANSIN

The youngest, the most attractive, and the most fashionably stylish of the informants in this study, Suwŏn-mansin is also the most educated. She is a college graduate, having attended Sŏrabŏl College of Arts in Seoul. English words in popular usage among certain college-educated Korean women and in glossy women's magazines pop into her conversation with an ease characteristic of old habit.

Her mannerisms vary readily with the occasion and situation, and usually very convincingly. At home, in the strictly domestic and personal sphere, she is calmly proprietary and managerial. In more public domains when she is performing in her professional capacity as a shaman, she is often extremely coquettish in a manner reminiscent of traditionally trained *kisaeng*. In the presence of some men, she can also be quite willfully seductive. She appears almost relentless in her expert titillation of men; she seems smugly and unabashedly aware of her sexual attractiveness. When the client for her *kut* is male, she interacts with her client more frequently and intimately in the course of the *kut* than when the client is female.

A captivating dancer and a stirring chanter, she often leaves her audience at *kut* spellbound in open-mouthed appreciation. Improvising at times, she dances with the confidence of one who knows she is good. When her low-keyed, almost hoarsely husky voice hits a high pitch in the chant, she is electrifying. Her inspired musicians come alive and punctuate their own music with gusty shouts of "*Chotta'a* ("Bravo")!"

Suwŏn-mansin is also the only shaman who sought me out and volunteered herself as an informant. I first met her in 1971 at Kuksadang where I had gone to meet another shaman who failed to keep her appointment. Perhaps to mollify my disappointment, the mistress of Kuksadang who had arranged the aborted meeting invited me to stay for a *chaesu-kut* ("*kut* for good luck") scheduled for that afternoon. When I asked about the possibility of meeting and perhaps later interviewing the shaman performing the *kut*, the shrine mistress expressed her doubts as to her suitability. "Sure, you can meet her," she said, "but I don't think she will be a good one to interview. She lies and exaggerates a lot and thinks she is very special just because she went to college. But the truth is, she is not very bona fide; she improvises a lot in her *kut* if she is not with *ch'ŏngsong-mansin* ("expert shamans who act as consultants"). You will get inaccurate information on Korean shamanism from her." I reiterated my wish to meet her and stayed to watch one of the most aesthetically stimulating *kut* performances I had seen.

The *kut* lasted almost five hours, ending just as dusk engulfed the city below. I was eager to meet the shaman, but the shrine mistress said the shaman and her coterie would be busy for another hour putting their paraphernalia away. Instead, she guided me into the pathway leading to the fertility rock farther up the mountain. Barren women come to pray for conception there. We were halfway up the path when the shrine mistress's young son came running to tell his mother that Suwŏn-mansin wanted to see her. I started to follow, but she motioned me to go on up to the fertility rock as she hurried toward Suwŏn-mansin, now sitting under a tree just outside the shrine. I could not hear them but kept them focused in my view. Soon the shrine mistress motioned me to come to them.

With a look of misgiving, the shrine mistress said: "Suwŏn-mansin wants to meet you. She wants you to study her." I was pleased but a little confused by Suwŏn-mansin's smile; it bordered uncomfortably on being a smirk. She apparently felt no hesitation. She offered full cooperation. She then demanded to know if my dissertation would be published as a book. Not knowing why she asked but impressed that she knew the process by which doctoral dissertations sometimes metamorphosed into books, I told her that it was a possibility. "Good," she exclaimed, "you make sure yours gets published, because I have a request. I want you to run a full photo of me, dressed as a shaman, on the first page of your book. The caption should read:

This is Suwŏn-mansin, the abandoned wife of O XX, a son of a bitch and a bastard.

She went on: "I hear he has an American wife and a child. . . . He went there to study, huh! I want you to run my picture in your book. I want to haunt him in America. He thinks he is so safe there from the shame of me. Huh! I want him to feel utterly ashamed. I want him to see pictures of me in all the bookstores in America!" She spoke with menacing vehemence.

I warned her that I could not promise such an outcome as a condition of our interview. By now we were encircled by a throng of curious people. Leaning toward her, I whispered if I might visit her at her home for our interviews. Her response was: "Why not now?" She insisted that her helpers would be at least another hour getting everything packed. What did I want to know? Did I have my pad and pencil ready? Or a tape-recorder, maybe?

For about an hour, Suwŏn-mansin talked almost without pause, totally engulfed in her own flood of words, seemingly unmindful of the snickers and open protests from her retinue when she embellished her accounts too elaborately for their comfort and own recollections. Certainly, much of what she said during the hour sounded fantastic. I had to strain constantly for internal consistency.

Suwŏn-mansin lives in a lower middle-class residential neighborhood, not far from the Independence Gate and only a bit farther from Kuksadang on Sŏnbawi Mountain where she performs all her major *kut*. Houses are very irregularly numbered in her neighborhood, so that having her address was of little actual help. I inquired of neighborhood storekeepers and finally located the house, but the woman who claimed to be Suwŏn-mansin was a stranger to me. After some embarrassed explanation on my part, the shaman pointed to a spot higher up the hill and said I must be looking for the other Suwŏn-mansin. She instructed me to ask storekeepers along the way for the house of Suwŏn-mansin "the younger" ("*chŏlmŭni*"), "the pretty" ("*eppuni*"), or "the stylish" (*mŏttchaengi*).

I regretted not having done so from the start, as my Suwŏn-mansin had told me to do just that. These adjectives were obviously routinely used to distinguish the two shamans in the same neighborhood, but because she had beamed with such undisguised pleasure as she insisted upon them for locating her, I had thought she was bragging. All during the first summer of fieldwork with her, I remained at a loss to know when she was fabricating and when she was not.

Though the house is badly cramped into a small lot, it is the only two-story house in the neighborhood. It is painted bright blue—a most unusual color for a house in Korea. Inside, the layout is typically Korean, an L-shaped structure cradling a small courtyard. Immediately to the right, a narrow stairway leads up to the second floor. Though there were men there, the women, including Suwŏn-mansin, were dressed only in their undergarments. A very young soldier in uniform sat patiently at the edge of the *maru*, as though he were not part of the scene. Suwŏn-mansin seemed both surprised and pleased to see me, and at once introduced me to those present. I had met some of them already at the Kuksadang *kut*. After a while, an old woman came in with a bundle of candles, incense sticks, and a few golden melons (*kŭmch'amoe*).

Putting on her outer garment, Suwŏn-mansin preceded the old woman and the soldier to the second floor, inviting me to come along. The entire second floor consists of a room, about ten by twelve feet, which served as a shrine, and a veranda crowded with flowering plants. Once on the second floor, it was difficult to realize one had just come up from the floor below. The two floors represented two different orders of phenomena.

On the first level, there are five small rooms, including the kitchen. Suwŏn-mansin and her adopted infant son occupy the inner room (*anbang*). Her two widowed aunts and their four daughters, who double as live-in servants and nursemaids, occupy the remaining rooms. Suwŏn-mansin would like her daughter to live with them also, but her in-laws refuse to let her. All during the summer of 1971 she was in a bitter struggle with them over her daughter's custody. Her daughter wants to live with her and runs away from her grandfather's and uncle's place whenever she can, but the uncle or his henchmen always take her back.

The *anbang* is crowded with the usual status-symbol items: television, electric fan, telephone, and an oversized stereo cabinet with many records of popular Western and Korean songs. In one compartment of the stereo cabinet is a stack of Pet condensed milk bought no doubt on the black market for her three-month-old adopted baby. Suwŏn-mansin has remained very secretive about the circumstances of the baby's adoption, except to say that she "relieved an unwed mother of her burden."

When she is with the baby, she gives it very little peace. She is constantly playing with it, sometimes undoing the diaper and fondling his penis, calling everyone to look at the "little chili pepper." When the baby spits out or otherwise loses the pacifier, she immediately shoves another into his mouth and commands someone to wash the other. She personally supervises all the bottle washing and formula making. She is completely absorbed in the baby. At the least sign of fuss from the baby, she calls in one of her nieces or aunts to carry the baby on her back and take it for a walk.

On my first visit I got off to a poor start. Suwŏn-mansin wanted to talk about American movie stars and other celebrities on whose love lives she wanted the latest "scoop," but I had no new information. Disappointed but apparently determined to salvage some of her expectations of me, she put on a jazz record and asked me what kind of music I liked. What were Americans dancing to now? Would I like to dance with her? I could not satisfy her on any of these. She seemed a little dispirited but began to tell me of her own likes and dislikes and how she had studied singing, dancing, and drama at Sŏrabŏl College of Arts; how her singing in the traditional manner of a shaman has ruined her once fine contralto voice; and how even now she goes to cabarets occasionally just to watch others dance, though her possessing spirits, jealous of her diversion from them, silence the band music so that she sees a roomful of people dancing to no music at all. As she talked about herself, the oversized, elaborately gowned and coiffured Western-style doll on the dresser, the wardrobe full of the latest style of Western clothes, popular records, and stacks of women's magazines, glossy and pulpy, all made more sense as part of her surroundings.

Professionally at her peak in 1971, she was much in demand by other shamans and had a fairly constant stream of clients calling on her at home. But she frequently found seeing clients an onerous task, and kept them waiting for long periods before seeing them. She sometimes chainsmoked two or three cigarettes before meeting her waiting clients in the shrine room. By contrast, she enjoyed performing in large *kut*; she hoped that her fellow shamans would make her a *ch'ŏngsong-mansin* ("expert shaman who does consulting"). She wanted to dispense with the daily routine of seeing clients for divination.

When I last saw her in 1973, she had made a number of major changes in her life. She was still very much engrossed in her adopted son, talking to him constantly of growing up big and taking care of her in her old age. Though her own daughter was now living with her, Suwŏn-mansin clearly preferred her adopted son. She let her daughter drop out of school in the sixth grade, saying she does not think a college education particularly useful for women. During the winter of 1972/1973, her former husband had returned to Korea for a visit, bringing their three sons who had been with him in Honolulu. On this occasion, he invited Suwŏn-mansin and their daughter to participate in the family and lineage reunion. She was immensely grateful to her ex-husband for this residue of good will toward her and wanted me to look up her husband and sons in Honolulu, but her in-laws would not divulge the address. She bitterly resented this slight and was determined to "show them." She would become wealthy and have her in-laws grovel before her, she declared. During the summer of 1973, she was actively pursuing this goal.

Encouraged by her ex-husband to quit the shaman role if possible, she took a giant step in the winter of 1972/1973 toward actualizing a long-standing desire to change her occupation. In partnership with a man who had been a regular client for *kut*, she purchased a cabaret on Chongno, one of the busiest streets in downtown Seoul. She also transformed her personal appearance. Since becoming a shaman, she had always worn her hair parted in the middle and in a traditional *tchok*. Now, she had her hip-length hair cut just below the shoulders and had it waved, as befits a cabaret proprietress. When seeing her shaman clients she wore her hair in a modified *tchok* that others called *sinsik-mŏri* ("new style hairdo").

Suwŏn-mansin no longer saw her shaman clients after supper but spent the evenings at the cabaret, not to work as a madam but to "see how things are going." She usually watched from an obscure booth but emerged at whim to interact with those customers who struck her fancy. She was also attending a language school to "brush up" on her Japanese, as many of the cabaret customers were Japanese male tourists. She enjoyed visits to the cabaret immensely. There in the cabaret, with hair done up in a becoming French twist, false eyelashes securely in place, her face made up extravagantly but tastefully, and her cigarette in hand, Suwŏn-mansin, the shaman, was totally eclipsed by Suwŏn-mansin the proprietress.

The interior of her house has also been remodeled since the summer of 1972. She has moved the altar from the second floor to the *anbang* where it is concealed behind a newly installed pair of sliding doors. Her daughter and adopted son sleep in this room now, while she sleeps upstairs. The second floor is now a Western-style sitting room/bedroom, though it lacks a Western-style bed. She receives all her non-shamanistic callers, including me, in this room. Judging from its interior decoration, one might easily mistake it as her daughter's room.

Suwŏn-mansin desperately wants her venture in the cabaret to succeed so that she can quit her shaman's role completely. She feels that 1973 and 1974 will be crucial years for her and is a little afraid that she may not be able to maintain her dual role as a shaman and an entrepreneur. She wants to send her adopted son to Seoul National University; she has already purchased a complete set of encyclopedias and children's books—on monthly installments—although the second birthday celebration was only a short while before.

Suwŏn-mansin was born in 1937, the fourth child and the only daughter of seven children. Two elder brothers who immediately preceded her did not survive infancy, and her eldest brother was ten years her senior. Her lineage was moderately wealthy, having enough resources to send her father to Seoul for both his high school and college education during the Japanese colonial period. It was an extraordinary feat both in foresight and in material resources for a rural Korean family in the early part of the century. Nevertheless, her lineage and family were deeply grooved in tradition, and her father was married to a woman several years his senior when in high school. She remained with his parents in Suwŏn, Kyŏnggi-do, the seat of his lineage, while her husband was in school, seeing him on his periodic visits and during vacations.

Suwŏn-mansin was born in the house where her ancestors had lived for an untold number of generations, until recently the only tile-roofed house in the village. By the time of her birth, her father had a modest civil service job with the central government and was subject to periodic transfers. Her mother accompanied him on these transfers, returning to the ancestral house in Suwŏn with the children during school vacations.

Although a girl, Suwŏn-mansin says her birth was welcomed and her growth, watched with a great deal of anxiety, because two older brothers immediately above her had died during infancy. Her grandparents were so concerned about her health that they insisted her father go to his new assignment without his family until Suwŏn-mansin was a bit older. In the meantime, they secured the service of a distant kinswoman as a nursemaid for her. Even then, the grandparents hovered about her so much that both the nursemaid and her mother lived each day in dread of something happening to Suwŏn-mansin. Suwŏn-mansin proved a delight to her grandparents and a relief to her caretakers, for she was healthy, though badly spoiled. She claims she was an exceptionally lovely looking child, and in fact she was; she still has many photographs taken during her infancy and delights in showing them to people.

According to Suwŏn-mansin's aunts, their brother, Suwŏn-mansin's father, was a man of few words who was humble about his college education and government position. Even with his wife, he was unerringly a gentleman, addressing her in the respect form of speech and treating her as he would an elder sister. He was also a filial son, but did not know much about the management of the family and lineage land holdings. As a result, Suwŏn-mansin's grandfather had to supervise all their agricultural production long past the usual time for informal retirement. He always made sure that his son's family did not want for anything, by supplementing the latter's salary with rice and other farm products the year round. The old man was apparently an equally doting grandfather. Commemorative photographs of Suwŏn-mansin's one hundred day anniversary and first birthday anniversary celebrations show a broadly smiling elderly gentleman propping up his granddaughter, with the help of his wife, behind an elaborately laden table.

Suwŏn-mansin's life continued much the same way as she grew up. During the summer her family returned to Suwŏn to live with the grandparents, except of course her father, who could not leave his job. In her grandfather's village, Suwŏn-mansin had greater freedom of movement and more playmates than in her own household and neighborhoods, but she was still isolated by special treatment accorded her by the villagers, adults and children alike. As her grandparents were the wealthiest farmers in the village, the penumbra extended by their social status kept her shielded and privileged throughout the village and beyond. As Suwŏn-mansin herself put it, "I grew up *not* knowing what it was not to have my own way or not to be the most privileged."

During this period, her mother gave birth to two younger brothers, but they did not diminish the attention Suwŏn-mansin received from her grandparents or her mother's anxiety about incurring her parents-in-law's displeasure by the way she was rearing her daughter.

Suwŏn-mansin's family continued the pattern of accompanying her father as he was transferred from one post to another in different parts of the country. In 1944 when she was seven, her father was assigned to a post in Seoul. World War II was at its midway point, and Japan's war efforts were beginning to severely strain resources. In Korea, the Japanese colonial government was intensifying the Japanization of Koreans which had begun in the 1930s. It now compelled enrollment of school-age children, including girls, in elementary schools as an aspect of the assimilation program. Very probably, Suwŏn-mansin would have been sent to school even if such a program were not in effect, as it was becoming relatively commonplace by this time for girls to attend school in urban areas, especially Seoul (cf. W. K. Han 1970). In any case, she was enrolled in school at age seven. At about this time or shortly afterward, her older brother died under mysterious circumstances involving the Japanese police.

Suwŏn-mansin liked school and did acceptable work in the classroom, but she excelled in singing and acting. She was, she says with pride, in every play that her class or school put on for the parents. Her mother came to every performance, of course, and faithfully attended all the parent-teacher conferences as well. Her mother made sure that her classroom teachers received gifts at the beginning and end of each semester.[1] She has less happy memories of her relationships with peers at school, however. Many did not like her, and though she tried, she could not get into any of the cliques. She attributes her peers' rejection to their jealousy, indicating she was always better dressed and brought more delicious lunches to school than they. She did fare better, however, with her teachers. She was often their favorite.

Her mother gave birth to yet another healthy younger brother, but Suwŏn-mansin almost gleefully recalls that she retained her central position in the family configuration. She explains that it was because she was "just the kind of a child that adults delight in." She was coaxing and sweet-talking in her manners with adults, especially with the important ones. She was cheerful and pretty, and, by her own admission, could turn her charms on or off as it suited her. If she failed to get her way through charm, she recalls, she used to pout and sulk until she prevailed. She used the same technique also to expose servants that "abused her." She never directly "tattled" on them but if one of them did not comply with her demands, she would sulk and pout until cajoled by her mother to explain her reasons.

She was taught no domestic skills during her childhood. Neither was she taught to manage servants appropriately. She says the servants used to call her a "fox" behind her back. Certainly, the image she creates of herself as a child at this stage is that of a brat much dreaded by the household servants, if not by her mother as well.

Once enrolled in school, it became the primary and all-encompassing focus of her life whether at home or at school. Upon graduation from elementary school at thirteen, she sat for examination both at E. Girls' High School and B. Girls' High School. She was rejected by the former, a first-rate school, but accepted by the latter, which was not so prestigious. She did not mind the rejection, for she was more interested in the performing arts and athletics than she was in academic subjects.

Her grandparents continued to be important in her life, as the family still spent school vacations with them, and they in turn visited her family during the school year. One of her fondest memories of her grandparents is of helping her grandmother slip out of the house through a small side door at night after her grandfather had retired, so that she might attend a *kut* or visit a *mudang* for divination. Her grandmother loved these activites and became almost childishly happy whenever she stole out of the house in this manner. Her grandfather usually found out about it though, and there was thunderous shouting and scolding issuing from the *sarang-bang* all the next morning while everyone moved about as little as possible and kept absolutely quiet.

Suwŏn-mansin's memories of her peers in the village are less happy. She does not remember having had any really good friends in the village, in her own neighborhoods, or at school. She sometimes managed to get close to one or another girl for brief but intense periods of friendship, but they always, she recalls, retreated back to their own cliques without her.

Suwŏn-mansin remembers her high school years in post-Korean War Seoul as an exciting and exuberant period in her life. Although only an average student academically, she was a school favorite on both the basketball and volley ball teams and was often cast in lead roles in school dramas. Moreover, she proudly declares, she was one of the pacesetters for the entire student body—one of the "bad" popular girls who were tolerated by teachers. For the first time, she had her own clique of friends. But high school too had its constraints.

She despised having to wear a school uniform which permit-

ted little individuality in dressing. She used to look through
fashion magazines and Sears catalogs from America with a consuming passion and secretly frequented theaters to take in as
many foreign films as she could. Doris Day was her idol. Since
high school students were not allowed to attend theaters without
permission from school authorities and parents, she disguised
herself to look older for these escapades. She had an insatiable
interest in things foreign, she says. She used to cook Western
dishes for her friends, much to the chagrin of the old servant
charged with looking after her while she was finishing school
away from home. Her parents had retired to Suwŏn during her
junior year in high school.

In Suwŏn-mansin's own opinion, her most outstanding feature during high school and college was her physique. She says:

> I had the most fantastic body. . . . Even in high school, but
> especially in college. . . . In those days, it was fashionable to
> have a tiny waist and a huge bosom . . . I remember my friends
> had to pad their shoulders and their breasts, but not me. I had a
> natural body build that a well-fitted, one-piece Western dress
> showed off to a dramatic advantage.

Evidently her physical attractiveness did not go unnoticed. She
met her future husband at a college sporting event when she was
twenty and a sophomore at Sŏrabŏl College of Arts, where she
was majoring in the performing arts. A popular athlete himself,
he played soccer for his school, the College of Engineering, Seoul
National University. They fell passionately in love and were constant companions for the next three years. To her, these courtship
years with her husband represent the pinnacle of her life. In fact,
she would really like her life to be one long protracted courtship.
Although she had no sex education either from her mother or
from school, she says, she had picked up an assortment of information on sex from friends, magazines, and films. What she had
not yet learned, she adds with a smirk, she learned from her
boyfriend, her future husband.

To her, sex seemed the most natural sequence to falling in
love, and they engaged in premarital sex almost from the start of
their romance. At twenty-three, just before graduation, she found
herself pregnant.

Suspecting that their daughter might be involved in a romance that might not result in marriage, Suwŏn-mansin's family

made one very serious attempt to arrange a marriage for her while she was a junior in college. Although she had had an understanding with her future husband from the beginning of their relationship that they would eventually marry, she went along with her family's attempts, partly out of curiosity. She met the prospective groom in a prearranged encounter with both family representatives present. She thought the man ugly, and refused to give the matter a second consideration. Now, in the face of confirmed pregnancy, she could not avoid considering marriage, although it had been her ambition and plan to pursue a career in acting after graduation. At least, she was marrying her lover.

Neither she nor her boyfriend considered induced abortion as an alternative, although it was a common, if illegal, practice among Korean women in 1960. Her boyfriend considered marriage the only solution. It was a matter of informing their respective families and persuading them to consent to their marriage. The groom's family could only comply, being of impeccable *kamun* ("lineage reputation") and prominence in their region. Her parents were grateful that the groom's family was willing to save their daughter from a permanent disgrace.

Because of the very suddenness of the marriage, Suwŏn-mansin's family was unable to provide a lavish wedding or a substantial dowry, as might have been expected of them. As it were, Suwŏn-mansin had gone to her wedding ceremony practically from her graduation ceremony. Following the marriage in Suwŏn, she was taken to her husband's household in South Ch'ungch'ŏng Province, installed under the supervision of his elder brother's wife, and left. Her husband had been doing his mandatory military service since he graduated from college the year before and had to return to his unit shortly after the wedding. Suwŏn-mansin was resentful at being "abandoned and exiled" in a strange household in a region famous for its ultra-conservatism and traditionalism.

For Suwŏn-mansin, all the strain she had anticipated in the role of a rural housewife descended upon her the moment she arrived in her husband's household, which consisted of her father-in-law, her elder brother-in-law, who was the town magistrate, his wife, and their nine children. Her mother-in-law had died some years previously, and her husband's younger brother was in Seoul going to school. An elder sister was long ago married out.

Suwŏn-mansin's sister-in-law was very nice at first, acting as solicitously as if she were a mother. She apologized about their provincial ways, saying, "You are from Seoul and educated in modern ways. You are not used to country living," and treated her as if she were a special and an important guest. Even so, she found life in the country totally frustrating. Sometimes, just out of sheer boredom, she dressed up in some of her best Western-style dresses and realized that half the women from the neighborhood were fighting for a good peephole in the fence to have a look at her. After all, few women there wore anything but the traditional clothes, and certainly no decent married woman went about with exposed calves in her father-in-law's presence, as Suwŏn-mansin did. Her only relief from the monotony of rural life was her husband's occasional visit.

Suwŏn-mansin found her sister-in-law (and women in general in the area) terribly old-fashioned. The way her sister-in-law kept house and cooked reminded her more of her grandmother than even her mother, many years older than her sister-in-law. Suwŏn-mansin missed the city life with an anguish. There were foods that she craved which were simply unavailable in the country. She was amused by some of the regional customs that she found quaint, but no activity interested her enough to participate. As for household chores, Suwŏn-mansin felt neither inclined nor knowledgeable enough to perform. She sent instead her old maidservant to help her sister-in-law, while she lounged in her room reading magazines or experimenting with facial make-up or a hairdo. Her husband had been against bringing the old servant with them, but she had been insistent. Now, the old servant was a constant reminder to everyone that some misfit event had taken place in the household. No one in her husband's household knew quite how to treat her, nor did she know how to fit into the hierarchy of the household. But her presence saved Suwŏn-mansin from the drudgery of the kitchen. She says with unmistakable pride in her voice that she never once cooked a meal during the two or more years she lived with her sister-in-law.

Under the circumstances, her sister-in-law's initial attitude of solicitude changed quickly, becoming almost hostile after Suwŏn-mansin miscarried the baby that had brought about the marriage. Though Suwŏn-mansin conceived again almost immediately, her situation in her husband's household did not

change. Suwŏn-mansin thought she would go mad with boredom and her sister-in-law's exasperatingly correct behavior toward her. She could no longer talk to her sister-in-law; there was
no response beyond a polite and perfunctory acknowledgment of
having been addressed. Even her old servant began to balk at the
awkward situation, often siding with her sister-in-law. Suwŏn-
mansin recalls: "The old hag got to muttering: 'It's a wonder they
don't send you back to your *ch'injŏng* ("natal family")." In fact,
Suwŏn-mansin wanted very much to go back to her own family,
but says she was afraid to ask. She begged her husband but he
put her off each time, saying that he would be out in no time at all
and that they could then move to Seoul where he expected to get
a job.

According to Suwŏn-mansin, her sister-in-law was a very
competent mistress of the household. She did everything with
dispatch and certitude, with scarcely a ruffled note in her voice,
whether it was putting up the winter's supply of *kimch'i*, the
annual stock of soy sauce and bean pastes, serving her father-in-
law his meals, or living with a younger sister-in-law who refused
to "fit in." She was adored by their father-in-law, respected by
her husband, and praised by others. She never raised her voice to
any of her numerous children. Suwŏn-mansin was jarred to see
that her own husband felt a deep affection for her. She had been
like a mother to him, especially since the death of his mother, and
even now she seemed to value his peace of mind above her own.
As far as Suwŏn-mansin could determine, her sister-in-law had
never said an unkind word about her to her husband. She resented her sister-in-law's virtuousness and felt frustrated by it.
She felt that her sister-in-law's behavior misled her husband to
make light of her own complaints about living there. Her sister-
in-law's serene contempt for her tormented her, and she sometimes stayed in her room for days at a time to avoid her. She felt
they had come from different "worlds" and there could never be
any overlap between the two. Suwŏn-mansin was thoroughly
miserable.

On their first wedding anniversary, Suwŏn-mansin and her
husband went to her natal household for a prolonged visit. She
felt like a prisoner out on a temporary pass; she did not want to go
back. Her husband insisted that it would look bad for his sister-
in-law if she were not to go back, and her parents, eternally

beholden to their son-in-law and his family for having "taken her in," agreed with him. She felt utterly trapped. No one understood her predicament and misery nor wanted to help her out of it. Finally, they agreed on a compromise: she could return to give birth to the child with whom she was already several months pregnant.

If her husband had remained home after marriage, he might have been able to function as an intermediary, interpreting his family and helping Suwŏn-mansin cope more acceptably. As it was, she had been abruptly transplanted among virtual strangers about whom she had little more than preconceived and stereotypic notions of rural people. To quote Suwŏn-mansin: "I was scared. . . . I had no one, not even my husband to counsel me (t'airŭda). . . ." She saw her in-laws and their neighbors as backward people in need of modernization, and thought sincerely that she could help them in this endeavor. She had completely mistaken her sister-in-law's expressed recognition of her modernity as an endorsement of her superiority and made no responding move to adjust and adapt to their ways. As a result, her relationship with her sister-in-law and, by extension, others was now tense with polite but mutual hostility. They were locked into an impasse. Both women waited for her husband's discharge from the Army to rescue them from each other. In the meantime, Suwŏn-mansin pined for the city life and the acting career she had abandoned in its inception. She longed for the company of some of her classmates; she was sure none had suffered her exiled fate.

Upon his discharge from the Army in 1962, her husband obtained a position as an engineer in Seoul and moved her and their son there, much to everyone's relief. Shortly afterward, Suwŏn-mansin gave birth to her daughter, with her mother in attendance. Her mother now felt free to visit her and help her with major, seasonal housekeeping events as well. For the first time since her marriage, Suwŏn-mansin felt happy. In retrospect, she describes this period as having been idyllic. But it was not to last. They had no sooner settled into their "home, sweet home" (her own English expression) tan'ga-saenghwal ("nuclear family living") than the stream of visitors from her husband's home town began. The visitors were not limited to relatives; everyone from her husband's home town who had business in Seoul came

to stay with them, sometimes for prolonged periods. Furthermore, her sister-in-law sent one after another of her children as
they became of age to attend high school in Seoul. With so many
extraneous persons regularly a part of the household, it was
impossible for her to arrange her life with her husband and
children as a "romantically happy modern family" modelled after
the American family of Doris Day movies.

She felt despondent in her frustration. She recalls: "I had just
escaped from a prison-like married life (*kamok-sari-kat' ŭn-sijip-
sari*), and now we were going to be the satellite unit of the *k'ŭnjip*
("the main household"). . . ." She was aware, of course, that
none of these occurrences was exceeding the conventional expectations in the relationship between the main household and its
branch household. It was simply not an aspect of life she had
envisioned for herself and her husband. She was afraid to complain too strenuously to her husband. All he ever said was, "Well,
I can't tell them they can't come." More and more frequently, he
came home just in time to avoid the curfew at midnight. She
turned to a female cousin living in Seoul and poured out her
emotional pain, but all her cousin did was to point out that it was
a very common problem.

Perhaps wanting to ease his wife's pain which he apparently
sensed but felt helpless to cope with himself, Suwŏn-mansin's
husband urged her to accompany him to the Catholic church
which he had begun to attend recently. Although not particularly
inclined to religion, she gladly accompanied him to church, as it
gave her an opportunity to do something exclusively with her
husband. His relatives would have no interest in participating
even if invited; they were Buddhists, as her family were. About
three years later in 1966 when she was twenty-nine, Suwŏn-
mansin agreed to be baptized in the Catholic faith with her husband. In the meantime she had had two more sons.

Her religious conversion apparently failed to bring about a
fundamental change in her attitude toward the still constant
stream of visitors she had to cope with at home. She saw them as
intruders who destroyed her happiness and life. "No matter how
hard I tried to regard them lovingly (*kopkye-poda*), my eyes burned
only with the fires of indignation (*nun-e-puli-nada*)." Now with
four children, she always felt overworked and fatigued, although
she had a housekeeper and an errand girl. Her health began to

deteriorate, and in late 1966 she had to have her appendix removed.

She had a normal post-operative recovery in the hospital, but upon discharge developed a "paralysis of her stomach and intestines" that required re-hospitalization. Once in the hospital, however, her symptoms disappeared spontaneously and completely, leaving the doctors perplexed and unable to diagnose. As soon as she was discharged, the same symptoms recurred: dizziness, clammy skin, nausea, and inability to pass gas or stool. She was hospitalized several times with the same complaints, and each time, the same thing happened. Her hospital expenses were taxing the family resources. It was about this time she had her first hallucinatory experience. Retrospectively, Suwŏn-mansin identifies this and the symptoms that had required her post-operative hospitalizations as her first round with *sinbyŏng*.

She was urinating one day when she saw a giant. He grabbed her long hair and flung her out across the courtyard. Family members, roused by her screams, found her sprawled in the courtyard with both shoulders dislocated. They took her to a hospital to have them set but when she returned home, they again became dislocated. She claims the experience was repeated three or four times. Unlike the "paralysis" of her stomach and intestines, these symptoms were more concrete and everyone became more concerned. When she became increasingly unable to manage her household, it became a financial necessity to move her and the children back to the main household in the province. Her own mother, who had often helped out in the past, could not do so on any long-term basis. She had her own parents-in-law and husband to look after, as well as a new daughter-in-law to supervise. For a while, her husband tried to manage with the help of servants sent up from his home town, but Suwŏn-mansin's strange behavior made it very difficult to retain them.

Back in the main household, Suwŏn-mansin continued to display her various symptoms and neighbors began to suggest that she might be possessed. They urged her sister-in-law to have a *kut* rather than waste money on ineffective modern medical care. Her sister-in-law, being a devout Buddhist, hesitated at first but in the end acquiesced. When Suwŏn-mansin learned of it, she was outraged. She asked instead to see a Catholic priest. A local Catholic priest was prevailed upon to make regular visits and offer prayers but the effects were not lasting. In the meantime, Suwŏn-mansin formulated her own ideas of how she might be cured, and petitioned to go on a pilgrimage of traditionally holy places in Korea.

Although they had strong misgivings, her husband and in-laws agreed to let her visit Kyerong-san, a mountain famous as the headquarters of numerous indigenous religions, many of them healing cults.[2] They were afraid to refuse her lest she die with a grudge against them for a last wish denied. Nearly half a year later, Suwŏn-mansin returned from her pilgrimage, weighing only thirty-two kilograms. She had lost eighteen kilograms during her absence. Her husband and his family were at a loss to know what to do next. Unable to finance her "cure" any longer, they formally requested her natal family to take her back. She had been married about seven years at the time.

Her younger brother who had come to fetch her was shocked at the condition of his once beautiful sister and deeply angered with his brother-in-law for not having revealed her true condition to them earlier. They had known of her illness but had not been given any indication of its actual severity or bizarreness. He took Suwŏn-mansin home and began to nurse her personally when, after about a week, she sat up and asked for a watermelon. Although it was early for watermelons, they found one for her. As soon as Suwŏn-mansin saw it, she "clapped her hands" and dashed out of the house dressed only in her underwear. Taking a short cut through the mountain, familiar to her from childhood and thereby successfully evading her pursuers, she went to the railroad station in town where she boarded a train for her husband's home town. Upon arrival there, she went straight to the police station and demanded to see the police chief. She warned him that even though he was a Christian he must authorize a *kosa* ("a shamanistic ritual of sacrifice"), to be performed within the next three days. Otherwise, something horrible would happen to his police station.

Annoyed by the rantings of a crazy woman, they threw her out bodily into a throng of onlookers who had gathered about the entrance. As she staggered to her feet and began to walk away, the crowd followed her, throwing stones at her. Bleeding and weak from excitement and lack of food, she stumbled and fell several times. She drank from the muddy puddles in the road. All the while, she kept telling the crowd that she was the daughter-in-law of such-and-such household. No one paid her heed. Finally, a friend of her husband recognized her and notified her in-laws. They came and amid much wailing took her home. Three days later, she says, the police station burned down to the ground. When the word spread, people poured into the house requesting her services. Though she refused, her in-laws were humiliated and demoralized.

Her husband rushed down from Seoul and tested her with two wrapped light bulbs, one white and the other red. Each time she correctly guessed the color of the bulbs, thoroughly disconcerting her husband. He began to wonder if she was after all supernaturally possessed, rather than just insane. Following the experiment, however, Suwŏn-mansin became hysterical and began to curse everyone, including her long-suffering father-in-law. They were now completely convinced that she had gone mad. They tethered her to a post, having first tied her with a rope, and notified her natal family. On seeing her tethered like a dog, her brother wept and asked to have her untied so he could take her home. But before anyone could stop her, she dashed out of the house and, jumping into the stream nearby, swam across it. Once on the other side, she alternately lamented that no one had given her her *naerim-kut*, and stopped passersby to tell them their fortunes with a leering grin.

Her brother had barely gotten her back to their own home in Suwŏn when people flocked in from all around to seek her service, lining up outside the house from an early hour. Among them were some people she had known since childhood. She thought they might have come for a social call, but they too wanted her professional service. She realized then that she had become an outcaste—a person labeled as a shaman—and felt crushed by it. The entire household was upset with the disruption caused by the callers.

One evening her brother took her aside and confided that he could no longer countenance what was happening to her or to their family, including his young children. Shoving a packet of sleeping pills across the floor between them, he begged her to take them all. She understood. Obediently, she took the lot, but she says she failed to die. After the episode, she felt she could not stay in her natal household any longer. In asking her to take the pills, had not her brother already asked her to leave them so that their hands would not be forced to cast her out themselves? Though it was the wrong season for it, she dressed in her best winter brocade outfit and stole out of the house with 180 *wŏn*. Once entrained for Seoul, she bought a pack of chewing gum and counted the change. She had exactly thirty *wŏn*. She knew she had no one now; she had to make it on her own, she realized, for the very first time in her life. She decided to become a *mudang*. Had she not failed to die? There must have been a reason for that. The year was 1968.

On arrival in Seoul, she went to a cousin who rented out a room to a *mudang*. She stayed with this cousin for about a year, working with her tenant-shaman mostly on divinations. As she became better known, other shamans began to ask her to perform in their *kut*. She earned a good income and was able to indulge herself in some aspects of the city life that she enjoyed, but she missed her husband and children terribly. She tried to contact her husband through the firm where he had worked, but he was no longer there, they said. Then rather unexpectedly, her in-laws got in touch with her in late 1968.

They had relocated completely to Seoul and, having bought a large house, invited her to return if she wanted. She could, they said, keep her shaman role, if she kept it outside the household. She was very grateful. She had not seen her husband or children much in the past two years or so. She agreed to their condition and returned to them eagerly. Her husband was distant but very kind toward her. Her children eyed her from a safe distance. Only her daughter approached her hesitantly. Still, Suwŏn-mansin was hopeful of making a family life once again. Then, one day not long thereafter, her husband failed to come home. He did not return for several days. Finally, she was told that he had left for America. It seemed that her husband had been negotiating to go to America for a long time, long before the family relocated to Seoul. It had not been certain that he could obtain a visa, but once he had it, he left without delay. Of course, every adult in the household knew, except Suwŏn-mansin. She was enraged. How could he leave her without giving any inkling of such a momen- tous event even on his last day at home? She felt utterly betrayed. For the time being, though, she resolved to stay with her in-laws. She wanted first to save enough money to buy a place of her own;

she would then move out with her children and have no more to
do with her treacherous in-laws.

But her husband and his family had other plans for the
children. About a year after his departure, her husband sent for
the three boys to come to him in Hawaii, where he had established himself. Suwŏn-mansin became hysterical with this second
betrayal, but it was to no avail. The boys left, saying a sober
goodbye to their raving mother. Suwŏn-mansin decided to move
out of her in-laws' house with her daughter, but they would not
let her take the child. She simply stole out at night with the child,
but her in-laws "kidnapped" the child back the very next day.
When I first met Suwŏn-mansin in the summer of 1971, the
custody fight for the child was still going on unabated.

Suwŏn-mansin fared better in her professional life. When
she first assumed the *mudang* role, both her own and husband's
family had been relieved. She was no longer a constant source of
potential catastrophe for them so long as she functioned effec-
tively as a *mudang*. Her brother came up periodically to check on
her progress and was not ungrateful for the relative anonymity of
Seoul. It enabled him and his family to deal with Suwŏn-mansin
in a separate compartment from their lives.

Of her own subjective experiences during this time,
Suwŏn-mansin says she was as much frightened of her prophetic
abilities as she was excited by them. She was always sensitive
about not having had her official initiation as a *mudang*, and
carefully restrained herself not to exceed the bounds of her
abilities in dealing with her clients. Then one day she did an
impulsive thing which put to test the validity of her claim to
supernatural possession in a dramatic way. She was on a country
road on her way home from a *kut* with a companion when a jeep
appeared on the road. She found herself blocking it and telling
the handsome [she used this English word] middle-aged pas-
senger to get out. She told him:

> You dress well and look like you might be of *yangban* stock, but
> the truth is your dead father's corpse is facing northeast, and
> there are snakes nesting at his feet. Your father's grave will
> bring you bad luck. . . .

Stunned both by the very extraordinariness of the encounter
and the fact that he had very recently buried his father—a fact he
felt she could not have known—the man became upset but also

very intensely interested. He protested that he had hired a re-
nowned geomancer who selected the most auspicious site within
a six-mile radius of Taech'ŏn for his father's grave site. When she
told him to check for himself, he asked her who would pay for the
expenses. Without hesitation, she told him that if wrong, she
would pay the entire cost. The gentleman told her and her companion to get in, and they picked up a couple of laborers en route
to the grave. He promised to double the amount if she were
correct. When she realized that he had truly "called her bluff"—
that there was no getting out of it now—she was, she says,
thoroughly scared. For one thing, she had very little money with
her. Whatever could have possessed her, she wondered, to provoke a perfect stranger into such a bizarre contest?

> When the laborers actually began to dig at the foot of the grave, I
> sat in a gulch nearby and began to cry and shake . . . I was
> terrified . . . I had no idea what made me say the things I had.
> . . . Everything going about me seemed so unreal and eerie. . . .
> About an hour or maybe later, the man came to where I sat
> huddled. He was shivering like leaves in the wind. He bowed to
> me on the ground and asked me to come with him. . . . Sure
> enough, there, wrapped around a leg of the corpse was the
> molted skin of a snake. . . . The man called me sŏnsaeng-nim
> ("honored teacher")—the first time anyone called me that in my
> life—and asked me to tell him where to bury his father. . . .
>   I told him to go up higher on the hill and showed him where
> to bury his father. . . . I told him that if he did as told, his fortune
> would change for the better in a dramatic way within the year.
> . . . Months later, he brought me 11,000 wŏn (about $300) and
> told me that after his father's reburial, the court case regarding
> land ownership which had been pending since before his
> father's death was finally settled in his favor. . . . He has been a
> regular customer ever since.[3]

Following the episode, she became completely confident of
her supernatural "gift"; she felt omnipotent, she says. She had
the longest uninterrupted seizure of ecstasy of her experience.

> I was completely preoccupied with my mudang activities. No-
> thing else mattered. I forgot all about my husband, children,
> and family. . . . All I cared about was that I should get healthy
> and be the most important mudang in Seoul.

She began to study shamanism seriously. When she realized

that, unlike Christianity which provides a place for childless believers after death, believers in the Buddha and *mudang* had to
depend on offspring for a place to go after death, she was moved
to do something about it. She started to petition the Korean
government in writing about the pitiful conditions of the poor and
old Buddhists and *mudang* who had no children and requested a
land grant. She wanted to create a community where childless old
people of Buddhist and shamanistic religions could live with
younger followers of the same religions in fictive kinship relationships. She thought her community might be modelled after the
industrial village complex of Pak Changno-kyo;[4] members could
then have a place to work and live *and* the assurance of being
remembered by the survivors on occasions of ancestral rites.

She also began to keep a diary in which she recorded her
thoughts about the future development of the utopian community for childless old folks, her impressions of clients she saw,
descriptions of their problems, and her counsel to them. She also
started work on a procedural manual for various shamanistic
rituals as she had learned them. In still another notebook, she
wrote down the historical development of shamanism in Korea as
she got it from various sources. She had been disappointed that
there was no established doctrine in shamanism as there was in
Christianity and Buddhism. Realizing, however, that the task she
envisioned was too big for herself alone, she tried to interest other
mudang in her efforts.

> I thought the first thing I had to do was organize the *mudang* into
> a group, like the Christian churches. There must be three
> thousand *mudang* in Seoul alone. We could collect membership
> dues from them to finance the project; after all, a *mudang*'s
> money is easy-come, easy-go. There is a proverb that says, "He
> who expects a free handout is a *mudang*'s husband." We could
> just as easily give the money to our organization. . . .
>
> Most people think that Christianity is the strongest religion
> because they build fancy churches and go around saying that
> their god is the only true god. But the truth is, many Christians
> come to a *mudang*; you won't find a *mudang* going to a Christian
> priest or minister. . . . Buddhism and *mudang* have ways of
> comforting Koreans that the Christian religion does not have, no
> matter what they say. . . .
>
> So, I wanted to organize *mudang* and establish a doctrine of
> shamanism, but nobody was interested. Every *mudang* I talked

with said that she was unfairly treated by the world, but everyone also thought my ideas were insane. . . .

Still, I tried to read whatever I could find on shamanism to understand why it is so despised but at the same time so widely followed. . . . It's been with us from the beginning of our society, but none explained why the contradiction existed.

She eventually became discouraged and abandoned ideas of organizing any practicing *mudang* or petitioning the government further to do anything for childless old people. She nevertheless continued to keep her diary. Although she never kept her promise to let me read these diaries and other manuscripts, she once showed them to me. They are neatly stored in a box inside a locked drawer.

Her disappointment with her fellow *mudang* led to a disenchantment with her own *mudang* role, but her practice prospered and drew her into an ever-widening network of clients and professional colleagues and ancillary workers. Once, for example, she was asked to participate in a very large scale *chaesu-kut*. When she arrived at the house, a semi-Westernized Korean mansion in an exclusive new neighborhood, she was shocked beyond her "senses" to recognize in the patroness a former classmate at Sŏrabŏl College. She was having the *kut*, her friend explained, to ensure good luck for her husband's business. Suwŏn-mansin says she returned from that *kut* and wept bitterly for days. Her friend who had been almost inconspicuous in their college days was leading just the life she had always dreamed of living herself and was so far from ever realizing. Worst of all, after the initial shock of mutual recognition, her old classmate had treated her completely professionally. As she put it, "It was as if the person I was and continued to be was no longer visible to others. To them, I was a *mudang*, period."

She wanted desperately to give up her *mudang* role. There was some money saved; she could perhaps go into some kind of business. She missed her husband and children achingly and felt sick with envy when she saw young lovers or young families having fun at an outing. She realized that not all of her friends were comfortably off like the *kut* patroness. Some were harassed by their many children and looked prematurely aged from the burden of their domestic role. Still, she envied them. They had husbands for whom they could worry and on whom they could depend. She felt utterly alone. If she brooded over her fate, she worked herself up into a convulsive state of hysteria [her own expression in English]. She began to plot a way out of the *mudang* role and back into proper society.

She had no employable skills and, being a female in her mid-thirties, she could not have found a job even if she had had such skills. She thought of operating a small restaurant. Her natal family was pleased and willing to help financially. On the day the final papers were to be drawn, she set out for the restaurant with her brother. Dressed in a new outfit made for the occasion, she was halfway there when she fainted on the sidewalk and had to be carried home on her brother's back. Once home, however, she woke up as if from a nap and told her maid to rip apart the blue silk skirt she had on and make it into a *k'aeja* [a type of traditional warrior's outfit worn by *mudang* during *kut*]. She realized anew that she was a person marked by the spirits; she was afraid to disregard them now. She decided to have her *naerim-kut* as soon as possible and was about to prepare the costumes necessary for it. It was at this point that the invitation mentioned earlier came from her husband's household to return to them. It had come just at a time when she thought she had no more doubts about her supernatural calling.

Later, in reaction to he husband's departure for America and her in-laws' refusal to grant her custody of her daughter, Suwǒn-mansin again resolved to make the most of her *mudang* role and thus to "get even with them [her husband and his family]." In this manner, almost five years after first experiencing *sinbyǒng*, Suwǒn-mansin had her *naerim-kut* in 1971. For the occasion, her brother not only donated a whole pig for the ceremony, but came up from Suwǒn to attend it in person. According to Suwǒn-mansin (and the *tang* mistress did not deny it), her *naerim-kut* was one of the most elaborate held at Kuksadang in many a year. Shortly afterward, Suwǒn-mansin performed her first official *kut* at Kuksadang and has since been a frequent and popular shaman among her colleagues. She does many *kut* on referral; that is, she performs in *kut* sponsored by other shamans' clients.

Since the initition ceremony, her relationship with her brother has become even closer than before. They learned during the ceremony that Suwǒn-mansin was possessed by her older

brother who had died mysteriously while in the custody of the
Japanese police in 1944. His ghost explained that he had been a
boxer and, had he lived, might have become a champion professional boxer. But he was tortured to death by the Japanese police
for hitting a Japanese police officer. It had not mattered that the
officer had provoked the attack. Her brother's ghost wailed and
wept as he talked about his grievous death. He had died without
achieving either his professional ambition of becoming Korea's
champion boxer or his personal goal of being a filial son to his
parents. His ghost now charged them, sister and brother, to put
his soul at ease, Suwŏn-mansin by being the best *mudang* possible
and his brother by mending his casual manner of living and
taking a serious role in sustaining the family and lineage. As the
eldest surviving son he must guide the other brothers.[5] Then,
turning to Suwŏn-mansin, her brother's ghost said that she of all
people in the family understood how he felt to have died such an
unfulfilled person, for she too has been betrayed by life. That is
why he had come to her; now he would not be so forlorn.

After her initiation, Suwŏn-mansin says, members of her
natal family seemed to accept her *mudang* role more openly; she
now visits them occasionally. Still, she feels that there is a wall of
sadness that separates them from her.

> I know that their sympathy for me comes from their heartbreak.
> . . . and that saddens me. I feel myself set apart even from my
> own family when I hear my immature nieces and nephews say,
> "We can't go visit auntie in Seoul because she is that thing." I
> really would like to die at times like that. Yet, I know I can
> always depend on my brother to bail me out if I am in trouble or
> need help. . . .
>
> Even so, he cannot really understand me. You, though you
> say you are trying to understand how I became a *mudang* and
> what it's done to me, you will never understand me. . . . You
> see, there cannot be any real understanding between the pos-
> sessed and the non-possessed. . . . The possessed have had
> experiences that the non-possessed cannot begin to com-
> prehend no matter how they try. At best, they can only see what
> your possession is doing to you and to them [her family] so-
> cially. They cannot really understand your inner feelings or
> experiences. They cannot be expected to either. So, there can
> never be a full communication, only tolerance and pity on their
> part. . . . I told you that my brother once asked me to die. . . .

She wept copiously as she recalled that incident and quietly lamented that perhaps if she had not been brought up so ignorant of the ways of *mudang*, she might have recognized her illnesses as symptoms of *sinbyŏng* and saved herself and her families the anguish they all went through. She adds: "You might say that I have worked out my own *mudang* destiny *chasu-sŏngga* ("by one's own hands")."

Although her health has improved considerably since she assumed the *mudang* role, she claims to suffer periodically from a recurrence of some of the old symptoms. Having always been athletic, she finds poor health terribly depressing. The most agonizing aspect of these recurring symptoms, she contends, is that her spirits will sometimes commandeer her body without letting her know, so that her body does things independently of her mind. At other times, she says, she gets weepy for no reason at all and gets into a melancholy slump that lasts for days at a time.

> I just sit and stare into the distant space; I remember my child-hood days and hot tears begin to sting my eyes. . . . Sometimes I don't even know I'm crying until tears plop down into my lap or the floor.

It was at such times that she used to go barhopping for relief. With a small laugh, she adds that she is the only *mudang* she knows of who did that for escape.

Asked if she has any male companion, she denies it and volunteers that she has not had sexual intercourse since the first time she left her husband's house. Asked then whether, like other *mudang*, she had felt sexually uninterested in her husband, she accused the other *mudang* of lying. She claims it was the most satisfactory aspect of her relationship with her husband but that as soon as she became ill, he would have nothing to do with her. Her face distorted by anger, she remarked, "He must have been saving himself already for that American wife of his!"

She finds escape in other forms of self-indulgence also. She has an impressive wardrobe both of traditional Korean clothes suitable for her *mudang* role and of Western-style clothes for non-professional occasions. When she dresses in Western clothes she sometimes looks as though she might have come from a fashion show. Her greatest comfort, however, derives from her real estate transactions. She is extremely proud of the house, bought with her own money, and of other properties.

Even with her substantial economic assets, she claims to be terribly insecure and lonely. When her clients hurry home to their families at the end of a *kut*, she feels her loneliness in the marrow of her bones. Although her two aunts look after her every conceivable wish and need at home (and her nieces are not likely to completely forget her generosity to them), she dreads old age and says she has had nightmares about growing old alone. She feels better now since she had adopted a son.

Suwŏn-mansin is completely enamored of this boy and raises him exactly as she described her own upbringing. By 1973 when I last saw the child, she had succeeded in spoiling him so thoroughly that her aunts wondered aloud in her presence about the consideration she is likely to receive in old age from a child so spoiled and self-centered. Suwŏn-mansin appears oblivious to such observations. For her, he represents the opportunity to recreate, however belatedly, the family she has lost by becoming a *mudang*. He is going to grow up and be to her all that her real sons cannot be. She says that no one will think lightly of her now that she has a son. Her entire hope for the future hinges on him. This becomes especially clear when one observes the preferential treatment that she gives him over her own daughter.

Ironically, it was only after Suwŏn-mansin had already adopted her son that her in-laws allowed her to have her daughter. She appears very happy to be near her mother and is constantly alert to her every wish. Suwŏn-mansin, on the other hand, is rather indifferent towards her. While she does not in any way abuse her daughter, the only positive and kind words she says to her have to do with the way she can soothe or otherwise care for her adopted brother better than anyone else. As a result, she has made her adopted brother her primary concern. The girl appears determined to reach her mother's heart, it seems, through the adopted brother.

I was surprised to realize in 1973 that Suwŏn-mansin's daughter had not been to school during the 1972-1973 school year. When I asked Suwŏn-mansin about it, she brushed the question off by saying that a college education had done nothing for her. "All that girl, or any girl, needs is a good husband; and you don't need schooling for that," she explained.

I asked Suwŏn-mansin if she ever thought of remarriage. She thought my question the most hilarious she had ever heard. Breaking into a falsetto laugh, she said: "You haven't learned anything about *mudang* from two summers of interviewing me, have you?" Though she dismissed my question without a direct response, it seems that she would like to remarry if she could, for she added that she sometimes resents the fact that her professional and household head role deprive her of her femininity.

> I feel uncomfortable having to give up being coquettish, dependent, trusting, and looked after by a man. . . . When I have to argue with the tax collector or haggle with porters, I become masculine. . . . It makes me feel confused. I want to be a woman, soft, but I am always having to act like a man. . . .

Adopting a son has apparently also altered Suwŏn-mansin's views about the inescapability of the shaman role quite radically. Strengthened, seemingly, by the symbolic social significance of having a son and the more definite shape of a full-fledged household made possible by it, she began to reassess her *mudang* role and decided to ease out of it and move into an entrepreneur's role during the winter of 1972-1973. However, since her *mudang* role is the only reliable source of income, she could not discard it suddenly and completely. She was also still mindful of her previous experience in trying to shed the *mudang* role. She wanted to make the transition carefully and with sufficient overlap of the two roles to permit her some maneuverability, should there be signs of supernatural retribution. Suwŏn-mansin still very firmly believes she will never be able to sever completely the relationship with her brother's ghost and other possessing spirits without incurring some catastrophe for herself or her son. (She did not mention either her daughter or her natural sons.) At the same time, she feels she can keep the spirits placated by being more attentive to them.

During the summer of 1973, Suwŏn-mansin was so completely preoccupied with the day-to-day state of the cabaret business that she frequently appeared distracted in transactions with clients. If clients lingered too late into the afternoon, she became visibly impatient. Beads of sweat often appeared on her forehead; she also tended to impersonate angry and impatient spirits. If clients called while she was in the process of transforming herself, by means of make-up, hairdo, and clothes, from a *mudang* to a modern cabaret proprietress, she instructed her aunts and daughter to say she was not in and would not be back until the next day. She was now spending most evenings in the cabaret, except when she had to perform *kut*. Since she and her partner have hired out the management of the cabaret, it is not necessary that she be there. She obviously finds the night life of the cabaret exciting and altogether to her liking.

Suwŏn-mansin is prayerfully hopeful that the cabaret will be a huge money-making success. She feels it is her last chance at "making it really big" and showing her ex-husband and in-laws "where they can go," as well as establishing a life with some semblance of normalcy and approximation to her earlier dreams of a "sweet home life." She is fully aware that in the hierarchy of the Korean society, the role of a cabaret proprietress is not much above that of a *mudang*. Just the same, she points out, the role of an entrepreneur is closer to the center of the society than that of *mudang* which is definitely external. And once inside, she shrewdly explains, wealth can buy one considerable social prestige, especially today. She then adds, almost breathlessly as if she were afraid that her possessing spirits might act in some retaliatory manner to her, "Of course, I shall always serve my *momju* ("the main possessing spirit," i.e., her brother's ghost) and other spirits. I would just like to get out of the 'headachy' daily rounds of seeing clients for divination. I would like to be able to do just the *kut* on referral from other *mudang*. . . ."

*

7

DEACONESS CHANG

BRIEF CHRONOLOGY OF DEACONESS CHANG'S LIFE

1920	Born, the third child and second daughter
1929	Grandfather died
1930	Family emigrated to Kyoto, Japan
	Enrolled in school for the first time
1935	Withdraw from school in the fifth grade
	Sent to work in a factory to help support the family
1939	Married through parental arrangement
1940	Began to experience first serious role strain
	Returned to old job at the factory
	Husband quit job in Osaka and found work near home
	Became pregnant
1941	First child, son
1943	Second child, son
	Accompanied husband with children in move to Osaka
	Lived happily in nuclear household situation

1945	World War II ended
	Family repatriated to Korea
	Husband returned to Japan to sell property
1946	Third child, son
1947	Father-in-law went to Japan to bring husband back but returned alone
1947	Rumors confirmed that husband had Japanese wife and son
	Husband still promising to return to Korea
	Deaconess Chang's health and then that of eldest son deteriorated
	Told to pray to *Ch'ilsong* for cure; effective
1949	Husband returned from Japan, empty-handed; factory had failed
1952	Hallucinatory experiences; *sinbyŏng* diagnosed
	Naerim-kut held
1953	Fourth child, son
1956	Eldest son converted to Christianity
1957-1958	Family business (mill) failed; family moved to Seoul
	Began to hear voices again
1961	Husband converted to Christianity
	Confrontation between Deaconess Chang and family over *mudang* role
	Deaconess Chang exorcised and converted to Christianity
	Abandoned the *mudang* role and assumed that of a deaconess

DEACONESS CHANG

A diminutive woman looking much younger than her age, fifty-one years old in 1971, Deaconess Chang dresses becomingly in

Western-style clothes. Most Korean women her age who "do not go out into public life" but dress non-traditionally usually wear a style of clothes that is a hybridization of the Western and the Korean styles.[1] Deaconess Chang says she is more comfortable in Western clothes than in Korean ones: having grown up and married in Japan, she has been accustomed to Western-style clothing for daily wear for most of her life, she says. She also wears Western-style shoes.[2] By her manner of dress, she sets herself apart from others.

Her hair is bobbed and waved. It may possibly be dyed as well, as no gray shows. Her still pretty face is subtly but carefully made-up to enhance the whiteness of her skin. She faithfully shields her face from the sun with a parasol, and whenever she walked with me, she tried to keep me shaded as well. She regarded my brown skin with sadness and sympathetically lamented that living in Hawaii made it inescapable. She admired my white, even teeth and confided bashfully that when she was young it had been the fashion to have one's teeth, even the perfectly normal, gold-capped. Her entire upper front teeth are gold-capped.

Personable and delicately mannered, she is regarded as modest and charming by members of her prayer group, all members also of her church—The Pure Evangelical Presbyterian Church. The prayer group meets daily for worship, except on Sundays when they meet at the church. Attendance at the prayer meeting varies from day to day, but the core of the prayer group, consisting of four deaconesses, is unfailingly present at each meeting. They meet in one another's home on an irregularly rotating basis at about ten in the morning when husbands and children have been sent out to work and school and the house has been put into some order. These prayer meetings last about two hours and are occasionally followed by lunch served by the day's hostess. I first met Deaconess Chang at one of these meetings.

A dedicated member of the group, she sometimes walks three to five miles one way to attend meetings. In fact, her presence is so regularly relied upon that when she does not appear on time, the others hold up the meeting for at least fifteen minutes. In the afternoon, she makes rounds of sinbang ("visiting the faithful") either alone or with other members of the prayer group.[3] She occasionally accompanies her husband, also a deacon, on his own rounds of sinbang.

The morning prayer meeting begins with a brief prayer by one of the deaconesses, followed quickly by hymn singing and scripture reading by the entire group. This formal phase is comparatively short. The marathon session of individual prayers which follows generally lasts for two uninterrupted hours. Each woman takes her turn at prayer, reporting in impassioned detail all the pains, injustices, and temptations she has suffered as well as giving thanks for happy events since the last meeting. Usually, suffering and pain are the dominant themes, and their exorcism the main activity of the prayer group. They moan, groan, and wail as though their entrails were being ripped open. They sob paroxysmally, sometimes pounding their chests with clenched fists as if to break loose the grief dammed up inside. Their emotions are so intense that they sometimes lurch forward under their force. It is a rare member who finishes the prayer meeting in the same spot where she began. Their seating arrangement alters throughout the meeting by their shifts of knees and thighs that seem to draw them closer toward an unseen presence.

During this phase of individual prayers, the remaining group serves much like the chorus in Greek tragedies: they pick up phrases from the supplicant's prayer and chant them in refrain, punctuating the supplicant's pleas and confessions with "Amens" and "Hallelujahs" or supplying their own commentaries addressed to the Almighty God but always for the benefit of the supplicant. Everyone's eyes are tightly shut throughout this phase. When everyone has had her turn, one of the deaconesses leads the group in a collective prayer, summarizing the vicissitudes of life just expressed and asking for continued strengthening of faith and courage to live yet another day on the narrow path they have chosen to His Kingdom. Collective hymn singing, followed by a benediction, ends the meeting. Some members leave immediately; others linger for a more informal visit with one another. Usually, they are subdued but cheerful with one another following the meeting.

I was initially invited to these prayer meetings by my hostess, one of the four deaconesses. After attending a few of these meetings, I found them too time consuming to continue, although they revealed much insight into the psychological lives of the women involved. By way of explaining my decision not to attend their meetings any more, I told them of my doctoral fieldwork with shamans. They were keenly interested and asked many penetrating questions. Some days after the incident, I was approached by them and asked if I would be interested in studying the life history of a former shaman whose "soul has been saved from the Devil by our merciful Lord, Jesus Christ." The person they had in mind turned out to be Deaconess Chang, one of the four deaconesses of the prayer meeting group. She had once been a financially successful shaman with a respectable clientele for about ten years.

Her eldest son, now an Army chaplain, was the first to be converted to Christianity, followed by her husband and other sons. Her own conversion came much later after a protracted battle "between Christ and the Devil" for her soul. It had required the physical destruction of her shamanistic altar by her husband, sons, and Elders from their church while she sat cowered and enraged, unable to stop them. She describes her experiences which led to her conversion to Christianity as having been far more horrifying than her earlier experiences of being possessed by shamanistic spirits.

The prayer meeting group urged me to study her case. After all, should I not study also how the Christian God, in His infinite love, can save even those once possessed by Satan himself? Frankly, they felt Deaconess Chang's conversion history was far more worthy of my study than the life histories of ordinary shamans. Apparently the idea to suggest this to me had evolved in one of their prayer meetings. I welcomed the proposal but was uncertain how Deaconess Chang felt about it. I learned later that she was accustomed to having church and family members use her testimony of conversion in proselytizing. One or more members of the prayer group were always present when we began our interviews so that I felt severely constrained. I thought I sensed a similar constraint on her part. During the second summer of fieldwork, I was finally able to see her alone from time to time, away from both her family and church peers. At one of these private sessions, when we were talking about her early years of marriage in Japan during World War II, she stopped in mid-sentence as if it were too much to continue. We had been talking casually, almost mundanely, so that I was unprepared for the tears that streamed down her carefully made-up face. Soon, she simply surrendered herself to silent but helpless weeping.

Though I could not see her face, now buried in her lap, I could see her shoulder blades jerk spasmodically as she drew gasping breaths between sobs. When her tears were spent, she pulled herself together and smiled faintly in apology. "I'm being used by both Satan and God. . . . My poor body and soul are the arena of their power contest. In their battle to possess me, neither God nor Satan has any pity for me. I just can't take it sometimes." She did not try to dry the tears that again welled up and coursed down her cheeks. After a long silence, she added that she needed the constant prayer of her fellow believers to keep Satan at bay.

Within the bounds of politeness, I tried many times to extract an invitation to visit her home in the evening but I failed. As a result, I never met her husband or any of the three sons who live at home. Her eldest son, the chaplain, lives with his wife and son near the DMZ where he is stationed. It was this eldest son who was the main motivating force behind conversion to Christianity, first of his father, then brothers, and ultimately of his mother. I was particularly anxious to meet the eldest son, for, even in absence, he influenced the daily life of his parental home to an unusual extent, especially their religious activities. Although Deaconess Chang mentioned several times that this son wanted to meet me, we never managed it. Because she had no telephone at home and I was often doing fieldwork, arranging a meeting during his usually brief and often unannounced visits home posed some difficulty.

Since giving up her shaman role, Deaconess Chang has had no income-generating job. However, she is actively and conscientiously engaged in her voluntary work as a church deaconess. She is rarely at home during the day, attending prayer meetings in the morning and making her rounds of *sinbang* in the afternoon. She frequently receives urgent telephone calls requesting her presence and prayer in the home of a sick church member or one of the family.[4] Such requests come largely from female members of the church and not infrequently surreptitiously, since their husbands may be non-believers. In such cases, Deaconess Chang must act clandestinely.

Economically, Deaconess Chang is dependent on her husband and sons. Her husband, aged fifty-nine (1971), supplies sesame seed oil to inexpensive restaurants and earns some money; however, their major sources of income are rental units in their house and their sons. Their eldest, the chaplain, aged thirty (1971), their second, a house painter, aged twenty-eight, and their youngest, an office clerk, aged eighteen, all contribute to the household purse. Their third son, aged twenty-five, lives at home, as do his two unmarried brothers, but does not contribute to the family income as he is still in college. In fact, he constitutes a major expense for the entire family. Deaconess Chang's mother-in-law, eighty-one years old and nearly blind, also lives with them.

Their house is at the peak of what was, as recently as the Korean War, a well-forested mountain where fox roamed. Now it is completely covered with houses which seem to give grudging concession to the snaking alleyways that lead to doorways in the most random fashion. The place is another large urban "squatter-ville." Their house appears exceptionally large, but the exterior is somewhat misleading. Inside, the U-shaped house is shared by three families. Deaconess Chang's famiy live in the center unit. Each unit has two connected rooms and a kitchen. The water pump and the outhouse are communally used. Deaconess Chang, her husband, and his aged mother share one room, while her three sons occupy the other room.

The rooms are terribly crowded but immaculately kept, as is the communal courtyard. Two walls in their sons' room are lined with books on a variety of subjects. A good portion of the books are college texts and apparently belong to the third son, but Deaconess Chang claims that all her sons are avid readers. She feels considerable guilt that the college expenses of the third son are keeping the second son from marrying. At twenty-eight, he is well past the usual age for marriage. (He was still unmarried at age thirty-one when I last inquired in 1973.) All of the sons are devout churchgoers and, according to her, their gratitude to God for saving her from the Devil, i.e., from her *mudang* role, is so boundless that they consider no personal sacrifice too great to make for her continued salvation.

Deaconess Chang was born in 1920, the third child and second daughter, to parents who were among the poorest in an economically depressed village just north of Pusan, a port city in southeastern Korea. By the time she was born, her parents had already lost their first daughter and were eking out a precarious living by hiring out their labor and taking in an assortment of odd jobs. They had little land of their own and could not get enough sharecropping. Her mother supplied wine houses in the vicinity with bootlegged *makkŏlle* ("rice wine") and took in sewing to supplement further the family income. Her parents were patient people who worked hard and bore their grinding poverty without complaint. They were filial to her grandparents and were trusted laborers who enjoyed a good reputation in their own and neighboring villages. Looking back, Deaconess Chang supposes her parents must have welcomed her birth but not without worry about feeding another mouth.

Her family lived in a small, thatched, mud-walled house; it was always immaculately kept, as she recalls, with lots of flowers around the soy sauce and bean paste crocks in the summer. Her grandmother cared for her most of the time, she thinks, since her mother was always busy helping her father and grandfather with farm work, hiring out to other people, or taking in piece work. She cannot recall anyone in her natal family ever reminiscing about her infancy, though her mother occasionally remarked that she and her brother had been docile. Her own clearest memories of early childhood are of her older brother. She used to hang about him, longing for him to include her in his play. He sometimes let her play with his homemade tops or other toys in the courtyard.

After a reflective pause, she shifted to her mother and grandmother and remarked that both had been ordinary women who had the misfortune of marrying into an impoverished household where the men knew no other occupation than farming or any means of increasing their land. Both women had faced their lot in life with quiet determination and pride and did the best they could to keep the household going within the limits imposed by their sex and their husbands' relative lack of material, social, and personal resources.

Despite the "pinched" feeling their poverty gave to their life, her early childhood remains in Deaconess Chang's mind a time of joy. In talking about it, she stopped often, arrested in her private reverie, and laughed or dabbed at her eyes with her handkerchief. She remembers, for example, that her grandmother or mother used to station her on the threshold of the kitchen door to guard it against chickens. Or sometimes they gave her a huge reed-woven fan to shoo away the flies from food being sun-dried. She says she took all her assignments very seriously and did not budge until told. She remembers weeding the tiny vegetable patches about the house with her grandmother who teasingly complained that she pulled as many vegetables as weeds.

No one in her family was given to violent tempers; she was never harshly treated by anyone in the family—and sometimes very tenderly. Every summer, her grandmother dyed her finger-nails and toenails with the crushed petals of touch-me-not balsam flowers. Her grandmother was lavish with praise, at times point-ing out to her mother and neighbors what a bright and dutiful child she was. Her grandmother thought her very quick-witted and fast with her *nunch'i* ("social sense"). She was proud that her granddaughter learned so readily how to be attentive and respect-ful, particularly to elders and men.

In 1929 when Deaconess Chang was nine, her grandfather died. His funeral, though shamefully modest, left the family utterly destitute. Her father decided to migrate to Japan where he had heard that wage labor was easily obtainable. He saw no other way of breaking the vicious cycle of poverty. Deaconess Chang was ten when the entire family, including her grandmother, moved to Kyoto, where they lived for the next fifteen years.

She remembers feeling mildly curious and at the same time dreading the steamer trip across the Korea Strait to Japan. She simply trusted her elders to look after her. She had never gone any further from her village than the nearest market town and in truth had no idea what to expect, although she knew it would be different, having heard some of the tales of villagers who re-turned from Japan.

Once in Kyoto, the family moved into an urban Korean ghetto where they spoke Korean, ate Korean food, wore Korean clothes, and generally lived as though they were still in Korea.

In a short time, her parents found janitorial work in a medical clinic nearby. Her mother did the sweeping, mopping and other general housekeeping chores indoors while her father did the heavier chores, maintenance work, and kept the grounds clean. At home, her grandmother kept house for them as before, but with increasingly greater assistance from Deaconess Chang. The entire family adjusted well to Japan, although she remembers her grandmother constantly worrying about the health of the family. She believed firmly, as most Koreans do, that when one changes

drinking water—moves to a different region — one is susceptible
to ailments during the adjustive period.

Deaconess Chang and her brother were enrolled in school for
the first time in their lives. She spoke no Japanese and felt timid
about going to school at first. But there were many other Korean
girls in her school, and she soon came to love it. She had also
worried about being three to four years older than most of her
classmates, but because she was so petite, it did not become a
problem. She was almost always at the top of her class. When she
was in the fifth grade, however, her schooling came to an abrupt
end. Her family needed her support, and she was placed in a
factory. She was fifteen and understood the necessity of it, but
felt bitter she could not have waited one more year when she
would have graduated. Her brother, who did not do so well, went
on to graduate from high school.

As with school, Deaconess Chang found her factory job socially comfortable, because she worked mostly with other Korean
girls, though her supervisor was Japanese. The most important
person, her forewoman, was a Korean.

She has no particularly outstanding memories of her teen
years in Japan. She liked the country and their urban life, but life
at home continued much as it had in Korea. She was praised for
her good behavior which everyone described as becomingly Korean and modest. Such praise-giving adults would often lament
that a good Korean girl like her was becoming rarer to find and
that she would be a "prize catch" as a daughter-in-law for some
lucky family one day.

As she became of marriageable age, she was in fact much in
demand by many of the Korean families in the area with marriageable sons. Most of the prospective grooms were good risks,
although her brother had objected to one of them for some reason
now forgotten. In 1939, the year she was nineteen, Deaconess
Chang married the man her family had selected. He was, at
twenty-seven, much older than the other candidates and well
past the marriageable age. He also had a number of younger
siblings still largely dependent on him, a considerable liabiity in a
prospective groom. But her parents felt these disadvantages were
more than compensated by his character. They knew his parents
and had watched him mature into a responsible adult and dutiful
son. Besides, they told her, an older man would appreciate her
more.

Neither her family nor his was very well off, but they observed tradition by getting a go-between to negotiate the marriage agreement. They were, however, too poor to mark the occasion with a public feast. Within a short time after the betrothal, Deaconess Chang was married in a modest traditional wedding ceremony. She had no dowry. According to her, a dowry is not customary in Kyŏngsang Provinces where both she and her husband come from. She took only *insa-ot* ("gifts of clothes one presents on the occasion of first meeting") for the members of her husband's household when she went to live with them.

When marriage negotiations first got underway, Deaconess Chang's husband was working in Osaka, though his family lived in her neighborhood in Kyoto. An important part of the negotiations was a promise by him that he would quit his job in Osaka and find work in Kyoto when he got married. Howver, circumstances did not work out so that he could change jobs; consequently, he remained at his job in Osaka and came home once or twice a month. Deaconess Chang was unhappy about this but endured it quietly at first, thinking it a temporary condition. It soon became apparent though that her husband was not making any serious attempts to find a job nearer home. Today perhaps the suggestion might be made that she should have gone to live with her husband in Osaka, but in those days such an idea never occurred to anyone, including herself, she says. She was after all the eldest and, at the time, the only daughter-in-law; her proper place was with her parents-in-law.

Whenever her husband came home, she felt overcome by shyness for a day or so, but she felt inwardly ecstatic to have him home. She adored her husband and found it painful to see him leave each time, especially as she did not always know when he would be home again. She longed to ask but was too shy to do so outright when the time came. As a result, she developed the habit of always examining the shoes lined up in the entrance hall of the house whenever she returned from being out, to see if her husband's shoes were there. She remembers that the disappointment did not grow lighter with time. She got a very heavy feeling inside when she did not see his shoes, particularly if it was time for his visit. Worse still, however, was having to conceal her disappointment lest other members of the household find out. If his shoes were there, though, she greeted him and conversed with him as she had seen Japanese women do with their husbands.

Deaconess Chang points out that while this was not traditionally a wifely behavior in the presence of parents-and sibling-in-law, she had liked the Japanese custom and decided to follow it. Her parents-in-law did not object. At first, her relationship with her husband was much as depicted in a Korean proverb, she says, "By day, like seeing a stranger; by night, like seeing a lover."

As it was the custom of Kyŏngsang Province according to Deaconess Chang for a daughter-in-law to follow in her mother-in-law's ways without question, she fully expected to have to change her ways if necessary to conform to her mother-in-law's patterns. And at first, she had no serious conflicts with her mother-in-law, but when she demanded that Deaconess Chang take complete charge of her three young brothers-in-law, she felt it excessive and grew resentful. She wished that her mother-in-law had had a daughter; surely, she would have understood the needs of a young woman better if she had. Without her husband at home, she had often felt lonely and estranged among her husband's people. Now she felt periodically overwhelmed by her responsibilities as well. She says:

> I had known his family slightly because we all lived in the same neighborhood, but I found it pretty difficult to feel affectionate toward his family members. . . . They felt like strangers to me, and my husband was not there to bind us. I felt like I had quit my factory job for a new job as a housemaid in my husband's household. . . .

She feels that she had married too young, that living with in-laws would have been less difficult the first few years if she had been a little more mature. Still, she contends there are some undeniable advantages in living with in-laws. If one finds favor in the eyes of one's parents-in-law, then one receives much praise and recognition from them and, by extension, favor from one's husband. Also, when one begins to have one child after another, it is nice to have a mother-in-law who can help with their care. Deaconess Chang recalls that while her body used to ache at times from her household tasks, it was satisfying too to have the approval and appreciation of her in-laws. Her parents-in-law used to "sing my praise to my husband" when he came home.

Her mother-in-law was very pleased with her. In fact, she was no sooner established within the household than she was given complete charge of it. It was as though the mother-in-law had been waiting impatiently to retire from her mistress' role. At first, Deaconess Chang was flattered by the responsibilities entrusted to her, but she soon found them also quite overwhelming. Her mother-in-law did not even wash her own clothes, much less help with the work involved in caring for her three still very young sons. Deaconess Chang says of this period:

> Thinking back, I can see that I was lacking in many ways, but I did mind my mother-in-law scolding me whenever I did something not quite right, especially since she did not help me at all with any of the work . . . and she was still relatively young and robust in health.

Insofar as tasks were concerned, Deaconess Chang found the care of her father-in-law's clothes the biggest challenge. He always dressed in the traditional Korean clothes, including *turumagi* ("overcoat") in the winter, as did the majority of Koreans his age in the Korean community. Traditional Korean clothes have to be ripped apart at the seams for each washing and resewn after each washing. She says she would like to have back the hours she spent doing that as a young bride. Still, she feels she had been fortunate in that both her mother-in-law and mother had come from the same province in Korea, for their ways were not radically different.

She found her father-in-law congenial and gentle. He still handled the family finances, so her husband turned over his earnings to him; and she received housekeeping money from him as needed. She recalls:

> He was not stingy. . . . My father-in-law loved me and consulted with me on all important matters concerning the household. . . .

Still, if she felt no particular oppression from her parents-in-law or husband, she did not have any freedom of action either. Towards the end of the first year of her marriage, she began to feel unbearably exploited by her in-laws and neglected by her husband, who still worked in Osaka. Although she continued to discharge all the responsibilities given her, she felt burdened with a nagging sense of futility and had to struggle to keep her resentment suppressed. Finally, she made a dramatic appeal to her husband to find a way to live at home so that she might feel a little like his wife, not just a maid-servant in his household.

Her husband was surprised and distressed, but no change came about.

Deaconess Chang, who had always enjoyed good health, began to fall ill sporadically about this time with an assortment of symptoms that ranged from diarrhea to indigestion and heart palpitations. Her body felt leaden, and she found it difficult to perform her usual tasks. She decided to return to her old job and asked permission of her parents-in-law. She was afraid she would go mad if she did not get away from the household at times. By then she had made the household tasks relatively routine, and she thought she could handle both. Besides, her mother-in-law could do some of the work, she thought. Her parents-in-law were unhappy with her decision but acquiesced. She told them she felt too stifled (*taptap-hada*) just staying home. Besides, the family could use the extra income.

Once back on the job, Deaconess Chang felt much healthier, though she was now combining two roles. She faithfully turned over all her wages to her father-in-law. Still, they became increasingly uneasy about her working outside. Though they said nothing, she knew they did not like her habit of stopping at her mother's place en route home from work. Several months after she returned to work, her husband quit his job in Osaka and set up his own business in Kyoto near home. He now lived at home. Deaconess Chang was thoroughly gratified and quit her job when she discovered that she was pregnant. Her eyes awash in tears and her hand concealing the smile on her lips, she confides that her husband used to "sneak" her favorite foods into their bedroom at night and watch with great satisfaction as she relished them. She thought at the time that the worst period of her married life was safely behind her.

During the fourth year of their marrige, circumstances of World War II led the Japanese government to abolish all small factory operations and to consolidate them. Her husband's glass factory in Kyoto was shut down, and he had to return to Osaka. This time, she accompanied him with their two sons and lived in a nuclear family situation for the first time. They remained in Osaka for two years until the war ended. Despite the fact that those were the harshest war years in Japan, Deaconess Chang recalls this period as perhaps the happiest one in her entire married life.

The conclusion of World War II brought this happy period to

an abrupt end. Frightened by rumors that if they did not repatriate immediately to Korea, they would not be allowed to take any of their belongings with them, both her natal family and her husband's decided to return to Korea at the earliest possible moment. Thus, within less than two montsh after the Japanese surrender, Deaconess Chang and her family returned to their native village in Korea. Her husband, anticipating difficulties in making a living in Korea, had brought with him a motor capable of running a grain mill. That proved an astute move, for the harvest season was at hand when they returned to Korea. By December of 1945, they were fairly well established near the mill situated between their native village and the nearest market town.

Rumors came with later repatriating Koreans that it was now possible to sell properties that Koreans had owned in Japan. Deaconess Chang's husband decided to return to Kyoto to see if he could sell his old glass factory, as he needed more capital to set up a similar operation in Korea. So, late in December of 1945, he found a way to re-enter Japan, leaving the mill in the hands of his father and younger brothers. He did not expect to be gone very long, returning by spring at the latest.

Once in Japan, however, it was difficult to sell the factory at a reasonable price; so, he resumed production, thinking that in an operating condition he might have an easier time of selling. In the meantime, he sent home letters assuring them of his forthcoming return, but at the same time explaining that he could not return until his mission had been accomplished. Had he not risked his very life returning to Japan? There would be no second chance.

In 1947, almost two years after her husband had left for Japan, her father-in-law went to Japan on a smuggler's boat to bring him home, but returned alone. Her husband asked for a little more time: his factory was just beginning to make a little money and if he could stay just a little longer, he was sure to return to Korea with a "tidy bundle."

Deaconess Chang felt heartsick. Her father-in-law also confirmed rumors they had been hearing that her husband had a Japanese wife and a son. Deaconess Chang sank into a black despair. It had been all she could do to endure her longing for him and to manage the mill and the household in his absence, thinking that he too was toiling for them.

> I had never expected that he would send his old father back to
> Korea alone . . . and then to have the rumors I had tried to
> disbelieve confirmed by his own father! . . . I understood that a
> man cannot live without a woman for such a long time, but it did
> not make pain any the less for me. I had been suffering from
> poor health since I gave birth to my son, my third, and now it
> really took a turn for the worse. . . .
>   When he finally returned home in 1949, he thanked me for
> having served his parents well in his absence, but it couldn't
> wash everything away. The heartache I suffered had gone too
> deep for that. . . . Do you know that he returned empty-handed,
> leaving his Japanese wife and son behind?

Between her father-in-law's return from Japan in 1947 and
her husband's return in 1949, her eldest son also became sickly.
He had no particularly obvious symptoms; he seemed just to wilt,
like his mother. Her concerned mother-in-law consulted a *mudang*
in a nearby villge and was told that their illnesses were due to
their neglect of the *Ch'ilsŏng* spirit which was accustomed to being
served in their household. Until her husband's generation,
Deaconess Chang's husband's lineage had continued precariously through an only son for four generations. When her
mother-in-law was first married, she had been told to give bi-
monthly devotional rituals to the *Ch'ilsŏng* spirit to grant her
multiple sons. For three years, her mother-in-law prayed to *Ch'ilsŏng* without failure on the first and fifteenth of each month, after
she had carefully purified herself by bathing, shampooing, and
changing into completely clean clothes. She had been blessed
with three sons as a result, and now she urged her daughter-in-
law to continue the custom in order that both she and her son
might achieve good health. The *mudang* also intimated that
Deaconess Chang might be suffering from *sinbyŏng*.
       Deaconess Chang remembered that a *mudang* her mother-in-
law had consulted in Japan when she became periodically ill
towards the end of her first year of marriage had given similar
advice. At the time, she had ignored the advice and even now felt
disinclined to accept it. She in fact resisted it, and both she and
her son became very ill. Following her decision not to invite any
spirits to possess her, she suffered severely from insomnia,
anorexia, and malaise. She lost so much weight that people did
not recognize her. Her parents-in-law called in a modern doctor,
but he could find nothing wrong with her. They tried Chinese

herbal medicine, but it had no better results. Deaconess Chang says: "Of course, no one knew at the time that Satan was sitting inside me. How could anything cure me of Satanic possession when the only cure is faith in Jesus Christ, our Lord?"

Finally, under the stress of poor health and her husband's continued absence, she acquiesced. The *mudang* insisted that it was no longer sufficient to pray twice a month: she must draw water from the well before anyone else had touched it and, placing three bowls of it on a table in the family courtyard, pray to *Ch'ilsŏng-nim* every day. It required a lot of energy and devotion to do this daily, but she was determined to do anything for her son's health and, secondarily, her own. She performed this ritual for five years without missing a single day, continuing even after her husband's return from Japan in late 1949.

In the meantime, as predicted by the *mudang*, she and her son gradually regained their health. Retrospectively, Deaconess Chang thinks this episode of illness was her second encounter with *sinbyŏng*, the first having been during the first year of her marriage and the third, when she again fell gravely ill shortly after her husband's return. She explains:

> The first signs of possession come through bodily afflictions.
> . . . And as your afflictions grow worse, you want to invite the
> spirits in so that you may have relief. . . . Then, too, people
> around you keep suggesting that you're suffering from *sinbyŏng*.
> . . . I'm supposed to have kept saying, "I'm your grandmother-
> in-law. I have brought you the spirit of *Ch'ilsŏng* to look after the
> family. Let me in." I have no recollection myself of saying such
> things. . . .
> People began to say that I should become a *mudang*, or else I
> would die. At first, I fought off all such suggestions. I said I
> would do the daily ritual three times a day but that I would not
> serve the spirits in my body.

This time, her mother-in-law became impatient with her chronic illness and her stubborn refusal to accept the call to become a *mudang*. Still, Deaconess Chang resisted, thinking she preferred death to being a *mudang*. However, when she found herself on the "threshold of death," she says she began to think a little differently.

> I asked myself, "Who will recognize my struggle to resist the
> possession of spirits if I die in the process of it?" When I reached

the point in my illness of being a walking dead, my mother-in-law and others in the household began to treat me as if I were already dead. They no longer tried to find ways to cure me. . . . They sometimes obliquely suggested that I was feigning my illness. I realized I was all alone in my struggle, that my pain was not really shared by anyone else. . . . Eventually I decided the most important thing was to regain my health, whatever the cost. One day I openly requested my father-in-law to give me his permission to have my initiation *kut*. He refused. He said there had never been a *mudang* in his lineage and he was not going to start one now; he did not care if it was his mother's ghost which possessed me. . . . Though people think nothing of seeking service from *mudang* when they are in need, they just as readily point their finger at a *mudang* and her family. My father-in-law was not going to have the family stigmatized. . . .

Finally, my condition deteriorated to the point where people were saying that I was dying because my in-laws refused to give me my *naerim-kut*. Frightened herself by my rapidly worsening condition, my mother-in-law appealed to my father-in-law to let me live. She argued that life was more important than *kamun* after all. My husband said nothing either for or against it. I think he blamed himself, at least in part, for my condition. Having left me alone for four anguished years, he could not now tell me to go to my death to save his face; still, he was overcome with shame before others. In any event, I had my *naerim-kut* in a grotto near a famous waterfall near our village two or three years after my husband returned from Japan.

Unlike most women who are possessed by supernatural spirits, Deaconess Chang claims she did not behave in the bizarre ways that often led people to mistake them as insane. Her supernaturally-imposed afflictions were limited to physical conditions, and so some neighbors were surprised by her initiation. Once she had her offical initiation, though, the spirits opened up the "gate of talk" in her and she was able to "serve the Devil" with facility. She began to make prophetic statements and find lost objects for people. Soon, paying clients flocked to her. Then one day, as she sat alone, the Devil—the reference she now uses to refer to her possessing spirits—told her to stop her prayers on behalf of her eldest son. Puzzled, she asked Satan—another term she now uses to refer to shamanistic spirits—and was told that her eldest son had another source of protection on which he depended and did not need her prayers and devotional rituals.

With an expression almost of awe, she says, "Now, isn't it amazing how the Devil knows such things so well!"

At the time, however, she had no way of knowing what the Devil was talking about. They had no relatives or even a family friend in Seoul who might look after her son while going to high school there. So she waited anxiously for his return home during the summer vacation to find out who might be looking after him.

On his arrival home for his vacation, her eldest son did not bow to the altar of shamanistic spirits as was customary for her children to do when they had been away from home. Surprised and annoyed, she pointed this out to him. Quietly but firmly her son replied that he had not forgotten it; he was not going to bow to "Grandmother" any more.[5] Angered by his impertinence, she demanded to know why and was told that he was a Christian. The Bible, he said, forbade worship of idols; consequently, he could not bow before her altar. Deaconess Chang says:

> Then I knew what the Devil had meant when it said I should stop praying for my eldest son. I could feel my whole body just flushing with anger. I moved toward him as if to attack and began to berate him. Thus began our spiritual battle between mother and a favorite son. . . .
>
> To this day, it surprises me how a mother could change the way she feels about her favorite son so completely and abruptly as I did. . . . My son became repulsive to me. I found him ugly. I didn't even want to look at him. I wanted him out of my sight. When he ate, I watched every spoonful that went into his mouth and begrudged every morsel that he took . . . after having worried all year about how and what he was eating in Seoul! I just did not want to have anything to do with him. . . . He had brought home a bundle of dirty clothes from Seoul; I did not want to wash them for him. The Devil was so strong that even when I finally decided that I should do the laundry for him, I could not. I put the laundry in a large basin and started to lift it up to place it on my head, but my arms refused to go above the shoulder. After many tries, I finally told my mother-in-law, "Mother, I cannot do this laundry." She had to carry it to the stream and do it herself.

Deaconess Chang says that she gave her son absolutely no peace thereafter. She demanded to know why, when she had become a *mudang* in order to save him from his illness, he chose to go against her. The Devil in her was so enraged by her son that he kept her in a constant state of agitation. She could neither sit nor lie still for a moment. What is more, she could not keep her hands off her son, a half-grown man by now. She slapped him in the face and beat him with a broom, but to her absolute fury, all he did in response was to call out, "Chu-yŏ, Chu-yŏ ("Master, Master," i.e., Christ)." He made no move to get out of her way no matter how hard or long she beat him. She says she got so furious once that she rolled across the length of the floor several times, screaming abuses at him and telling him to get out of her sight.

Some days later, he informed her that he would be returning to school in Seoul. She knew the semester did not begin for almost another month but said nothing. When the day of his departure came, she refused to cook his supper for him. Instead, she sat all afternoon, facing the wall. Her mother-in-law, realizing tht she would have to cook if her grandson was to eat anything before leaving on the evening train, went into the kitchen to prepare the evening meal hurriedly. There was not enough time for her son to finish his meal after all. That bothered her, but she still refused to say goodbye to him. She did not feel that he was her son and did not care if she never saw him again. When he had bid everyone goodbye, he opened the door to her room where she still sat facing the wall and, bowing deeply, said, "Mother, stay in peace. I am now taking your leave. I shall think of you every single day." (Deaconess Chang broke down at this point and wept so hard and so long that we had to terminate the interview for the day.)

Her husband, heartbroken himself over the development of events that was robbing his son of the respite he had come home for, followed his son to the station. Calling him to his side, he told his son:

> Son, I cannot take either your side or your mother's side in this battle between your spirits. Just remember what a devoted mother she used to be to you; she is not in her right mind now. It is her p'altcha and ours. You must not feel rejected or injured by the way she behaves towards you now. Now, go well.

Many years later, Deaconess Chang's husband confided to her that no experience in his life before or after that event had been so difficult for him—not even leaving his Japanese wife and son permanently in Japan.

Deaconess Chang's children had accepted her assumption of

the *mudang* role seemingly without noticeable trauma until that summer. She says she cannot be positive, as she was too preoccupied to pay close or prolonged attention to her children during the first years of her practice as a *mudang*. Her mother-in-law looked after them with help from her other daughters-in-law. The boys might have gone to their grandmother and/or aunts with their woes of being taunted by neighborhood children for being the children of a *mudang*, but she has no recollection of her children complaining to her. Her sons were generally very docile and obedient. For her part, Deaconess Chang tried to consider her domestic role before her professional one. She saw clients only during hours that did not interfere with her domestic duties. She rarely went away overnight for *kut*. She was determined that no one should be able to say of her that, being a *mudang*, she neglected her parents-in-law, husband, and children. In fact, by 1956 when her eldest son left to attend high school in Seoul, they had settled into a stabilized routine. The Korean War had been over for some time then, and between the grain mill and her *mudang* practice, they had an adequate income for a reasonable life even though her husband's various business ventures since his return from Japan had all been disappointments.

In Seoul, her eldest son had been befriended by a classmate who was a devout Christian. At his invitation, her son had gone to his church one Sunday and heard the minister preach coincidentally on the evils the Devil worked through *mudang* and other superstitious practitioners of false religions. The minister exhorted his congregation to resist temptations to resort to "those doers of Satan's work" when they were under stress, but rather to hold fast to their faith in the Christian God, the only true God, for He was capable even of ridding *mudang* themselves of their Satanic possession. Her son became excited; he had not known that the *mudang* role was escapable. He had always quietly endured the fact that his mother was a *mudang*, for he thought she could not help it. In the course of the year, he became a baptized Christian and resolved to convert his entire family, including his mother, to Christianity. That the role of *mudang* was *not* irreversible was a revolutionary idea to him. That summer, he went home determined to save his mother.

Now back in Seoul early after his heartbreaking encounter with his mother, he renewed his resolution to save her. He would match his mother's devotion to *Ch'ilsŏng* with his own. Rising at daybreak, he prayed daily for five years without interruption for a way to bring his mother to Christ. She was converted in 1961.

In the meantime, Deaconess Chang related in a sob-choked voice, she could scarcely contain her rage. Her son's refusal to bow before the altar and his denouncing of her spirits as false gods was profane enough, but he had also replied calmly that he was disobeying her out of his filial devotion and duty to her. To her, that reply was insufferable; she says it sat "in my throat like a fishbone caught sideways." Awake or asleep, she says, she could not forget it or forgive him for it. She hated him, once her favorite child. Continuing, she adds:

> It wasn't just my son I was so cold to. I kept my husband at a distance too. I found body contact with him for whom I had pined day and night for four years chillingly repulsive. I forced myself to submit to him sexually, but it was an ordeal. . . . By and by, we stopped having sexual intercourse; we did not resume it until after we both became followers of Christ. . . .
>
> You know, when the Devil possesses you, he works to make sure that your husband fails at everything he tries his hands at. The Devil is very jealous of the *mudang*'s husband; but more important, if the husband makes a good living, he is more likely to put up a real opposition to his wife's possession by the Devil. . . . So, in order to prevent the husband from making an effective opposition, the Devil works overtime to make sure the husband fails in everything he tries. The Devil's message to the *mudang*'s husband is: "Be idle and be fed." That is why there is a proverb that a *mudang*'s husband eats without working. You will find most husbands of *mudang* unemployed, not because they are by nature lazy but because the Devil makes sure that they will fail in everything they try. . . . Otherwise, the Devil cannot "talk big." Ours was no exception; everything my husband tried turned sour. So we had to sell everything and move up to Seoul the second year that my son was going to high school here. In such ways, the Devil gains domination of the whole household. Why, even my mother-in-law used to quail before me when I was in possession state with her mother-in-law's ghost! The entire family obeyed me except my eldest son after his conversion.

Still, Deaconess Chang feels that she could not have been unreservedly committed to her *mudang* role, for she recalls that she was always asking of herself, "How did I get to be a *mudang*? How can I get rid of my possessing spirits? Is there really no way out, as they say?" She was always preoccupied with lamentation and ashamed to be in the company of others. She is convinced today that her spiritual possession had been willed by God to test her son's faith, because he had already been elected to become a minister of Christ.

Although it had meant leaving behind her established clientele, Deaconess Chang agreed to move to Seoul where her husband thought chances of employment or starting another business would be better for him. In spite of repeated failures, her husband never gave up his efforts to sustain his provider's role; and she felt she should go with him. She did not want another separation. Besides, she says, her practice was diminishing due to the interfering effects of her son's prayers. So, leaving the grandparents in the care of the younger sons and their families, they moved up to Seoul, where she set up her shamanistic practice anew. Her eldest son came home to live with them in a small house with two rooms and a kitchen, all in a row.

Deaconess Chang's practice inconvenienced the rest of the family, for they had to vacate the premises, especially her husband and older sons, in order not to hinder her. Within a few months, she was able to support the family on her income alone. Then her eldest son's constant prayers began to interfere with her own effectiveness. Furthermore, he was "sneaking" his younger brothers to church. Every morning, he rose as early as his mother and went to church to pray while she performed her daily devotional ritual at her altar. Repeatedly, mother and son found themselves on a collision course; her tirades against him became almost a daily routine that upset the rest of the family and made them tense and nervous. In the meantime, she began to hear her grandmother-in-law's voice telling her to go back to the province and have a *kut* in order to strengthen her possession. So, she went back to the grotto and staged a *kut*.

During the *kut*, she could feel the spirits invading her and possessing her. She felt her shoulders pick up in rhythm with the drum and cymbals; she was dancing as of old. She was feeling fantastic, "out of myself."

> You are in a state of ecstasy; there is no other way of describing the feeling. . . . When you are in that state, you can clearly see

the ghosts and spirits that possess you; you know what their
voices should sound like, what they should say . . . it all just
comes to you. . . .

So strengthened, she returned to Seoul, feeling she could not
only resist her eldest son but also subdue him as well. Instead,
upon arrival home, she fell gravely ill and remained sick for four
days. Her eldest son nursed her devotedly while looking after his
father and younger brothers. The second day of her illness, her
eldest son was in the kitchen cooking supper when his father
came in. It was a Tuesday. He spoke to his son in hushed tones:

> Son, there is no help for the situation we are in. I am going to
> forsake everything and accept your God. Things cannot get any
> worse.

The son was overjoyed; this was the first positive result of his
five-year vigil in prayer. He was nearly beside himself with disbe-
lief. When he realized that his father was serious, he asked his
father to join him in a prayer of thanksgiving right there in the
kitchen. The next day, Wednesday, the father joined the son and
attended the evening service at the son's church; he thus joined
his son's crusade to save his wife from the Devil.

Deaconess Chang did not know of her husband's conversion.
On Wednesday evening she had difficulty sleeping and was feeling even worse than the day before. When she finally dozed off,
she had a dream from which she woke feeling troubled. It was
like no other dream she had ever had.

> I was going someplace and realized I was being followed by two
> men with knives. They were coming after me. I was scared; I
> didn't know where to run for my life. Then I saw a red brick
> building surrounded by a brick wall. I knew somehow that I
> would be safe from my pursuers if I could get inside the wall of
> that building. I started to run for it. When I got there, I saw three
> guards at the gate. Before I could ask them to let me in, they told
> me to hurry and let me slip through. Once inside, I realized
> there was someone else there. It was an old man with a beard—I
> know now that it was Jesus himself—but of course I didn't know
> it them. He was seated next to a desk; I went up to him, and
> addressing him as Grandfather, begged him to save me from my
> pursuers and snuggled into his bosom. He patted me like a child
> on my back and told me not to worry. Somehow, the pursuers
> had caught up with me and began to pull at me to drag me away

from the old man. Just then, the old man pulled open a drawer and took out a very fat bundle of money. Quickly counting the money and wrapping it in a bit of cloth, he handed it over to my pursuers. They let go of me and walked away. Feeling safely rescued, I turned to watch them go and saw four retreating figures where there had been only two before. (Of course, as you know, the Devil always appears in four.) They were covered with scars both on their faces and bodies. I felt so utterly safe that I began to taunt them to catch me if they could. They gave no response but kept walking away, and I woke.

She knew the dream was a message to her, but she could not figure out who her pursuers were or who her rescuer was. If it had been her *momju*, it would have been a female, she thought. She went over every step in the *kut* she had recently performed in the grotto, thinking that the dream was trying to tell her what she had done wrong there. Otherwise, she would not be sick. She could not come up with a satisfactory interpretation. The next day, her illness took a turn for the worse.

The same night, her third son had a dream which he felt extraordinary enough to relate to his eldest brother. An old man had appeared to him in the dream with a Bible and said that if he wanted his mother to be saved from the Devil, all he had to do was to read the Bible one hundred times from cover to cover. If he did, the old man promised, his mother's soul would return to her. The two brothers had no doubt now that the younger brother's dream was the sign of encouragement and approval from Christ himself. They informed their father of the dream, and the three decided that the time had come to chase out the Devil from their mother and the house. On Saturday morning, Deaconess Chang's husband went into his wife's sick room, and sitting by her bed, told her:

> Listen. Don't say a word. From now on, do exactly as I say. We have tried your spirits but you keep getting sick again and again. . . . Let's try something different. Let's give up all this superstition and the Devil's work and accept Christ.

Deaconess Chang says she was so shocked that she felt unable to breathe. She had never expected such a suggestion from her husband. She wanted time. She asked him who was going to carry on the ancestral rites if he became a Christian. She demanded that he consult with his parents before doing anything so drastic. He pleaded with her, "Trust me just one more time. I will accept all the blame and responsibility. All you have to do is follow me." She could not sleep that night. The next day was Sunday, and she knew something big was going to happen. She got up early and cooked breakfast, the first she had made since becoming ill a few days earlier. The younger children were all scrubbed clean and were barely able to keep still. It was obvious that they were going to church with their eldest brother and father. They had been afraid to go to church before because whenever they did and got caught, they had been beaten by her. But today, with their father in tow, they did not fear their mother. She saw that they were united as one against her but did not say anything. When they left the house, she too set out.

She went to see an older *mudang* she sometimes worked with. Having heard her tale, the older *mudang* shocked her by telling her to go along with her husband if she had already tried everything she could to win them over. There was nothing so pitiful, the older woman lamented, as a woman without a "master [i.e., husband]," like herself. Deaconess Chang felt angry with the old *mudang*. She had come looking for succor and for ways to destroy the hold Christ had on her son and now on her husband, and the old woman was telling her to become a Christian. She felt worse than before. She could not return home. She had no strategies to combat the onslaught she knew was waiting for her at home. She roamed the streets while two voices, arguing in her ears, made her dizzy with confusion. One voice told her to go home and fight it out with her family; the other one told her to disappear without a trace. Finally, fatigued and having no money, she decided to return home and confront the family.

The gate was left ajar and the house was silent, but she saw enough shoes there by the veranda to indicate about twenty people inside. She left and returned a little later, but this time she was greeted with hymn singing loud enough "to blow the roof off the house." She left the house a second time, feeling annoyed because she wanted to lie down. She did not feel she could fight off such an unfair match, especially just then. When she returned for the third time, there were no extra shoes and the house was quiet. When she opened the door, her eldest son sprang to his feet and welcomed her with outstretched arms and the crowd in the room burst into hymn singing as if on cue. They had hidden their shoes in the kitchen.

Deaconess Chang became hysterical and screamed at them to shut up and leave. Then, speaking in the voice of her possessing grandmother-in-law's ghost, she pounded the floor and wept until she felt her "innards had been squeezed out." One of the deacons moved forward after a while and, embracing her firmly from behind, said, "All you have to do is cast out the Devil and embrace Jesus Christ, our Lord. Then all will be well. You have nothing to worry about. . . ." The rest of the crowd chimed in with their chorus of "Amen, amen."

Deaconess Chang says she looked up at this point, but could not see anyone except her family although she could hear the voices of the others.

> I went up to my husband, looked him squarely in the eyes—something I had never done in all the years of our married life—and demanded to know what the meaning of all this commotion was. . . . I felt like slapping him silly in the face, but my son intervened by coming between us. "Mother," he said, "we are praying for your soul. We are praying to have you saved from the Devil. Please calm down, Mother."
>
> I turned on him and slapped his face repeatedly, as if I were turning over rice cake dough, all the while screaming that I had become a *mudang* for his sake in the first place. He didn't try to avoid the blows; he kept his face lowered and kept saying, "Mother, hit me to your heart's content. This is the last time you will do it. Hit me, Mother, hit me, please, all you like."

Others intervened to separate her from her son, and suddenly she felt overwhelmed with fatigue. She felt her body go limp, and instantaneously the church people raised their voices in hallelujah and exclaimed that they had seen the Devil exit from her body. They had exorcised her, they said. They rose as if on command and began to dismantle her altar and toss it out into the yard where someone had already started a fire. The bonfire burned brightly, and the entire neighborhood turned out to watch the drama. Drained of her possessing spirits, she felt lifeless. From where she sat leaning against the wall, she could see everything but felt helpless to stop it. She knew then, she says, that her time had come to an end. She finally understood the meaning of the dream related earlier and the omen of the spoiled rice. It had been her custom each year to put the year's first harvest of rice in a bowl and place it on the altar as a thanksgiving to her spirits. This year had been no exception, but a strange thing had happened. A few days after she placed it there, she found worms crawling out of the bowl. Lifting the lid, she discovered that the rice had turned black with mold; it had spoiled.

When her altar and all her other shamanistic paraphernalia had been destroyed, most of the church people left, leaving behind only a few of her son's friends from his theological seminary. While her son made her bed and carried her to it, his friends and her husband went out to the kitchen to prepare supper for her. She could not eat for trembling; her body shook violently. Forming a circle about her, the little group prayed for her, each taking a turn. She remembers most vividly that she was above all afraid. She now had neither her possessing spirits nor her son's God. It occurred to her, she says, that it would be nice not to have to be a *mudang* if somehow she could be sure that rejecting the role would not bring "the roof down" on their heads. The group stayed with her all night, someone staying awake to guard against the return of the Devil to repossess her.

Next day at dawn, her son carried her on his back to his church for the early dawn prayer meeting. It was snowing outside; the date was 27 November 1961. Everyone in the church came forward to welcome her. She remembers feeling embarrassed and confused. Thereafter, the entire family except the youngest child went to daily pre-dawn prayer meeting. On the third morning while she was at the prayer meeting, she began to "see" a replay of all the injury she had done over the years to her eldest son as if she were seeing a motion picture. She began to weep in atonement. She felt as though a dam had burst inside her. When she had finally stopped crying, she realized she was there all alone with just the minister. Everyone else had gone. She felt light. She was ready to accept her savior, Jesus Christ.

Her tendency toward weepiness came upon her unexpectedly for the next six or more years.

> I am sure I bothered people a lot with my crying. Sometimes I didn't even know that I was crying until I felt my shoulders heaving.
>
> Even now, on Saturdays, I feel just a little sick. The Devil still tempts me. So, even when sick, no, especially when I am feeling sick, I go to church. I always feel better afterwards.

Deaconess Chang says she suffered indescribable physical afflictions during the transition period which followed. All the old symptoms which had plagued her during her *sinbyŏng* episodes recurred even after she received baptism. Her migraine headache returned to befuddle her mind, while her eyelids swelled up and sties recurred to make her vision hazy. She suffered from paroxysmic attacks of chills and fevers that left her exhausted. Her extremeties felt as though she were being pricked by a thousand needles. She was sure at times that her palpitating heart would burst right out of her chest. Her list of symptoms is endless. She says that Christ tested the firmness of her faith for five years by visiting these afflictions upon her. Each time, her eldest son and husband prayed over her until they had successfully exorcised the Devil from her and carried her safely through another temptation.

Deaconess Chang's younger sons were no less pleased with her conversion to Christianity than their eldest brother. They did not have to put up with her clients or the constant conflict between her and their eldest brother whom they adored. They could attend church not only openly now but in her company. As for her husband, after witnessing and participating in the exorcism of the Devil from his wife the first time, he has become a stout believer in Christianity and is today an active deacon and leader in their church.

During the initial phase of her conversion following her exorcism, her eldest son and husband arranged with the church minister to have someone with her continuously when the family could not be with her. She feels she might not have been able to resist repossession by the Devil without the prayers and support given her by her vigilant fellow Christians in their daily visits. She thus finds tremendous personal satisfaction in holding daily prayer meetngs in the homes of fellow members of her church and in visiting those individuals who request her prayers. Having once been possessed by the very Devil and been rescued through exorcism by fellow Christians, she is regarded by other Christians as especially potent in her prayers. She is in great demand by them for *sinbang*. In addition, as a deaconess and the mother of a young minister sufficiently strong in his personal faith to have saved his mother from Satan, she is one of the foremost leaders in the church. Their church now provides the framework within which the entire family participates actively, each extolling the others to keep fast to the faith. Deaconess Chang declares she is now happiest when she is meeting with her prayer group. She then adds, almost wistfully, "Of course, a woman is happiest when growing up under her parents. . . . You know, the Christian God is also a jealous one; you must be faithful."

As for the future, she had neither specific plans nor hopes for herself and her family. She merely reiterates time and again that she and her family are committed to serving the will of their Master, Lord Jesus Christ. She considers it a sign of insufficient trust in God for human beings to make plans for their own lives without being open to and attendant upon the Lord's will for them. She adds that God works in mysterious ways but always for the good of His children. Then, almost as an after-thought, she adds that she does not wish to live with any of her daughters-in-law; she simply does not wish to impose life with parents-in-law on any of her daughters-in-law.

Today, she is heralded by her fellow believers as a chosen one, saved by God from the very clutch of Satan. The special designation allows her to function much as she used to as a shaman in ministering to those in need of her potent prayers. She enjoys the prestige and social support that she receives from her fellow Christians and family members but at times wonders if she has not been duped—if she is not being used by God and His servants, the members of her church and family. She feels that she is but a pawn caught mercilessly in the cosmic struggle between God and Satan, neither of whom pays much attention to her own suffering. But she is even more afraid of losing the support of her family and church.

8

AN INTERPRETATION:
SINBYONG AS A PATHWAY OUT OF IMPASSE

This book has brought together the biographies of six Korean shamans. As individual women, they come from very different social and educational backgrounds, time periods, regions, and personal experiences. But they also share some important personality traits and life experiences.

While six is admittedly too small a number of cases from which to make generalizations applicable to the rest of Korean women, I believe it is nonetheless instructive as a first step in that direction to look at these life histories comparatively for the common patterns that may provide explanatory cues for the questions I had when I started the study and also for discovering new questions to ask.

In terms of personal attributes, the six shamans had in common the following: (1) a high level of intelligence; (2) above average capacity for creative improvisation (they were imaginative and capable of improvising verbally, behaviorally, and in the use of available resources); (3) above average verbal fluency and persuasiveness; (4) strong goal orientation (they tended to be willful, self-centered, self-reliant, and self-directed); (5) keen sensitivity to intuitive cues of others; (6) calculating and manipulative interpersonal skills which enabled them to manage social situations strategically; (7) a sharp sense of justice in terms of their own standards; and (8) an above average repertory of aptitudinal and/or achieved dramatic and artistic attributes such as singing and dancing. In addition, all but one were exceptionally attractive in appearance.

In looking at these attributes in the institutional context of the shaman role, it becomes clear that they are the kinds of traits necessary to the convincing performance of the shaman role. They apparently serve as criteria for screening potential shamans and selecting for the shaman role individuals of above average intelligence, ability and appearance. (Ttongkkol-mansin is outstandingly homely.) Although it cannot be determined from this study, these traits may contribute significantly to differentiating between those who successfully become shamans from those who ultimately become identified as insane, following exposure to sinbyŏng.

If, however, these same traits are looked at in the generalized context of modern Korea which has become and continues to become rapidly industrialized and urbanized, it becomes readily apparent that these same attributes are equally well suited to and demanded by a large number of the increasing range of extra-domestic roles open to women for achievement. Would this circumstance siphon potential shaman recruits into these new career roles, thus perhaps undermining the continued strength of the shaman role in the life of Koreans? If so, who will take over the social functions now served by the shamans? Or will the needs for the shaman's services themselves change so that the shaman role will become obsolete? These questions are beyond the scope of this book, but it seems clear that the shaman role has traditionally been filled by superior women.

Another pattern common to all six shamans were the severe conflicts they experienced, prior to assuming the shaman role, between their individual sense of self and the definition of the domestic role they had to accept and enact. These conflicts were, for all of them, qualitatively different from the role conflicts that emerged subsequent to and in consequence of assuming the shaman role, in addition to the domestic one. All six shamans had inordinate difficulty in reconciling either cognitively or emotionally the discrepancies they perceived between social expectations of them as women and their personal goals and interests as individuals. They were critical of cultural norms others accepted as givens in their lives, were hypersensitive to cultural inconsistencies, and suffered from a deep and abiding sense of having been morally injured as human beings. This is unmistakably implied in their experience of *sinbyŏng*, the possession sickness from which they all suffer, and made more explicitly evident in the philosophies they espouse in the practice of their shaman role and the fulfillment of family obligations after assuming the shaman role.

Sinbyŏng is not only an experience common to all six shamans but it is also the most significant personal experience of their individual lives. It is the experience through which they make the transition from being helpless housewives trapped in the impasse of a double bind to being shamans who transcend the natural (culturally defined) limits of being a woman, who have a system of social support independent of their domestic role, who have economic autonomy, and who have clear professional identities in the larger society. *Sinbyŏng* therefore demands special attention.

Sinbyŏng literally means sickness brought on by spirits and refers to a range of somatic, mental, and behavioral symptoms similar to those the six shamans in this book have experienced and displayed during their pre-shaman phase. As a rule, possession state is the most important indicator and also the most dreaded symptom of *sinbyŏng* because it makes the diagnosis of supernatural call to the shaman role inevitable. *Sinbyŏng* will last as long as necessary, folk beliefs would indicate, to convince the victim of the need to accept the shaman role, or it is terminated when the resisting victim dies. As was the case with Wangsimni-mansin, P'yŏngyang-mansin, and Deaconess Chang, *sinbyŏng* can last twenty years or longer, its symptoms flaring up intermittently.

Again, according to folk beliefs, *sinbyŏng* is supernatural in it etiology but depends upon human response for its prognosis. While the victim is completely without personal blame, having been selected by predestination, she can, by accepting the shaman role, terminate its afflictions on herself and prevent them from being visited upon other members of the family, including descendants. The victim's family, on the other hand, can rescue the victim from unnecessarily prolonged afflictions of *sinbyŏng* by urging her to accept the shaman role in spite of the social stigma it will bring upon them all.

Since it is a common folk belief that spirits in search of human victims to possess are particularly attracted by those whose souls have been "fractured"—however slightly—by personal tragedies or exploitations others have caused them to suffer, families of *sinbyŏng* victims are placed in a socially embarrassing and psychologically defensive position. They are made vulnerable to the implied moral obligation to resuce the victim. Hence, when the decision is ultimately made by the victim, the family, or jointly for the victim to accept the shaman role, it can be perceived as having been altruistically motivated and often promotes a sense of new found solidarity as fellow victims between the shaman recruit and her family.

By coming to its full symptomatic flaring at just such times when interpersonal relationships of the victim with significant members of the family are at an impasse, *sinbyŏng* forces the adversaries to mobilize their efforts in collaborative attempts at rescuing the victim from the afflictions of *sinbyŏng*, thereby momentarily bypassing the unresolved conflicts which in the first place had locked them into the impasse. In the process, there occur changes in the power positions of various significant members of the family with reference to the shaman recruit, the transformation coming to a culmination when she assumes the shaman role. Everyone, including the shaman, seems to make a conscious effort to maintain the conventional social structure of the family, but it is in fact radically altered even when such efforts are successful in presenting a conventional facade.

Since the possessing spirits are often the ancestral ghosts of the shaman's husband and since, for those who believe in their reality, spirits in general are superordinate to human beings, the possessing spirits of the shaman occupy the apex of the newly formed triad in the family; namely, the spirits, the shaman, and the shaman's significant others in the family. Inasmuch as only the shaman has direct access to the spirits, in any disputes between the shaman and other family members, the spirits are likely to be in coalition with the shaman. Thus, *sinbyŏng* functions as a pathway out of an impasse in the relationships which can no longer be tolerated, and the assumption of the shaman role serves as a mechanism for stabilizing and maintaining the altered power positions in the family social structure. In other words, *sinbyŏng* provides a mechanism whereby the oppressed can turn the table on the oppressors with the latter's cooperation and support while the shaman role provides a mechanism for maintaining it or, failing that, of permitting the shaman a viable means of escaping from the family situation. The most remarkable feature of these strategies is that they are face-saving, blame-free pathways out of impasses, which leave no individual burdened with guilt.

The critical importance of the shaman's economic autonomy and the family's economic dependence on her in sustaining the reversal in power positions between the shaman and her previous oppressors in the family becomes indisputable in the life histories of these six shamans. It is especially evident in the cases of Suwŏn-mansin and Deaconess Chang. Not being able to bind their families through economic dependence, these two fail to secure on their own terms the social and emotional support of their families for their shaman role. Of course, in their case, their failure to dominate their families is partly due to the fact that their families do not validate the beliefs of shamanism. For *sinbyŏng* and the shaman role to serve the traditional functions in the service of the shaman, it is necessary for the families to hold shared beliefs in the supernatural. Further, it is apparent that the traditional ascription of outcaste status to shamans, which stigmatized their kin more inexorably than today, at once facilitated the shaman to retain her newly won dominance within the family and also forced her to give generally conservative counselling that would uphold the status quo. It severely limited the shaman's chances of expanding her power beyond her family and "engineering" the family into more favorable social positions by using the economic resources made available to her through the shaman role.

Today, with such social constraints much more relaxed through democratization of education, industrialization, and urbanization, shamans can, by careful strategy, use their economic resources to liberate their children from social humiliation to some degree and motivate them toward socially more acceptable life styles, as P'yŏnyang-mansin has done.

If these interpretations are correct, they hold significant implications not only for Korean shamans and women but also for women in other societies where they are striving for changes in their culturally defined roles.

To be speculative for the sake of it, given the new possibilities open to the shaman role and the present political anxieties of Koreans and the social confusion they are experiencing while undergoing industrialization, will the shaman role diminish or increase in Korea? Divorce is available to the Korean woman now, as are education, jobs, contraceptives, and marriages of love. Will Korean women seek other ways of managing conflicts between their self-images and cultural definitions of them besides the traditional ones of becoming a shaman, a nun, or committing suicide? And if they do—and many are doing so—how will Korean women justify these new strategies culturally? Without the traditional, culturally sanctioned projection to the supernatural, how will they justify changes in their role definition? Will they use some abstract concepts like justice or equality between the sexes? How will Korean women cope with personal and individual responsibilities implied in those new decisions? Where will they go for support when they feel discouraged or guilty?

The six shamans in this book have shown that, given socially acceptable justification and a role which assures economic viability, Korean women can deviate from the convention and shape their own and their children's destinies to a significant degree. How will Korean men deal with the emerging modern Korean women who seek similar goals through secular roles outside the family? Will modern Korean women and men opt for collaborative changes in the traditional, cultural definitions of the male and the female? Of the family? Or, will they take the competitive and combative route to ultimate negotiations for new definitions?

For these and other questions raised, it would be desirable to do comparable studies of Korean housewives without outside careers as well as of women who combine other professional roles with family life.

APPENDIX A:
REVIEW OF SELECTED LITERATURE ON SHAMANISM

In the literature of shamanism, both Western and Korean, one encounters a relative wealth of material of shamanistic rituals, functions of shamans, and functionally oriented explanations of the existence of shamanistic institutions. By contrast, there is a paucity of information on shamans as individuals; that is, on their pre- and post-shaman life histories. Such material as does exist on personality structure, role recruitment process, and subsequent role maintenance focuses almost exclusively on the question of the shaman's psychopathology or normalcy. Furthermore, the material is marked by strong differences of opinion among researchers about the phenomena of shamanism. These opinions may be classified roughly into four categories: (1) the shaman is a pathological personality; (2) the shaman is a "healed madman"; (3) the shaman may be either a pathological or normal personality; and (4) the shaman is a normal or even a super-normal personality capable of reformulating and thus of providing clients with a new synthesis of world views.

According to Lewis (1971:179), the historically earliest, and perhaps the strongest established opinion in the study of shamanism, is that it is an "institutionalized madhouse for primitives" and the shaman is a "conflict-torn personality who should be classified either as seriously neurotic or even psychotic." In an early study, Wilken (1887) attributes the origin of Indonesian shamanism to mental disease, and Bogoras (1907:415), that much-quoted source on Chukchee shamans, describes them as generally extremely excitable, hysterical, and "half crazy" (cited in Lewis 1971:179-180). In subsequent years, this view has found a considerable following among noted scholars, many of them studying shamanism in very different cultures.

Kroeber (1952:318) states his position on the psychopathology of the shaman unequivocally: "The new extension [to his 1948 position] is this: Not only shamans—the professionally possessed or entranced or fraudulent—are involved in psychopathology, but often also the whole lay public of primitive societies." Another persistent proponent of this view is Devereux who characterizes the shaman as a severe neurotic or psychotic who serves his society as a "deputy lunatic" (1956:23 and 1961). Devereux argues—rightly as far as conceptual levels are concerned—that the fact that shamans serve culturally valued functions cannot be taken as evidence demonstrating their psycho-normalcy or absence of psychopathology. To prove this point, Devereux (1961:1089-1090) cites many well-known Western historical figures who were presumably psychopathological. Linton (1956, cited in Silverman 1967:21) is another noted anthropologist who regards shamans as psychopathological personalities.

These proponents of the equation, shaman=neurotic or psychotic, commit the same kind of conceptual and analytical error that Devereux charges to his opponents. As Handelman (1968:353) first points out and Fabrega and Silver (1970:471) later reaffirm, they fail to make the important distinction between the shaman's role behavior and the behavior which is directly traceable to personality dynamics of the shaman. Those who argue that the shaman is a psychopathological personality formulate their theory from analyses of the shaman's role behavior which was produced to conform to cultural definitions of the shaman; consequently, the validity of their equation, shaman=neurotic or psychotic, is at best questionable. Psychopathology of individual personality structure can be derived from role behavior *no more reasonably* than the question of psychonormalcy from role behavior appropriately performed.

More recently, Silverman refined the earlier formulation of

the equation, shaman=neurotic or psychotic, by specifying that shamans are similar to psychiatric patients of the essential schizophrenia, reactive type, that are seen in Western clinics. According to Silverman, there are no significant differences between acute schizophrenics and shamans in the "sequence of underlying psychological events that define their abnormal experiences" (1967:21). Unfortunately, Silverman applies to the shaman and the acute schizophrenic different modes of analysis, thus invalidating his conclusion on methodological grounds. As Weakland (1968:356) points out, Silverman considers shamanism as occurring "within and related to social contexts" but schizophrenia as "only a manifestation of *inner* psychic or mental organization. . . ." Again, as Weakland points out, neither does Silverman consider the possibility that the nature and etiology of acute schizophrenia itself may be viewed in terms of social interaction and behavior, as in fact he does with the outcome of schizophrenia, especially in the case of shamans.

Lebra (1969:221) who took life histories of the Okinawan shamans he studied and found their pre-shaman life marked by failure, especially in interpersonal relations and in achievement, concludes: "Observation, interviewing, and analysis of projective tests give ample indication of pathological thinking and acting among Okinawan shamans, and I feel quite sure that, in terms of general personality configuration, deviants are recruited for this role." He does stress, however, that "for the Okinawan shaman the greatest intensity of overt pathology occurs prior to taking office, especially what is termed the *taari* period" (ibid.:220).[1] While the successful shaman, he states further, achieves incontestable social adjustment through the role, she perhaps needs to retain some of the pathological traits in order to enact the shaman role successfully. He seems to suggest that at least in Okinawa there may be a correspondence between certain pathological traits and some attributes which are entailed in the shaman role.

Ackerknecht, who disputed the labeling of medicine men as pathological by anthropologists, holds a similar view, it seems, regarding the Siberian type of shaman whom he describes as a "healed madman." He writes: ". . . *shamanism is not disease but being healed from disease*. . . . The shaman after having passed through an autopathological state is autonormal. . . ." (1943:71. Emphasis in the original). At the same time, Ackerknecht, by pointing out that mental illness is not the only route to the shaman role, introduces the notion thereby that a range of variable personality types may be recruited into the shaman role.

Murphy (1964) does not deal directly with the question of the shaman's psychopathology; however, she strongly implies that the *practicing* shaman is, if anything, in excellent mental health. According to her, even those who had been suffering from mental disorder prior to their acquisition of the role of shaman find it a means of healing. Edgerton (1971:259-260) portrays his informant, a secularly and experimentally oriented Hehe ethnopsychiatrist, as a recovered psychotic, although he at no time identifies his informant as a shaman.

K. I. Kim, a psychonalytically oriented psychiatrist who has published extensively on Korean shamanism in the Korean language, and B.Y. Rhi, another psychiatrist but of Jungian orientation, who has also done considerable research on Korean shamanism, agree that shamans are recovered neurotics or psychotics. Both psychiatrists (K. I. Kim 1970, 1972a, 1972c, 1972d, and 1974 and B. Y. Rhi 1968) have reached these similar conclusions from their independent studies and perceive Korean shamanism as an institutionalized system of sublimation, which has both positive and negative effects.

K. I. Kim (1972a:89-90) in particular contends that shamanism encourages projection rather than intrapsychic insight and responsibility and thus sets into motion a vicious circle of promoting paranoid tendencies and then relieving the anxieties thus generated through further projection. Within the context of this circular system of sublimation, Korean shamanism, K. I. Kim maintains, exerts a positive influence on the psychological welfare of the people as a whole. He characterizes Korean shamanism as being humanistic and other-directed in orientation and having as its attributes such qualities as compassion, empathy, and high valuation of interpersonal harmony.

K. I. Kim (1970 and 1972d) and B. Y. Rhi (1968), who also agree regarding the functions served by Korean shamans, see them as primitive psychiatrists. With regard to their mental health, K. I. Kim (op. cit.) describes them as recovered neurotics or psychotics who use their own insights into psychological conflicts as a vehicle for treating others who are mentally ill, and achieve their psychotherapeutic effects largely through empathy and a process of identification with their patients.

K. I. Kim and B. Y. Rhi, who have been almost alone among Korean investigators of shamanism to be concerned with the issue of shamanic psychopathology, have also conducted research on folk concepts of mental illness as a natural extension of their interest in the problem.

B. Y. Rhi (1970:39), in his study of folk concepts of disease etiology, found that he could not determine conclusively whether Koreans distinguished causes of mental illnesses from causes of other types of illnesses. He did find some regional beliefs, however, which link mental illness of *women* to possession by a specific male spirit and *kwisin* ("ghosts or disembodied soul"). While B. Y. Rhi could not determine to his satisfaction that Koreans do not attribute physical illnesses to possession by spirits, he learned that the notion of mental illness as resulting from possession by spirits is an old one in Korea. He cites as his indicative evidence the record of a Yi Dynasty king whose insanity was attributed to spirit possession.

K. I. Kim and H. T. Won (1972) carried out a survey of folk concepts as to the etiology of mental illness and the preferred modes of treatment, using a sample population of 379 subjects selected from every province in South Korea on the basis of being older than fifty years of age and of living in remote rural areas. They learned that 82.4 percent of the sample population attributed mental illness to supernatural causation and/or psychological agony (*komin*). Of those who considered mental illness to have its genesis in supernatural causation, 59.4 percent attributed it to spirit possession, 21.3 percent to breach of taboos, and 9.7 percent to soul loss. As for treatment modes, 44.5 percent specified shamanistic rituals and about 27 percent favored other modes of folk therapy. An unspecified number of respondents also stated that some of the spiritually possessed are destined to become shamans, provided that they are possessed by good spirits and that they *recover* from their possession sickness through initiation *kut* (ibid.:97(33)). Most unfortunately, the authors do not specify the number of such responses they elicited. In the light of these statistical findings, it is interesting that all thirty women founders of new religions studied by M. H. Tak (1971) were specialists in curing the mentally ill and had themselves undergone experiences of spirit possession. In fact, twenty-five of them had formerly been shamans.

In studies in which K. I. Kim (1970 and 1972d) narrows his

focus of investigation to the possession sickness, *sinbyŏng* syndrome, utilizing his "psychoanalytical point of view," he concludes that the spirit possession syndrome has two distinct phases. In the first of what he calls the prodromal phase, K. I. Kim found the victims to be suffering from hysterical and/or psychosomatic symptoms. In the second phase which he calls the phase of depersonalization, K. I. Kim found the victims to be suffering from psychotic hysteria or schizophrenia. He suggests that the duration of the first phase may vary from several weeks to twenty years, although in some cases with acute onset the prodromal phase may be absent.

A case history of behavioral symptoms of a male shaman by Y. K. Kang (1970) parallels rather closely the description of the characteristics of the female shamans studied by K. I. Kim (1970 and 1972d) in both the prodromal and depersonalization phases. B. Y. Rhi and associates (1970) studied three female mental patients and discovered that folk concepts of mental illness colored their ideation considerably. All three had pre-psychotic life histories with characteristics which very closely resemble Lebra's (1964) Okinawan shaman informants; namely, their lives had been marked by interpersonal conflicts and failures. In a recent publication, K. I. Kim (1974) gives perhaps the most complete life histories available in the Korean language on two female shamans and concludes that shamans are recovered neurotics or psychotics.

Sasaki, in his comparative study of the life histories of fifty-six shamans in Japan, found that only sixteen of the sample were shamans of the type that he calls "spontaneous," i.e., they did not acquire the shaman role through apprenticeship but through their experience of spirit possession. Of these sixteen, eleven showed signs of personality pathology, while the remaining five did not show such signs of psychopathology. Sasaki, therefore concludes that shamans are recruited from the ranks of both the psychopathological and the non-psychopathological (1969:239). Kiev (1972) also suggests that the range of variable personality types recruited for the shaman role encompasses both the psychopathological and the psychonormal. However, unlike Sasaki, Kiev rests his postulate on secondary sources.

One of the earliest to hold the view that the shaman is a normal personality is Shirokogoroff (1923:248). He maintains that the shaman must not only be in good physical and psychological condition but that, failing this, he must delegate his shamanistic duties to another who can subjugate the spirits. Shirokogoroff seems to suggest that to be effective a shaman must be in control of his role performance and that a psychopathological personality is unlikely to maintain such control consistently. Nadel, who characterizes the Nuba shaman as a potential "cultural broker" endorses this view very strongly: "No shaman is in everyday life an 'abnormal' individual, a neurotic, or a paranoiac; if he were he would be classed as a lunatic, not respected as a priest. . . . I recorded no case of a shaman whose professional hysteria deteriorated into serious mental disorders" (1946:25-37).

Both Opler (1961) and Honigmann (1967:340-342) support Nadel's view and oppose the views of Devereux and Kroeber, i.e., the shaman is psychopathological. Honigmann argues that "for all their florid, expressive role behavior that sets them apart from laymen in their community," the claim that shamans differ from their non-professional contemporaries by being psychiatrically disordered has not been sufficiently demonstrated (ibid.:341-342). Another who holds a similar view is Lewis, who disparages scholarly preoccupation with the matter of the shaman's mental health. He likens it to an attempt to evaluate "the whole of psychoanalysis in terms of the psychotic experiences of some analysts" (1971:184-185).

Boyer (1964) who gives brief biographical sketches of thirteen Apache shamans he studied, as well as extensive background data on tribal child-socialization practices, finds that none of the thirteen had been marked early as psychological deviants; nor were they considered by their culture mates to be other than typical. Furthermore, with the possible exception of one, none of the thirteen had been cured of illness by a shaman prior to assuming their professional role. Boyer strengthens his position that shamans are normal members of their society who display personality structure very similar to that of its typical members by supplementing his findings from the Apache with analyses of literature on Chukchee and Balinese shamans.

Boyer (ibid.:254) concludes that ". . . those who become shamans may be innately creative individuals who have more capacity than their culture mates to use regression in the service of the ego and, as a facet of this capacity, are more able to convincingly employ conscious and unconscious impostureship. If this hypothesis be valid, it would be logical to state that, in contrast to Devereux's contention, at least some shamans are less afflicted psychopathologically than their culture mates." Boyer suggests, it seems, the possibility that the shaman is not only a normal and typical member of his society but mentally healthier than his culture mates. Since, however, Boyer characterizes all three societies studied as suffering from an hysterical personality disorder, his position on the normalcy of the shaman becomes equivocable.

In a study comparing Zinacanteco shamans with non-shaman Zinacantans on a variety of social and psychological dimensions, designed specifically to link psychological measures with those derived from social and cultural factors, Fabrega and Silver (1970) find no significant differences between the two groups. If anything, the investigators find the shamans to be super-normal members of their society, who among them display greater variation in personality structure than the non-shamans. Handelman (1967) who provides one of the more detailed shaman life histories depicts Henry Rupert, a Washo shaman, as a man who is not only non-pathological in personality structure but is adaptive, innovative, and independent. Rupert's grasp of reality is sound: he is given to experimentation and does not practice any healing technique in which he does not have confidence. The life history of this successful shaman in a society undergoing rapid sociocultural change challenges those scholars, such as Devereux and Kroeber, who see the shaman as a pathological personality who is rewarded with the shaman role in certain societies. Unfortunately, similarly detailed life histories of other Washo shamans are lacking.

The categories of theoretical positions reviewed above may be diagrammatically illustrated as follows:[2]

There are four ways in which cells A, B, C, and D may be combined in terms of the mutually exclusive categories, non-pathological/pathological and pre-shaman/post-shaman. The view that the shaman is a pathological personality is represented by the combination of cells B and D. That the shaman is a "healed madman" is represented by the combination of cells B and C. That the shaman is a normal personality is represented by the combination of cells A and C. The theoretically possible combina-

	non-pathological	pathological
pre-shaman	A	B
post-shaman	C	D

Figure 1. Pathology vs. Non-pathology of Shaman's Personality

tion of cells A and D is *not* represented in any of the theories reviewed. The view that the shaman may be either pathological or normal rests on both the cell combinations A and C and B and D, depending upon the situation.

Having briefly reviewed some of the various positions taken by investigators on the subject of the shaman's mental health, I conclude that more basic to the study of shamans are good ethnographic accounts of them in the making, i.e., their experiences in socialization before and after they have acquired the role of shaman. Such descriptions would enable investigators to imbed the role in the totality of a shaman's life experiences. At present, with such exceptions as Handelman, Lebra, Nadel, Sasaki, B. Y. Rhi, and K. I. Kim, most investigators have studied their shaman subjects (1) outside of their professional role (e.g., Fabrega and Silver); (2) in their shaman role only; or (3) in their shaman role with the immediately pre-shaman phase as a part of the shaman role. In the first instance, they judged the normalcy/pathology of the role personality of the shaman in terms of the normalcy/pathology of the shaman's personality structure, as this was defined by a variety of instruments. Thereby they left unanswered the important question of how the shaman manages such role behavior as trance. In the second and the third intances, they equated the role personality of the shaman with his personality structure, coming up with either the pathological or non-pathological label, depending upon their judgment of the role personality "seen" through his role performance.

As a result, I concur with Handelman (1968:353-354) who writes:

Yet data on the development of shamanic character, of early and later socialization, of personal world view and philosophy, in short of the mind and personal experiences of the shaman, are essentially absent from the literature. . . . This lack is not crucial to structural-functional analyses of sociocultural units but is crucial to the study of the *psychology of shamans, role recruitment of shamans*, effectiveness of therapeutic techniques, and evaluation of the innovative creative potential of the shamanic role. *Without adequate life-history material, theorizing in these areas must remain hypothetical* [emphasis mine].

On the point that experience of disorder in some form is an essential feature in the recruitment of shamans and that the disorder must be overcome successfully before the shaman can assume the role (Lewis 1971:187), differences of opinion also appear, although they are not as radical as those which divide the scholars on the issue of the shaman's psychopathology. In the absence of adequate life-history material on shamans, this point cannot be resolved adequately.

THE FOLK VIEW OF THE KOREANS REGARDING SHAMANS

From the popular literature, my personal observation and memory, and informal conversations, it appears to me that the Korean folk concept of shamans does not concern itself with the issue of the practicing shaman's state of mental health. It does recognize, however, that during the possession sickness, *sin-byŏng*, the behavior of the potential shaman-recruit can be mistaken for that of a "crazy" person or *mich'in-saram*.[3] It also holds that a shaman-recruit, i.e., one who is possessed by spirits, can actually *become* crazy if she is not appropriately initiated into the shaman role.

A more pervasive and dominant stereotype of the shaman depicts her as a charlatan who exploits the weak, the oppressed, and the unsuspecting, much in the manner in which Americans talk of medical doctors as quacks and lawyers as shysters. This negative view, however, does not prevent people from seeking the services of shamans but perhaps only fosters an ambivalence towards them as a social category.

In general, Koreans regarded recruitment into the shaman role as an unfortunate (or even the most unfortunate) act of predestination over which human beings have no control. They point as evidence of predestination by supernatural ordination to the afflictions that befall potential shaman-recruits and that defy natural explanations or conventional remedies. The victims, it is believed, can be relieved of these afflictions only if they assume the shaman role. At the same time it is also believed that spirits possess those human beings whose soul/heart (*maŭm*) is already in a weakened state, i.e., under psychological stress.

The initiation rite which marks the transition from the afflicted victim to the shaman is called *naerim-kut*, a rite in which the possessing spirits are officially invited to descend (*naeri-da*) and enter into the novice. Thereafter, the relationship between the shaman and the possessing spirits is explicitly transactional: the shaman provides the spirits with access to human beings and their affairs and is in turn relieved of the afflictions which had plagued her before assuming the role and which can again plague her and/or her family if she neglects her role. When the shaman is not sufficiently dutiful to the spirits, they retaliate; when the spirits are insufficiently protective of the shaman, she challenges their right to possess her.

The relationship thus forged between the possessing spirits and the shaman is an exclusive partnership in that no other human being may enter it and form a triad without incurring retaliation by the spirits. A popular folk belief is that the assumption of the shaman role presages the ruin of the household or minimally makes of the husband less than a full man in the social sense. Just in terms of the time and energy it consumes, the relationship preempts all of the shaman's other relationships. In brief, the shaman role is regarded as incompatible with the normative domestic role of the Korean woman.

The Korean folk view on shamans has several interesting points of correspondence with the views expressed by various researchers of shamanism, as noted previously. These are: (1) the experience of disorder of some form is an essential feature in the recruitment of a shaman; (2) afflictions alone do not automatically make a shaman of the victim—they must be overcome; and (3) the relationship between a shaman and possessing spirits are transactional and mutually binding, as in a marriage. Further, the folk view, like the scholarly one, provides insufficient information regarding the typical pre-shaman life-history of a shaman but implies only that a potential recruit is prone to be under psychological stress.

*

APPENDIX B:

WOMEN AND FAMILY IN TRADITIONAL KOREA

Whether among themselves or with foreigners, when Koreans talk about themselves, they tend to preface their remarks with a discourse on their history, now in its 4309th year, *Tan'gi*,[1] in A.D. 1976. Koreans are inclined to feel that neither their national character nor their individual behavior can be fully understood without such historical references. Their almost obsessive preoccupation with history is particularly pronounced with reference to the Yi Dynasty, A.D. 1392-1910.

Osgood (1951), an American anthropologist, wrote: ". . . however much a modern Korean may seem encrusted with other beliefs, hidden Confucian values will show up beneath a scratch." Other observers of Koreans generally concur with him (Brandt, 1971; Crane 1967 and 1972; and Rutt 1967), although the Confucian values they speak of are fundamentally Koreanized, as explained in Chapter 1. Despite revolutionary changes which have marked almost every aspect of their lives, especially in the present century, the Koreans feel an abiding and deep sense of identity with their cultural past and make a conscious effort to perpetuate it.[2] Such cultural persistence is especially strong in the institutions of marriage and kinship.

The Japanese colonial government in Korea (1910-1945) which carried out massive and systematic deculturation programs among the Koreans usually stopped short of directly interfering with the traditional social organization of the family and kinship group. Hence, the family came to symbolize the ethnic identity of Koreans struggling to resist assimilation by the Japanese. The Korean family is therefore both the best repository of traditional values of the Yi Dynasty Korea and also the most potent institution through which the past participates actively in shaping the present and future cultural trends of Korea. Other factors which have significantly contributed to the persistent continuity of traditional values in Korea are, first, the long history of self-imposed isolation from other societies during the Yi Dynasty and, second, the predominantly agricultural and rural nature of the nation's economic life until after the Korean War, 1950-1953.[3]

When the founders of the Yi Dynasty overthrew the previous dynasty, Koryŏ (A.D. 918-1392), they had justified it in terms of moral reformation of the entire society. They banned Buddhism, the official state religion of the Koryŏ Dynasty, and imposed in its place the monolithic world view of Confucianism[4] as the state doctrine, the official ideology. The officials actively proselytized Confucian values among the people at all levels through education, legislation, edicts, and civil service examination and appointment systems, to mention but a few means used. The goal was to create a thoroughly stratified but perfectly integrated society. The numerous edicts issued and enforced by the government for this purpose resulted in comprehensive and sometimes drastic social reorganization, as noted in most standard Korean history texts. One writer, U-Chang Kim, describes the Yi Dynasty Korean society as "the code-locked society of Confucian discipline and obligations" (1976:6).

The official interpretations of Confucian precepts came to dominate and regulate every aspect of the people's lives from birth to death, including such seemingly trivial matters as the order and seating arrangement by which family members were served at meal time in ordinary households.[5] Everyone was to know who he was, where he belonged, and how he should conduct himself in all conceivable circumstances. If there were no proper manner of conducting an interaction, such relationships were to be avoided. An individual was to be guided strictly by the five basic classes of relationships recognized and defined by Confucian ideology in all his interpersonal relationships. Namely, the relationship between (1) ruler and subject, (2) parent and child, (3) elder and younger, (4) husband and wife, and (5) friend and friend. Each class of relationship was ranked in the order given here so that the social structure was conically shaped in what Nakane (1967) calls the inverted-V vertical principle of alliance.[6] In all five relationships, reciprocity was asymmetrical.[7]

Recognizing marriage and family as the fundamental institutions of a society, the reform-minded, founding fathers of the Yi Dynasty concentrated their efforts predominantly on rearrangement of the Korean family (Cf. P. C. Hahm 1967) as a basic step in reorganizing the society. To them, establishing and maintaining proper social organization of the family was a national policy and its implementation, an immediate necessity.[8] The household head was made personally responsible to the authorities for the behavior of all the members under his authority. In turn, he had absolute power over the life and death of individual members of his own household. The household was thus a corporate unit, with the head as its leader and the individual members as somewhat differentiated component units with no independently viable life of social significance. The behavior of any individual member was the business of every other member of the household. Predictable and conforming internal organization of the family was crucial to its survival and necessary to social order.

Ideally, intra-household, interpersonal dynamics in the traditional household were to be carefully controlled and managed by exacting strict conformity from everyone to the detailed and explicit role definitions formulated according to the Confucian principles of interpersonal relationships mentioned above. Spontaneity in interaction was to be discouraged, and, where it conflicted with the Confucian prescriptions, it was to be actively suppressed. If individual wishes and needs were juxtaposed with the collective needs of the household, they were expected to be routinely sacrificed to the corporate needs of the household. Maintaining these prescribed patterns of interaction within the household was further facilitated by spatial and occupational segregation of the sexes as additional strategies. The architecture of the house, whatever its scale, separated it into male and female spheres. Generally, the male quarters faced outward toward the external world while the female quarters were protected behind it and separated from it by a courtyard. Access to the quarters of the opposite sex was strictly governed and minimal. Division of labor by sex was such that it made them indispensably and mutually dependent, though segregated in actual activities.

Since Koreans observed clan exogamy, however, every household faced a potential crisis whenever a daughter-in-law had to be brought in. She could upset the established equilibrium of the household. She, the stranger, therefore had to be selected with the utmost care and assimilated with the minimum possible disruptions to the overall integration of the household. This was generally achieved by first making marriage a matter of negotiation between two households with little or no personal participation by the prospective mates, although their respective social and personal attributes were studied with great attention and care by both households. Second, women were made utterly dependent on socially recognized relationships to men for their own social roles and identities. Their existence was defined by reference to men and justified by their usefulness to them. Women were, for all their indispensability to the society, ancillary people and were readily replaceable as individuals. Proverbially, a traditional Korean woman's life cycle was divided into three major stages in terms of the men she had to obey at each stage. Before marriage, a woman was enjoined to obey her father; after marriage, her husband; and in old age, her son (O. Y. Lee 1967:137).

Third, even when women assumed certain roles, such as that of a bride or a daughter-in-law, her continued right to remain in such a role was contingent upon others' evaluation of her performance in that role. Thus women were not only socially tangential to men but were also contingent role actors who had to continually validate their roles in order to retain them. For example, women could not under any circumstance initiate divorce,[9] but a woman could be divorced on any one of the following grounds. These were: (1) if she does not serve her parents-in-law well; (2) if she has no children, particularly male; (3) if she is lecherous; (4) if she is too jealous; (5) if she has an incurable disease; (6) if she talks too much; or (7) if she steals (ibid.:137). Finally, women had no legitimate economic autonomy (J. S. Choi 1966). Also, and most important, women were socialized to consider acceptance and adherence to these conditions of their sex role as the highest virtue and privilege.

Dire consequences befell women who, either through accident of fate or lack of appropriate socialization, disqualified for the normative role of women, i.e., marriage, or were dismissed from it. It was culturally inconceivable for women to remain unmarried. Women whose occupational roles forbade them to marry or made it difficult to marry were genuinely pitied and regarded as social non-persons. And once married, women no longer had any legitimate claim on their natal households. The best chances for socially acceptable survival for individual women lay in completely identifying with the interests of their husbands and sons. The surest way for women's self preservation lay in self denial.[10]

That the attributes of traditional Korean women's normative role were difficult to satisfy, there can be little argument. Koreans themselves have always recognized it. The Korean essayist O. Y. Lee insists that Korean women married and continue to marry commandants rather than men (ibid.:137). K. K. Lee, a Korean anthropologist, expressed a similar view in more anthropological terms when he said: "In Korea, the husband and his family have the status of rights and privileges and the wife, the status of duties and obligatins." It has been equally widely recognized, as evidenced for example by the abundance of popular proverbs and folk tales on the subject, that the task of socializing daughters for the traditional women's role was complex and difficult.

Since, almost by definition of their role, traditional Korean women were perpetually caught in a double bind, their adequate and appropriate socialization involved learning to live with a double bind without becoming disoriented by it. Empirically, it meant that their socializers had to teach them (1) to accept the double bind as an intrinsic condition of their life, (2) to develop flexible and adaptive strategies for coping with conflicts arising from it and other sources, and (3) to be well versed in the repertory of role demands—rules about role enactment (Sarbin and Allen 1968)—in addition to the attributes entailed in their role per se. If, for example, the demands of the men or other superiors in their households and the duties and obligations of their role happened to be mutually contradictory, what should the women do? How could they cope with errant commands of their superiors and at the same time save themselves from dismissal? How could they prevent role deviance by others without damaging their "face"?

For the majority, being socialized to avoid the seven grounds for divorce and to avoid unnecessary self-disclosure to anyone in her husband's household was probably sufficient under ordinary circumstances. However, as the following folk tale illustrates, being literal and uncritical in one's role enactment did not guarantee one continued occupancy of one's role.

> Once upon a time a man said to his daughter when she was setting out to go to her wedding, "A daughter-in-law's life is very hard. She must pretend that she does not see the things that are to be seen, that she does not hear the words spoken around her, and she must speak as little as possible."
>
> So for three years after her marriage the girl spoke never a word. Her husband's family thought she was deaf and dumb, and so they decided to send her back to her father's house.
>
> As she went back riding in a palanquin, she chanced to hear a mountain pheasant call, and she said, "Dear pheasant! I have missed your voice these long years." Her father-in-law, who was walking beside the palanquin, was overjoyed to hear her speak and took her back to her husband at once. Then he sent his servants to catch the pheasant.
>
> As she cooked the pheasant the daughter-in-law sang, "The wings that protected me I will serve to my father-in-law. The nagging beak I will serve to my mother-in-law. And the rolling eyes will do for my husband's sister" (I. S. Zong 1970:189-190).

Once role conflicts emerged, it behooved the traditional women of Korea to manage them in such a way that they did not expose those responsible or blamable for the conflicts. They had to be apt at improvising—at transforming situations to prevent anyone from being compromised by the circumstances—and yet at achieving what needed to be done for the collective good of the household or the other person(s). Another folk tale aptly illustrates this point.

> In olden times early marriage was the rule, and very often the bride was considerably older than the bridegroom. Once a rather elderly bride was married to a child-bridegroom. She tried to treat him as her husband, but he gave her no end of trouble by his childishness. She was ladling rice out of the pot one day when her husband came and asked her to give him the burned rice at the bottom. She felt ashamed that her husband should be so childish, and so she snapped at him, "A gentleman mustn't ask for such things in the kitchen." Thereupon the boy

burst into tears. She was greatly embarrassed by this, so she picked him up and put him on her back and started to soothe him like a baby. Before long he stopped crying. Just then her husband's father came along. So she went to the door and told the boy to climb up the thatched roof where the gourds were growing. Then she said loudly, "Pick me a good ripe one, please." She did this to show her father-in-law that she had not been carrying her husband like a baby, for it if had been known she would never have been able to hold up her head again (ibid.:190).

The most critical attribute to be developed for successful role enactment by traditional Korean women was the capacity for judicious assessment of persons, events, and situations and for being able to differentiate the actual issues of importance from the apparent or officially staged ones in any given situation. Such an attribute was of course completely contradictory to the total obedience expected of them. Consequently, it was a trait that had to be cultivted discretely—almost in collusion between the socializer and the socialized. Notwithstanding, it was a highly prized trait in traditional women as the following legend demonstrates.

Kang, a simple village girl, was drawing water from the well one day when a general rode up on horseback. The day was hot, and the general and his men had been on a long journey. "Give me water to drink," the General said to the girl. . . . The girl Kang . . . filled a big bowl of water, freshly drawn from the well. But before she handed the bowl up to the great man, she plucked a number of tender green willow leaves and dropped them into the cold water.

The general took the bowl in his hands and began to drink. He was greatly annoyed when he found how the willow leaves got in his way. Instead of taking the huge gulps, which his thirst called for, he was forced to sip slowly.

When he had drained the big bowl at last, the General scolded the girl; but he spoke gently, because she was in truth of a jade prettiness.

"It was not very polite of this young person to throw leaves into my drinking bowl," the General said to Kang.

"It was only because I feared for the health of the Great General. . . . You were overheated and tired, honorable sir. With quick drinking you would have swallowed the spirits of sickness. You might even have died. It was to prevent this that I put the willow leaves into the bowl. They forced you to drink slowly with very small sips. Thus no harm could come to you."

The General said to himself, "This maid is as wise as she is beautiful." . . . Then he said to the girl, "I will make you my bride if you will but wait until the war ends."

. . . And who should that general have been but the famous General Yi, who later became King of our Dragon Backed Country (the Yi Dynasty Korea). . . . Now, of course, the King had many other wives also in his palace, as do all kings. . . . But they say he admired none as he admired his good Queen Kang. Her wisdom shed light upon his most troublesome problems of state, and he always consulted her. . . . (Carpenter 1973).

If these strategies failed them in managing their role conflicts, traditional Korean women could resort to discharging their role obligations unilaterally and faultlessly according to the highest cultural ideals, as did Queen Inhyŏn and Ch'unhyang, both famous for their virtues (Rutt and C. U. Kim 1974). Women could use their virtuousness to embarrass their role others to social conformity—and thereby to their social salvation—and elicit public support for their private plight.

In terms of life cycle, traditional women lived through three major stages: premarital life in the natal household; postmarital, patrilocal life; and retirement. Each stage was subdivided into more or less distinct period marked by a transition in the socialization of the women. The premarital stage consisted of infancy, childhood, and post-pubescence. The postmarital stage began with a period of mutual assessment and adjustment and progressed through periods of childbirth and apprenticeship for the role of household mistress; assumption of the mistress role; and acquisition of daughter-in-law and grandchildren. The acquisition of grandchildren initiated anticipatory socialization for retirement which followed the complete relinquishment of the role of the household mistress.

The birth announcement of a female infant no longer automatically solicits condolences in contemporary Korea. Traditionally, the reception a female baby received was less certain, depending primarily on her birth order. If she were the first born, she was less welcome than a son would have been, but she was benevolently tolerated as her birth augured well for her mother's ability to produce children. If her birth followed a succession of sisters uninterrupted by a brother, her arrival could be met with open hostility and/or outright neglect. Minimally, it would have embarrassed her mother. According to Moore (1911), it was not uncommon for female infants in the late nineteenth and early twentieth centuries to be named Sŏpsŏphabi ("regrettables").

Even in the best of circumstances, being born female constituted a liability not only to the self but to those, in particular the mother, on whom the infant was dependent for nurture and protection. This is not to say that daughters were regularly mistreated, nor that they were not sometimes indulged by parents and grandparents. Rather, the point is that even when parents and grandparents found delight in a female baby, their enjoyment of her was quiet and private. If they spoiled a girl baby, they did so almost surreptitiously. And for those with insufficient resources to support another life or without a son already, the birth of a daughter posed an excessive economic burden. Some parents sought relief from such predicaments by selling their daughters as permanently indentured servants (or slaves before its prohibition), as apprentices for the *kisaeng* role, or as potential wives.

After the first year, the greatest concern was focused on keeping the presence of the child unobtrusive, lest its disruptive behavior interfere with the formal and orderly conduct of interactions, particularly across the lines of generation and sex. Unless grandmothers, older sisters, or other child care-takers were available to share the mother's burden, the years between one and three or four represented a trying period for the mother. If a younger sibling followed and replaced the toddler at the mother's breast as well, management and socialization of the child was even more trying for the mother.

Assuming adequate cognitive and motor skills, a girl child between the ages of one and three or so began to be perceived as a potentially viable social being. She was introduced to adult food—masticated first in the mother's mouth in the beginning—and was weaned from the mother's milk. The process could be either gradual or abrupt, depending on such fortuitous factors as the arrival of the next sibling, supply of milk, the health of the mother and/or the child herself, and the general economic circumstances of the family.[11]

There was apparently no rigorous regime with regard to toilet training. In the initial phases, it consisted largely of increased sensitivity on the part of the mother or other caretakers in anticipating the elimination needs and timing of the child. At anticipated intervals, the child was held in a position conducive to elimination and encouraged to do so by a series of sounds intended to imitate the passing of urine or the grunting of the child in moving its bowels. Pants for children in this age bracket were made with a slit running almost the full length of the inner seams of the legs to permit "accidents" to occur with minimum chance of soiling the garment. As a rule, toilet training was not experienced as particularly stressful for either the child or the mother.

As a child grew older, its care was increasingly delegated to others, especially to older sisters, sometimes no more than two or three years older. Between feedings, the mother's interaction and contact with the child, especially a girl, became more perfunctory. Korean mothers enjoyed fondling and playing with their children, but more than occasional and fleeting indulgence in such activities, especially with a girl child, was discouraged and frowned upon. Most Korean mothers lacked time for such activities in any case.

Some broad objectives of socialization during this period were to satisfy the child's elementary needs for physical growth and safety and to keep its presence as socially unobtrusive as possible. As a result, caretakers, especially very young older sisters, were concerned primarily with consequences to themselves of not keeping their charges pacified and out of the way. A natural concomitant was that the child was subject to situation specific and situation accommodative socialization practices rather than to thematic socialization practices which hold constant across situations and caretakers. This difficulty in maintaining consistency and constancy in socialization derived basically from child caretakers being females who could not impose their own conditions on the social environment, especially when male members were present. For example, a mother who might be inclined to let a child cry out its frustration as a possible technique of discipline could not do so if it disturbed adult male members present. As disturbances occasioned by girls were less readily tolerated and girls were more subject to externally cued fluctuations in the care and socialization they received than boys, they tended to be more motivated to develop greater sensitivity, accuracy, and vigilance in monitoring the social climate of their environment than boys needed to be.

In situations of conflict between sisters and brothers, resolution was usually made in favor of the brothers as a matter of course regardlss of their relative ages or issues involved. At best, girls were cajoled and distracted with substitute consolation "prizes" whether it be mother's breast, being carried on her back, or being taken into the kitchen and given a rare snack. Not infrequently, girls were scolded severely for causing their brothers to feel annoyed without regard to provocations they might have received from their brothers. Also, as a girl child grew more capable of self-locomotion, she learned that there were areas restricted to her but not necessarily to her brothers.

By the time of her third or fourth birthday, an appropriately socialized girl was expected to know, if only intuitively, that: (1) women are inferior to men and, therefore, she is an inferior being; any claim she has at the present for preferential treatment rests on her relative immaturity and helplessness alone. (2) She cannot reasonably expect to appeal to, or be treated by, the same system of justice as that of the male. In situations of conflict between the sexes, men are right by virtue of their maleness while women are wrong by virtue of their sex. (3) Women are peripheral to their social environment and tangential to their men. Consequently, if she persists in egocentric behavior, she can only provoke intensified punishment. Neither can she make predictions regarding her social environment with her self as the reference point. Accordingly, she had best develop accurate skills for monitoring it in order to adjust and adapt to the changes in it. In other words, she must be quick in *nunch'i* ("social sense") and sophisticated in manipulative strategies to avoid being made an innocent target of social processes that do not discriminate among individuals, especially females.

Still, until the onset of puberty, usually between ten and fourteen, the Korean girl enjoyed a relatively carefree life. The intensive anticipatory socialization for marriage did not begin until her menarche. However, beginning at about age six or seven, she experienced a radical shift in her socialization. Explicit and formal recognition of human sexuality was culturally acknowledged and expressed in the concept of *namnyŏ-ch'ilse-pudongsŏk* [after age seven, one may not sit with a person of the opposite sex]. If up to now a girl had only had intimations of her sex-determined social inferiority, of the necessity to acquiesce to the male without recourse to objective justice, and of her irrelevance to the decision making processes, she could not escape them after age seven. They were communitcated to her explicitly. She was no longer casually tolerated for not knowing "her place" as a woman. Minimally, she had to be cognizant of sexual inequality and the consequences of ignoring the differences.

During this period, between age four or so till puberty, a girl was increasingly called upon to assume the duties of a surrogate mother toward younger sibling, if any, and to be the additional "hands and feet" needed by the mother to carry on her many duties. If she were a girl from a social class in which most of the menial tasks were performed by servants, then she had to learn other class appropriate skills and knowledge. As a rule, upper class girls were subject to more rigorous sex role socialization than girls from the lower strata where necessity for their labor made strict conformity to the ideal sex role an "on stage" behavior displayed as needed.

Nearly every utterance addressed to a girl during this period was prefaced with, "A girl must (or mustn't) . . .," and her socialization became highly elaborated in its particularities. After age seven, proper socialization required a girl to be spatially confined to the female spheres and naturally also to the company and activities of females. She was often threatened with the fear of not being sufficiently suitable to make a good marriage if she did not conform to role expectations and learned in the process to dread being unmarried or divorced as the worst possible fate for a woman.

During this period, a girl was expected to recognize also that an overt path to power and control in her social environment would always be denied her and that she must be continuously alert with *nunch'i* to avoid unpleasantness for herself and to exercise influence on her significant others by covert strategies. She should have learned, too, that a traditionally effective strategy for gaining influence and power over men (and female authority figures) and for keeping her personal self somewhat invulnerable to social attack was to be as faultless in her own role enactment as possible.

After the age of seven, female role socialization focused more on acquisition of skills in specifically female tasks, accompanied by increased restriction of movement and closer supervision. In families sufficiently affluent to dispense with their daughter's labor outside the house, girls were "locked up inside the gate," as the Korean expression goes, after age ten or so.[12] As a girl approached puberty, the family began actively to concern itself with the arrangement of a suitable marriage for her. In the meantime, her female role models imparted to her, ideally, such traditionally adaptive strategies as have worked for them in coping with difficulties generally associated with the domestic role of women. They counseled her that the first law of behavior for women was obedience; the best way to cope with men and persons of authority in general was *not* by direct confrontation since women had no authority but by covert management of the total social situation, including the key actors in it; and the best way to insure personal social security was to become indispensably useful to men and persons of authority in general.

In other words, by the time that a normatively socialized girl reached her puberty, she should have had in her repertory of role knowledge and performance skill the following. (1) Women are inferior to men. (2) Women must expect and acquiesce to the preferential treatment accorded males. (3) Women are subject to spatial constraints in movements. (4) Women must maintain proper social distance from men in their household and practice social avoidance with unrelated men. (5) Women must conceal emotions which are incompatible with their role requirements. (6) Women must cultivate covert strategies for goal realization, i.e., learn to "work the system with 'tongue in cheek' and eyes sharply focused on the system." (7) Women are married out to strange households where their reception is uncertain. (8) Women who are valued by men and the society are those who uphold cultural values by their conformity and commitment to their female role and therein lies the traditionally most reliable social security for women. By the time of her puberty, a girl should have had "mapped out" with enough detail and accuracy the existing sociocultural realities of her life and been motivated to learn effective mechanisms for maximizing her goals within these limitations.

In traditional Korea, the eye of the social onlooker was focused on the quality of the performance an actor gave in a specified role much more than on the actor as an individual. Therefore, what was of primary social significance and therefore valued above the individuality of the actor was the *role* and its "specified 'constancies of behavior'" that an actor in the role was expected to uphold (Nadel 1957:21). It was not expected that the role should be modified beyond its culturally sanctioned range of variance either according to the will of the actor or according to her capacities. Rather, it was the individual woman who had to be socialized—modified—until she acquired sufficiently adequate role knowledge and performance skill. Traditional Korean women were judged, above all else, for their faithful conformity to their roles.

As a consequence, so long as women performed satisfactorily in their roles, they as individuals were relatively free from social censorship. The quid pro quo relationship between the individual woman and society was well defined, and she was not called upon to support publicly her behavioral conformity with her psychological or moral commitment, although of course this was encouraged. This separation between the self of the individual and the part(s) she played in her social role(s) permitted detachment of her psychological and/or moral self from her roles; it facilitated performance in social roles by eliminating the moral question of self-role congruence to a great extent. It therefore made good adaptive sense for socializers of traditional Korean women to urge on them an almost mechanical behavioral conformity to their role(s). Such survival oriented anticipatory role socialization accelerated as girls entered marriageable age, two or three years past puberty.

Perhaps the single most important lesson to be conveyed to marriage-bound daughters was that when they entered their husbands' households, they should not, in fact had no right to, demand reciprocal role conformity from others. Furthermore, inadequacies or even absence of such reciprocal role conformity did not entitle them to suspend their own role performance. Theirs was not the right to criticize the improper or absent reciprocal behavior of their others; theirs was merely the duty to assume, if necessary, a phantom reciprocation of behavior where real reciprocation was lacking and to go on *as if* they were being reciprocated. In other words, marriage-bound young women had to learn that their individuality or personal demands intruded upon their role only at the terrible risk of self-disclosure and vulnerability resulting from it. However much their partners deviated from or failed in the expected performance of their roles, for women to improvise or deviate in their role enactment beyond the culturally permissible range was tantamount to placing one's individuality above one's social utility and accountability to the group. Suppression of self expression was a key socialization task for post-pubescent girls.

In post-contact Korea, i.e., the late nineteenth and the present centuries, post-pubescent socialization of women probably underwent more changes than that of any other stage. As Korean males' ideal of womanhood changed in accordance with their own rapid modernization, socialization for post-pubescent girls was also modified to accommodate these changing expectations. Increasingly, their socialization proceeded on a dual-track course. That is, they were simultaneously socialized on two seemingly contradictory courses: (1) they were socialized in the traditional patterns, almost more rigorously than before to keep the traditional patterns from eroding in the face of many new, competing patterns, and (2) they were socialized in such emergent patterns as seemed to produce the attributes demanded by the more desirable bachelors, although it was done in an ornamental fashion.

One technique evolved to facilitate such dual-track socialization was to keep prenuptial daughters under constant chaperonage while permitting them to attend schools or to work in the public domain. Families of means provided daughters with constant companionship of servant girls or post-menopausal kinswomen who accompanied them to and from all public places, including schools.[13] Working girls, like their earlier counterparts, the daughters of poor peasants, were relatively freer but they too were constantly subjected to mutual chaperonage and the controlling power of gossip.[14] They, no more than girls from upper classes, could afford to have their virginal reputation damaged if they hoped to make a good marriage. In short, the social organization of roles permitted prenuptial girls was such that the girls were under almost constant surveillance and thus subject to swift corrective measures if they deviated.

The traditionally short period between puberty and marriage was devoted to further refining role knowledge and performance skills, including what may be termed sex education. However, the following folk tale suggests that sex education for traditional Korean women might have been at best perfunctory.

There were once three sisters. The eldest sister refused to undress on her wedding night, because she felt too bashful. The bridegroom thought she must dislike him and got up and left the house, never to return.

When the second sister married she remembered her sister's failure. So on her wedding night she went in to her husband naked, carrying her clothes over her arm. He was astounded that she should behave in such an outlandish fashion, and he too left the house at once, never to return.

The third sister was very worried after her sisters' two failures, and so on her wedding night she stood at the door of the room and asked her husband, "Shall I come in dressed as I am, or must I undress first and come in naked?" Her husband was so embarrassed by her strange question that like the others he too got up and left the house forever (I. S. Zong 1970:194).

Traditionally, this period represented the last chance for daughters to interact with their families as an insider. Once the curtain rose, once the wedding ceremony took place, she was on her own. At best, her parents and kinsmen could exert only the most indirect influence on her personal welfare. Since a married women had no legitimate role in her natal household, if she failed in marriage it usually meant that she was permanently deprived of the only legitimate role through which she could participate in the society.

As already noted, the postmarital life of traditional Korean women was divided into five periods, spanning two life stages. The first, the "mutual discovery and adjustment" period, usually lasted about a year and was traditionally terminated by the bride's visit to her natal household. If she were pregnant at the time, she usually stayed there until after childbirth, as was the custom throughout most of Korea. Although it lacked a specific and designated term in the Korean language, the importance of this initial period was noted in other ways, also. The linguistic practice of addressing a new daughter-in-law as *aga* ("baby") by both parents-in-law was widespread, as was the attachment of the prefix *sae* ("new") to kinship and non-kinship terms of address and reference in regard to the bride during the first year. The bride was also permitted to wear clothes of fine material and colors not worn by married women beyond this period. At the same time, this was for the bride the probationary period during which she needed to establish a favorable reputation among her in-laws, kinsmen, and neighbors. She needed to learn also that any conflicts that emerged between herself and the other members of the household would be expected to be resolved in the others' favor. For example, if a normatively socialized bride entered a socially deviant household, the cultural norms at one level would have her support the deviancy of the household at the same time they would urge her at another level to correct the deviance discretely. On the other hand, if a bride were deviant, she would be expected to make such changes as would make her more acceptable or face possible divorce.

During this period, the bride generally made the transition from *sae-saekssi* ("new bride") to *ae-ŏmi* ("mother of a child") also. Koreans have long recognized this initial period as a difficult one in a woman's life, but the general cultural expectation has also been that it would be endured by most women. A popular Korean proverb, often quoted by Koreans, says: "There is no woman who cannot sustain married life for one year, and there is no man who cannot carry one *sŏm* (5.12 US bushels) of rice" (K. M. Yi 1962:412).

The apprenticeship period which followed had its own hardships for the traditional Korean women. An often repeated axiom among Koreans is that it takes a bride ten years of married life to stop longing for her natal household (Brandt, 1971:132). Since, traditionally, brides had no other role options, the axiom attests to the many difficulties which a bride normally encountered in achieving a sense of identification with her husband's (and ultimately her son's) household. The already quoted proverbial injunction that a bride should remain dumb three years, deaf another three years, and blind still another three years to weather the trials and tribulations of married life further supports this observation.

The apprenticeship period was probably more determinative of the traditional woman's particular place in the overall constellation of her husband's household composition than any other period. It was during this period that she could most fully demonstrate the extent to which she could actually validate her role within the household. It was during this period that she had to stabilize a tolerable pattern of relations with the other members of the household and bring about a routinization of her role enactment.

It was also the period when she had to secure the emotional

commitment of her sons, as a foundation of security for old age and an ongoing source of a sense of well-being. It was the period when she must gradually motivate her mother-in-law to formally relinquish her hold on the management of the household and transfer the role of the mistress to her. In other words, this was the period during which the traditional, married woman had her maximum opportunities to individualize her domestic role for the remainder of her life. This was the period during which she had to carefully lay the foundation for the informal power and influence that she would want to have subsequently over the household in general and over her husband and son(s) in particular. Throughout this period, she must compete with her mother-in-law for her husband's attention and access to him. Generally, however, the two women met on more agreeable grounds with regard to her son(s) and her mother-in-law's grandson(s).

The apprenticeship period varied in length, depending on the social class, region, and individual inclinations and attitudes and aptitudes of the mother-in-law and the daughter-in-law involved. The daughter-in-law who sought too actively to take over the mistress' role from her mother-in-law was severely criticized, as was the mother-in-law who withheld it too long from her daughter-in-law.

Once she assumed the role of the household mistress, the traditional Korean woman had some autonomy, especially in the management of the internal affairs of the household. Equally important, she was now finally "one of them." A woman who reached this stage was rarely if ever dismissed from her role through divorce.

Ultimately, when she acquired a daughter-in-law of her own, she had reached the pinnacle of the traditionally normative, domestic role of the Korean woman. She was now the dreaded mother-in-law in charge of launching her own daughter-in-law in a course of apprenticeship to succeed her and to continue the tradition of the household to the next generation. If, as a daughter-in-law, she had to do whatever was in the best interest of the household while being careful not to incur her mother-in-law's personal displeasure, now as the mother-in-law and the primary socializer of her daughter-in-law, she had to be careful not to have her mistress' role usurped too prematurely by her daughter-in-law. At the same time, she had to be mindful of the fact that when she retired, her welfare in old age depended to a considerable degree on the grace of her daughter-in-law.

Many women retained their role as the household mistress until long after they had become grandmothers. Therefore, retirement from the role of the mistress and the acquisition of the grandmother role did not necessarily coincide. But postretirement grandmotherhood was significantly different from pre-retirement grandmotherhood. After retirement she had no formal responsibilities; only privileges and such task-oriented roles as she chose to assume. Postretirement grandmothers generally focused their attention primarily on their grandchildren, indulging and loving them openly. This was the golden period of the traditional Korean woman's life cycle, the one which made all the preceding ones worth enduring.

*

NOTES

1. For a more detailed treatment of Korean shamanism and shamanism in general, see Appendix A.

2. For a detailed treatment of women and family in traditional Korea, see Appendix B.

3. For a selective review of literature on shamanism and on the question of shaman's psychopathology, see Appendix A.

4. W. J. Joe (1972:9-11) describes the *Mumun* people as double beneficiaries of the Scytho-Siberian culture and the agricultural culture of North China. According to him, the *Mumun* people brought the Bronze culture to Korea about 600 B.C. and assimilated the Neolithic people of the Korean peninsula who had produced the comb-marked *Chŏlmun* pottery. The bronze implements left presumably by the *Mumun* people have been found largely in Pyŏyang Province, with some in the southern part of the peninsula.

5. Buddhism was first introduced into Korea during the Three Kingdom period. It came first to Koguryo in A.D. 372, then to Paekche in A.D. 384, and much later to Silla during the reign of Nulchi-maripkan, A.D.

417-457. While Buddhism received a much warmer reception in the first two kingdoms than it did in Silla, all three kingdoms came to recognize it officially and to promote its propagation, especially among the elite ruling classes. Confucianism was introduced into Korea about the same time; however, its influence was largely on the reformation of the administrative organization of the government rather than on Korean religious practices (W. K. Han 1970).

6. The Sui Dynasty was founded in A.D. 589 and lasted for about thirty years. The T'ang Dynasty which succeeded the Sui lasted about three hundred years (W. K. Han 1970:75). One of the battles in which female shamans are credited with having given aid might have been the one waged by King Yong-Yang (A.D. 590-618) of Koguryo against the Sui in A.D. 598. The Sui army was defeated in this battle by the Koreans (ibid.).

7. One of the three Korean literary works referred to as "Palace Literature," *The True History of Queen Inhyŏn* or *Inhyŏn Wanghu Chŏn*, describes the trials of the Queen at the end of the seventeenth century Yi Dynasty, Korea. Unlike the other two in "Palace Literature" which were first-hand memoirs, *The True History of Queen Inhyŏn* was created as a work of art, a historical novel. As a historical novel, it makes relatively few references to the political background of the palace drama that it depicts. It focuses mainly on the life of the Queen as an individual. The original author of the story is not known, though speculations exist regarding the creator's identity. Today there exist at least four different versions of the story. For greater details on the background of the story, see C. U. Kim's introduction (1974:181-184).

8. Ch'ŏndism is also known as Tonghak, Eastern Learning, as opposed to Western Learning which began to penetrate Korea with the introduction of Catholicism and subsequent contact with the West.

9. Osgood does not define shamanism as he uses the term. Neither does he cite the source of his information. Consequently, it is difficult to know what books shamans of the period were ordered to submit to the government. These books might have included books of geomancy and fortune-telling by non-shamans such as *p'ansu* ("blind fortune-tellers").

10. Cited in Knez and Swanson (1968) and an important source for Akamatsu and Akiba (1938).

11. For a critical evaluation of Japanese scholarship on Korean shamanism by a Korean scholar of shamanism, see K. S. Ch'oe's "Re-

search Activities on Korean Shamanism in the Past and the Present," *The Journal of the Korean Association of Cultural Anthropology* (1970: III, 125-141).

12. Chosen Sotokufu, usually translated as the Korean Government-General, refers to the highest governing body in the Japanese colonial political structure of Korea.

13. Akamatsu and Akiba (1938:40) pose a slight problem by giving a second census figure of 10,344 shamans for the same year, 1930, from the same source, namely, Murayama, as reported in the *Chōsen Sōtokufu no Chōsa, 1930*. This figure gives us a ratio of one shaman per 1,837 in the population. My own opinion, based on my personal knowledge of the operations of township-level police stations of the period, is that both numbers 12,380 and 10,344, are conservative. I suspect that the survey did not extend into the outlying villages not within easy access to the police stations located in the town. That is to say, in the areas surveyed, the census is very probably accurate; however, it is strongly suspected that every village was not surveyed.

14. The conversion rate was two yen to the dollar according to the Japan Yearbook of 1911.

15. For a sampling of shamans' sessions with clients, see Harvey, 1976.

CHAPTER 2

1. Wangsimni is a section in a ward of Seoul. Literally, the term, *mansin,* means ten thousand spirits. It is used in conjunction with a place name as a geononym (see Lee and Harvey, 1973) to refer to and address shamans in an honorific manner. In speaking of shamans as a category or as individuals who are not present, the term *mudang* is used almost exclusively to refer to shamans. My exposure to the subculture of shamans had been so negligible during childhood that I did not know of this most elementary rule of etiquette. The wealthy and respectable matron whose family had patronized Wansimni-mansin's mother for three generations carefully drilled me on this fine point before she took me to meet Wangsimni-mansin and her mother.

2. I was frankly skeptical when first told this. Subsequently, I was

present at the Dragon Rite [*Yongsin-kut*] on the Han River when a police motor launch came charging toward the boat where the rite was in progress. The participants panicked and the boat tilted dangerously as they rushed to get off the boat before the police launch arrived. Soon, however, it became apparent that the police motor launch was there on a very unusual mission. It had come to deliver a large pot of chrysanthemums from the mysterious royal princess. I should add that police raids on shamanistic activities are commonplace and that all the shamans, including Halmŏni, had gotten into a frenzied state at the approach of the motor launch.

3. A shamanistic rite which honors the river dragons of the Han and insures a good harvest.

4. Halmŏni learned, some time after her marriage, that her husband had a sister who was a *mudang* also. She thinks he had been willing to marry a *mudang* and was uncensorious toward her because he had a sister who was also a *mudang*; however, she never discussed this with him.

5. *Sinkyŏng* means "nerves." *Manhi* means "plentifully," and *ssŏssŏ* means "used."

6. Halmŏni was astonished to hear this episode recounted. She had not known of this incident before.

7. The elementary schools estabished in the first quarter or so of twentieth century Korea were generally referred to as *pot'ong-hakkyo* which translates literally as "normal school." These were not teacher-training colleges.

8. Halmŏni used the expression, *maegi-ŏpkko, ch'imulhae-haesŏ*. Literally, the first expression means lacking any pulse, i.e., without any hope. The second, depressed, dejected, or melancholy.

CHAPTER 3

1. She is uncertain of the exact year of her birth.

2. A high-rise hotel built by a world-wide Japanese chain.

3. Public transportation becomes a nightmare generally after 10 P.M. If

they are not well on their way home before ten, those who live on the outer fringes of the city may find themselves still on the street after the midnight curfew. Curfew violators often spend the night in police stations.

4. Public education in Korea is now mandatory through the Middle School, i.e., the ninth grade. However, enforcement is not very effective, judging from the number of young people of school age on the streets during school hours.

5. Student assignments to public Middle Schools are determined by residential districts, but many parents still attempt to get their children enrolled in those Middle Schools which were prestigious before the allocation system became effective and which still enjoy a higher entrance record into similarly prestigious high schools.

6. The going rate for a simple divination was 500 *wŏn*. Namsan-mansin sometimes accepted as little as 100 *wŏn*. The exchange rate (official) at the time was 400 *wŏn* to the U.S. dollar.

7. Many Korean fathers come home late and dine alone. As a general rule, the best of everything is kept for the father, with the rice kept warm either on the stove or, in the winter, under covers on the warmest spot of the *ondol* ("heated floor"). In poor families, children eagerly await the return of their fathers who may leave some dishes unfinished. When he is done, the children may be permitted to eat the leftovers.

8. The first call, of course, was the one she received while still at the home of her first husband.

9. They had rented out their house after Mr. Kim's failure in the construction business.

10. The larger the *kut*, the greater is the profit margin for the shaman(s), generally speaking.

CHAPTER 4

1. It is the custom among Korean shamans to address and refer to the shaman who officiates at one's initiation *kut* by the fictive kinship term, *suyŏng-ŏmŏni* ("adoptive mother").

2. Korean people appreciate beautiful women, as other peoples do. However, extraordinary beauty in women is suspect in the folk view. In folk tales, beautiful women are often depicted as foxes in human disguise, and in general beautiful women are regarded as potentially dangerous. Beautiful women are believed by many to have been predestined for misfortune; they are thought more likely to become *kisaeng* or *mudang* than the average or homely looking women. Koreans do not regard extraordinary beauty in a prospective bride a desirable trait.

3. This elderly shaman is not the one who initiated P'yŏngyang-mansin; however, the two maintain a very close working relationship.

4. Her elder son was away in the Army at the time.

5. His use of the words *pakkat* ("outside") *sahoe* ("society") with reference to his job seems to suggest that he does not regard his piecework done at home as really a suitable job for a man and therefore for himself. Most Korean men would agree with him, but he seems also to be saying that so long as his engagement in cottage industry does not become public knowledge with regard to some inner reference group of his, he does not mind the actual tasks involved in his work. It is also of interest that his earnings are not touched for any household or school expenses; they are strictly for his own pocket money and for the "extras" like T.V. That is, his income is treated much like the incidental earnings of housewives in many Korean households.

6. *Maru* is a wooden-floored veranda of regular room size which connects two heatable rooms. Korean families do most of their informal living on the *maru* during the summer months.

7. I interviewed P'yŏngyang-mansin's mother for much of the information regarding her daughter's infancy and her own marriage.

8. *Sangmin* means ordinary people or the common people, but in actual usage, it has uncomplimentary connotations. For example, a common expression of insult among children and adults alike, especially during a quarrel, is to call the other the offspring of a *sangnom* ("a common bastard"). It is an insult only slightly milder than calling the other a son of a bitch.

9. The *pinyŏ* is perhaps the most conspicuous ornament in the shaman's hairdo when she is fully costumed for *kut*.

10. This part of the ceremony is referred to as *mugam-ssŭgi*, the wearing of shaman costumes.

11. The clapping of hands is understood as a signal that the person has surrendered to the possessing spirits, that she will not offer resistance to the spirits' use of her as their medium.

12. Until the reform in 1968, students took entrance examinations and were selectively admitted to middle and high schools according to their examination performance. The more prestigious schools scheduled their examinations earlier than the other schools.

CHAPTER 5

1. A chignon made of carefully coiled, braided hair and worn at the nape of the neck with a long rod ("*pinyŏ*") to hold it in place.

2. *Chŏgori-ch'ima* are the traditional Korean blouse and skirt.

3. Traditional custom permitted post-menopausal women to smoke, especially in informal situations.

4. Like many shamans I met, Ttongkkol-mansin refers to her main deity as "Grandfather"; among those who patronize shamans, this fictive kinship term is understood to refer to deities of the male sex.

5. She used the Korean expression, *chŏmjaeng* (a generic term for fortune-tellers). She did not single out shamans.

6. She used the Korean expression, *mudang-jil*. *Chil (-jil)* in Korean means the performance of a role.

7. This is a proverbial expression for total illiteracy, similar to saying "I can look at a circle all day and not know that it is the letter 'O'."

8. Literally, *minmyŏnuri* refers to a daughter-in-law who has not had her hair put up, a symbol of marital status. It is a form of adoptive daughter-in-law marriage similar to the Chinese *simpua* marriage that Wolf (1968) describes.

CHAPTER 6

1. Gift-giving by parents to teachers is a culturally accepted practice in Korea, although occasionally the custom is abused to bribe teachers.

2. For more details on Kyeryong-san, see J. S. Choi (1967:104-156).

3. I met this gentleman who independently told me about his first encounter with Suwŏn-mansin. His story supported Suwŏn-mansin's in all important details.

4. A revitalistic religious movement known also as the Olive Tree Movement, it was founded by Park Tae Sun and has come into prominence after World War II. It has built at least two self-contained, residential-industrial complexes for its followers. The first has a population of 20,000 followers of the movement. For more details, see Moos (1967).

5. I never received a clear answer as to what her two other brothers were doing. Once, when Suwŏn-mansin was not present, I asked her aunts about them. They gave me the evasive answer that they were idle ("*nolda*"). On the same occasion, they volunteered that their brother, Suwŏn-mansin's father, had died some time after Suwŏn-mansin became possessed. They asked me not to tell their niece about it.

CHAPTER 7

1. One of the ways that Koreans linguistically distinguish working women from ordinary housewives is by referring to the former as living a "social life" [*sahoe-saenghwal-hada*] and to the latter as living a "domestic life" [*kajŏng-saenghwal-hada*]. Generally, the former designation is restricted to women in professional or otherwise socially "legitimate" occupations, i.e., positions in formal organizations such as schools or banks.

2. More and more Korean women in all social strata are converting to Western-style or modified Western-style clothes for daily wear. However, most women still prefer Korean-style shoes for footgear; they are considerably cheaper and also far easier to slip on and off, a real advantage since Koreans do not wear shoes indoors.

3. Christians use this term to refer to the visits that they make with their fellow believers who are sick or otherwise shut-in at home and cannot attend church or prayer meetings. However, I could not find this definition in either the New Korean-English Dictionary by Martin et al. (1968) or in Kukŏ-taesajŏn [Unabridged Korean Dictionary] by Yi Hi Sŭng. S. Y. Yoon (1976:10) defines *sinbang* as meaning literally a "god-room" which, on Cheju Island, is used to refer to shamans.

4. One of the four deaconesses in the prayer group has a telephone. This telephone is in constant use as the nerve center of the group's communication network.

5. A kinship reference to female spirits.

APPENDIX A

1. *Taari* is an Okinawan term which refers to the afflictions, generally psychosomatic in nature, which strike the prospective shaman during the pre-shaman period (Lebra, 1966:37).

2. The idea for the diagram was first suggested to me by T. S. Lebra.

3. There are a number of folk terms which describe a mentally deranged or disturbed person in Korean. Some of the more common ones are: (1) *chŏngsin-nagan-saram*, one whose mind (or spirit or soul) has taken leave; (2) *che-chŏngsin'i-anin-saram*, one who is without his own mind (or spirit or soul); (3) *ŏl-ppajin-saram*, one whose spirit has been driven out or leaked out; (4) *kwisin-dŭn-saram*, one entered by (or possessed by) a ghost; and (5) *hollin-saram*, a possessed person.

APPENDIX B

1. From the year that the legendary founder and first king of Korea, Tan'gun, established Korea in 2333 B.C.

2. The government of the Republic of Korea designates living indi-

viduals who possess outstanding knowledge of its cultural tradition as Living Treasures.

3. According to a 1975 census (East-West Population Institute 1976:1-2), 51.5 percent of Korea's 34,688,000 people live in rural areas. Of the urban population, 40.8 percent live in Seoul, thus making Korea still a relatively rural society with the exception of Seoul.

4. The Confucianism that prevailed in the Yi Dynasty Korea was more accurately neo-Confucianism, as it was formulated by Chu Hsi of the Sung Dynasty, China, and subsequently introduced into Korea by An Yu, a Korean scholar who served for many years as an envoy to China during the Koryo Dynasty (K. P. Yang and Henderson 1958-1959).

5. See for example O. Y. Lee's (1967) essays: "Society as viewed from the Table," and "Two Solitary Islands."

6. Some scholars reverse the order of husband-wife relationship with that of friend-friend.

7. The relationship between friends is often regarded as the exceptional, egalitarian one; however, the principle of seniority superseded the egalitarian principle so that true equality was rare and difficult even between friends.

8. An example of the extent to which the government concerned itself with the maintenance of proper relationships among people is the custom by which men were banned from the streets at sundown. The streets were then open exclusively (in urban areas like Seoul) to women who could move freely without fear of recognition and also without regard to the spatial restrictions segregating the sexes.

9. A Korean woman may now initiate divorce, under the revised civil codes of 1967.

10. A culturally accepted, traditional injunction directed toward women on how to achieve the many desirable attributes of the ideal Korean woman goes as follows: "If one does not keep one's mind empty, then how will she be able to take in what comes to her mind from outside? In the final analysis, jealousy, hatred, and agony arise because one has not kept her mind empty. If one keeps her mind empty, it will have height and breadth so that she will be able to hear all matters fairly and comprehend them clearly. It is only if one arrives at this state of mind

that she can *'kill' herself and serve the society"* (J. S. Choi 1966:282 [emphasis mine]).

11. Most Korean mothers today report some stress in the weaning process. In my observation, when weaning becomes difficult, modern Korean mothers routinely resort to abrupt and prolonged physical separation of the child by sending it to the grandmother's house. Or, they rub their nipples with a variety of repellents, including chili pepper. Both methods are considered very traditional.

12. The traditional cultural hold on female socialization is still forceful, as demonstrated by the biography, not altogether singular, of a thirty-five year old Korean anthropologist. She was forbidden to venture outside the gate of her house after the age of ten and subsequently had to be "kidnapped" from her own house by an elder sister who aided her enrollment in a high school in Seoul.

13. My own mother went to high school in Seoul and subsequently to college in Tokyo in the latter half of the 1920s. In both instances, she resided in school dormitories or school-approved lodgings where space was provided for the girl servant who accompanied her. According to her, it was a common practice at the time.

14. I observed and interviewed a female Korean taxi driver in her early twenties for three consecutive summers between 1971 and 1973. Each working day, both her mother and father walked her to the garage where the taxi was kept and helped her get it ready for the day's business and stayed there until she drove out of the lot. At night, both parents again (when the father was feeling well enough) came down to the company garage to meet their daughter and stayed with her while she reported herself in before going off duty. Their explicit reason for doing this was to keep her reputation unsullied. To quote her parents: "She may be a poor working girl who had to resort to taxi-driving to support her parents and younger sibling, but she is a good girl who deserves a good husband. The least we can do is to make sure that the male drivers do not humiliate her with their off-color jokes or try to compromise her in any other way . . ."

*

GLOSSARY

Ae-ŏmi (애어미)
Mother of a child

Anbang (안 방)
Women's quarters

Chaesu-kut (재수굿) [財數]
A shamanistic rite invoking good fortune

Changgu (장구)
A double-headed drum pinched in at the middle, a drum shaped like an hourglass

Chasu-sŏngga (자수성가) [自手成家]
To establish oneself by one's own efforts; to develop a style of one's own

Che-chŏngsini-anin-saram (제 정신이 아닌 사람)
One who is not in possession of his own soul or spirit

Chesa (재 사) [祭祀]
A sacrificial rite; ancestor worship

Chiban (집 산)
The family, the household

Chiban-ŏrŭn (집산 어른)
Household elders

Chipsa (집 사) [執事]
A deacon or a deaconess in a Christian church

Chiruhaesŏ (지륵해서) [支離]
Past tense for *chirihada* (지륵하다). Tedious, tiresome, boring

Chŏ-ch'in'gu (저 친구)
That friend there. A reference to a third person present, generally among males

Chŏgori-ch'ima (저고려 치마)
Traditional Korean blouse and skirt for women

Chŏlmŭni (젊은이)
A youthful one

Chŏm (점) [占]
Divination, prognostication

Chŏm-jaengi (점쟁이)
A fortune teller

Chŏngsin-nagan-saram (정신 나간 사람)
One whose soul has taken leave of him

Chŏnse (전세) [傳貰]
A contract to rent a room(s) or a house or space with a deposit amounting generally to two-thirds of the price of the room, house, or space, to be repaid on leaving

Chuyŏ, Chuyŏ (주여, 주여) [主, 主]
Master, Master; Christ, oh Christ

Chuyŏk (주역) [周易]
The Book of Changes, a Chinese classic on divination

Ch'ach'aung (차차웅)
One of the terms by which kings of pre-historic Silla were called

Ch'ilsŏng (칠성) [七星]
The seven stars of the Big Dipper; the spirit of the Big Dipper, thought to influence fertility

Ch'imulhae-haesŏ (침울해서) [沈鬱]
Depressed, dejected, or melancholy

Ch'injŏng (친정) [親庭]
A married woman's natal household

Ch'ŏnsong-mansin (천송만신)
An expert shaman who works as a consultant to other shamans

Ch'ŏnja-ch'aek (천자책) [千字冊]
The one-thousand, Chinese character text, the most elementary Chinese primer

Ch'ŏnmin (천민) [賤民]
Despised people, persons who had despised and menial occupations such as execution, burial, butchery, tanning, and grave digging

Ch'ŏnyŏ (처녀)
An unmarried girl

Ch'ŏttchae (첫째)
The first

Ch'ohon-kut (초혼굿)
A *kut* in which spirits are invited to possess the shaman and thus enable the spirits to communicate with the living

Ch'onggak (총각)
An unmarried man

Eppuni (예쁜이)
A pretty one

Hako-bang (하꼬방)
Originally a Japanese word now commonly used among Koreans to refer to cardboard shacks

Halmŏni (할머니)
Grandmother

Hŏt'ŭn-sori (허튼소리)
Utterances which make no rational sense, as in a delirium

Hollin-saram (흘린사람)
One who is possessed

Hunjang (훈장) [訓長]
A village schoolmaster, a teacher

Hwan'gap (환갑) [還甲]
The sixtieth birthday

Kama (가마)
A palanquin, a sedan chair

Kamok-sari-kat'ŭn-sijip-sari (감옥살이 같은 시집사리)
A prison-like married life

Kamun (가문) [家門]
One's family, lineage, and clan; the reputation of such

Kasŭm-ap'ŭgi (가슴아프기)
Heartache, heartbreak, psychological pain, anguish

Kat (갓)
A Korean hat made of bamboo or horse-hair, formerly worn by
married men

Kat-sangja (갓상자)
A box for carrying *kat*

Kibun (기분) [氣分]
Feeling, sentiment, mood, frame of mind; atmosphere

Kil-takka-chul-saram-ŏpsi (길 닦어줄 사람없이)
Without anyone to soothe and smooth (the dead one's pathway)

Kimch'i (김치)
Pickled cabbage and/or turnips

Kimono (기모노)
Traditional costume of the Japanese

Kisaeng (기생) [技生]
A courtesan, a dancing girl, a professional female entertainer

Kiyŏk (기역)
The first letter in the Korean alphabet

Komin (고민) [苦悶]
Agony, anguish

Komo (고모) [姑母]
One's father's sister

Kopkye-poda (곱게보다)
To look upon favorably

Kosa (고사) [告祀]
A sacrificial offering to the spirits to avoid evil and attract good
fortune

Kungnyŏ (궁녀) [宮女]
A palace woman, a waiting woman

Kut (굿)
A shamanistic rite, usually consisting of twelve stages

Kŭm-ch'amoe (금참외)
A yellow melon famous for its sweet taste

Kwisin-dŭn-saram (귀신든 사람) [鬼神]
One who has been invaded or possessed by a ghost or spirit

Kye (계) [契]
A guild, a mutual assistance society, mutual benevolence group, a
credit union

Kkŏllŏng-i (껄렁이)
A good-for-nothing wretch

K'waeja (쾌자) [快子]
A type of traditional warrior's outfit worn by *mudang* during *kut*

K'ŭndaek (큰댁)
The main lineage household

K'ŭnjip (큰집)
See k'ŭndaek

Magi-ŏpkko (맥어 없고) [脈]
Lacking any pulse, without any hope

Majigi (마지기)
A patch of field requiring about one *mal* (말) or about eighteen
liters of seed rice, or about one thousand two hundred square yards

Makkŏlli (막걸리)
Rice wine, "rotgut"

Maknae (막내)
The last-born

Malmun (말문)
The gate of talk, i.e., the facile ability to talk

Maru (마루)
A wooden floored room

Marŭnŭn-byŏng (마르는 병)
A debilitating illness, a wasting illness

Maŭm (마음)
Mind, spirit, heart, idea, or thought

Mich'in-saram (미친사람)
A crazy or insane person

Minmyŏnuri (민 며느리)
A daughter-in-law brought into the household and raised as a
daughter and later married to a son

Miryŏk Buddha (미력부처)
A variant pronunciation for Mirŭk Buddha, i.e., Maitreya Buddha

Mŏttchaengi (멋쟁이)
A fashionable person

Momju (몸주)
The master or guardian spirit that possesses a shaman

Mudang (무당) [巫堂]
A female shaman

Mudang-jil (무당질)
To function as a shaman

Mudang-sŏbang (무당서방)
The husband of a shaman

Mugam-ssŭgi (무감쓰기)
The wearing of shaman's costumes by patrons to dance in one of the twelve stages of a full scale *kut*

Mumun (무문) [無紋]
Without design or pattern. Used with reference to pottery [*mumunt'ogi*] thought to be from the Neolithic Period in Korea

Myŏkkuk (미역국)
A kelp soup usually given to postpartum mothers

Myŏn (면) [面]
A county or a sub-county of *kun* [군 (郡)]

Naerida (내리다)
To come down or to descend

Naerim-kut (내림굿)
The initiation *kut* for the shaman candidate during which possessing spirits are invited to descend into the candidate

Namnyŏ-ch'ilse-pudongsŏk (남녀 칠세 부동석) [男女七歲不同席]
After age seven, the opposite sex may not sit together

Nim (님)
Esteemed, beloved

Nolda (놀다)
To play, to be idle

Nunch'i (눈치)
Tact, savoir faire, sense, social sense, perceptiveness, an eye for social situations

Nunch'i-pab (눈 치 밥)
Eating rice (meals) to which one does not feel rightfully entitled to; eating meals under the eyes of persons gauging the quantity one consumes

Nun-e-puli-nada (눈에 불이 나다)
Feeling enraged; burning of fire in one's eyes

Ŏl-ppajin-saram (얼 빠진 사람)
One who lacks his own soul, one whose soul or spirit has been taken out, one who is not in his own mind

Ŏmŏni (어머니)
Mother

Ŏrŭn (어른)
Adults, elders

Ondol (온 들) [溫 突]
The Korean under-floor heating system

Paekchŏng (백 정) [白 丁]
A member of the lowest class which once engaged chiefly in execution, grave digging, butchery, leatherwork, and wickerwork

Pakkat-sahoe (바깥 사회)
Outside society, the working world

Pinyŏ (비녀)
Ornamental hair pin used to hold the chignon [tchok], the hairdo of married women

Pujŏk (부적) [符 籍]
A talisman, an amulet kept by Buddhist or Taoist households

Pyŏng-kut (병굿)
A healing rite performed by shamans

P'altcha (팔자) [八 字]
The cyclical characters forming binomial designations for the year, month, day, and hour of the birth of a person; these are supposed to have influence on one's fortune, i.e., fate, destiny, one's lot in life.

Saemaŭl-undong (새마을 운동)
A government sponsored, nation-wide program begun in 1971 to rejuvenate the economically depressed rural villages of Korea

Sae-saekssi (새 색시)
A new bride

Saju (사주) [四柱]
The "four pillars" for the year, month, day and hour of one's birth which are supposed to influence one's fate. *Saju-tanja* (사주단자) is a letter to the house of the fiancée in which the Four Pillars of the bridegroom-to-be are written

Sanaun-p'altcha (사나운 팔자)
A harsh fate. See *p'altcha*

Sangmin (상 민) [常民]
The commoners

Sangnom (상놈)
An ill-bred man, a vulgar man

Sansin (산신) [山神]
See *sansilyŏng-nim*

Sansilyŏng-nim (산신령님) [山神靈]
The guardian spirit of a mountain

Sarang-bang (사랑방) [舍廊房]
The male quarters; a living room reserved for entertaining male guests, the party room, the room reserved for the exclusive use of males in a house

Sijip (시집)
The household of one's husband

Sinbang (신방)
To visit someone for the purposes of worship, prayer, or faith-healing, usually used by Christians in this sense

Sinbyŏng (신병) [神病]
Spirit sickness or possession sickness, indicative of supernatural notification to assume the role of *mudang*

Sin-chip'yŏtta (신 집 했 다)
Caught by spirits or fingered by spirits, possessed by spirits

Sinjang-nim (신 장 님) [神將]
A general of exceptional or divine ability; a powerful spirit

Sinkyŏng-manhi-ssŏssŏ (신 경 많이 썼 어) [神조]
To strain one's nerves a great deal, to be over anxious

Sin-naerim-kut (신 내림굿)
See *naerim-kut*

Sinsik-mŏri (신 식 머리)
New or modern hairdo

Sinsŏn (신 선) [神仙]
Taoistic supernatural beings or spirits

Sŏm (섬)
A straw sack holding 47.6 U.S. gallons

Sŏn'gwan (선 관) [仙官]
An official designation for palace shamans during the Koryo Dynasty
(A.D. 918-1392); another term for *mudang*; in Kaesŏng area, female
shamans of *yangban* origin were referred to as *sŏn'gwan*

Sŏnsaeng-nim (선 생 님) [先生任]
Honored teacher

Sŏpsŏphabi (섭 섭 하 비)
To be regretted, regrettable

Sojok (소 족)
A concubine's offspring

Sul (술) [戌]
The sign of the dog, i.e., the eleventh of the twelve earth branches
that corresponds to the period between seven and nine P.M.

Ssŏgŭn-tal (썩은 달)
A rotten month

Taegam (대 감) [大 監]
A guardian spirit; a house-lot god. Also, one of the six body guards in the Silla Dynasty

Tang (당) [堂]
A temple or a shrine

Tang-ajumŏni (당 아주머니)
Mistress or caretaker of shrines

Tan'ga-saenghwal (단가생활) [單家生活]
Nuclear family living, small family living

Tan'gi (단 기) [檀 紀]
From the year the legendary founder, Tan'gun, established Korea in 2333 B.C.

Tang-jigi (당지기)
A shrine keeper, usually male

Tan'gol-mudang (단골무당)
Hereditary shamans

Tan'gun (단 군) [檀君]
The legendary founder of Korea

Taptap-hada (답답하다)
To feel stifled, suffocating, oppressed, bored

Tarit-kut (다릿굿)
A shamanistic ritual performed for the dead to ease the ghost's journey to the other world, usually performed within forty-nine days after the death

Tasŏttchae-ya (다섯째야)
The fifth

Tchok (쪽)
A chignon

Toe (되)
About 1.8 liters

Tongt'i (동티) [動土]
Arousing the wrath of subterranean gods by disturbing the earth, referring generally to trouble brought upon self gratuitously. A variant of *tongt'o* (동토)

Top'o (도포) [道袍]
A Korean full dress attire in the olden days

Tultchae (둘째)
The second

Turumagi (두루마기)
Traditional Korean men's outer coat, overcoat

T'ahyang (타향) [他鄉]
Alien soil, a strange society

T'airŭda (타이르다)
To advise or counsel

Unmyŏng (운명) [運命]
Destiny, fate

Ŭinyŏ (의녀) [醫女]
Female physicians of the Yi Dynasty; they were selected from every province and trained in relatively easy medical skills, after which they were assigned to the free clinics for the needy at the Institute of Internal Medicine, one of three Medical Institutes established during the Yi Dynasty; they gradually assumed additional duties similar to those of *kisaeng* so that they came to be referred to as *ŭigi* ([   ]) also; they tended female patients in all social strata

Ŭp (읍) [邑]
Township

Yongsin-kut (용신굿) [龍神]
A shamanistic rite dedicated to the dragon spirit

Yangban (양반) [兩班]
The two civil and military upper classes of old Korea; the nobility

Yangmin (양민) [良民]
Good citizens

BIBLIOGRAPHY

Ackernecht, Erwin H.
1943 *Medicine and Ethnology: Selected Essays.* Baltimore, Md.: The Johns Hopkins Press.

Adams, Edward B.
1970 *Through Gates of Seoul: Trails and Tales of Yi Dynasty,* 2 vols. Seoul: Saham-bo Publishing Corp.

Akamatsu, Chijo and Takashi Akiba
1938 *Study of Korean Shamanistic Beliefs and Practices,* 2 vols. Tokyo: Osakayago Shoten. (In Japanese.)

Akiba, Takashi
1950 *A Field Study of Shamanism in Korea.* Tambaichi, Japan: Yotokusha. (In Japanese.)

Allen, Vernon L.
1965 "Conformity and the Role of Deviant." *Journal of Personality* 33:584-597.

Banton, Michael
1958 *Roles.* New York: Basic Books.

Barth, Fredrik
    1972   "Analytical Dimensions in the Comparison of Social Organi-
           zation." *American Anthropologist* 74:207-220.

Bateson, Gregory
    1972   *Steps to an Ecology of Mind.* New York: Ballantine Books.

Becker, Howard S.
    1960   "Notes on the Concept of Commitment." *American Journal of
           Sociology* 66:32-40.

    1963   *Outsiders: Studies in the Sociology of Deviance.* New York: The
           Free Press.

Bishop, Esabella Bird
    1897   *Korea and her Neighbors.* Reprint 1972 ed. Seoul: Yonsei Univer-
           sity Press.

Blumer, Herbert
    1962   "Society as Symbolic Interaction." In *Human Behavior and So-
           cial Processes.* A. M. Rose, ed. Pp. 179-192. Boston: Houghton
           Mifflin Co.

Bourguignon, Erika
    1976   " 'Possession' and 'Trance' in Cross-Cultural Studies of Men-
           tal Health." In *Culture-bound Syndromes, Ethno-Psychiatry, and
           Alternate Therapies.* W. P. Lebra, ed. Vol. IV of *Mental Health
           Research in Asia and the Pacific.* Honolulu: The University Press
           of Hawaii.

Boyer, L. Bryce
    1964   "Further Remarks Concerning Shamans and Shamanism."
           The Israel Annals of Psychiatry and Related Disciplines 2:235-257.

Brandt, Vincent S. R.
    1971   *A Korean Village between Farm and Sea.* Cambridge, Mass.: Har-
           vard University Press.

Brim, Jr., Orville G.
    1965   "Socialization through the Life Cycle." In *Socialization after
           Childhood.* Orville G. Brim, Jr., and Stanton Wheeler, eds. Pp.
           1-49. New York: John Wiley and Sons.

Burgess, Ernest W.
   1962   "Social Problems and Social Processes," In *Human Behavior and Social Processes: Interactionist Approach*. A. M. Rose, ed. Pp. 381-400. Boston: Houghton Mifflin Co.

Carpenter, Frances
   1973   *Tales of a Korean Grandmother*. Seoul: Royal Asiatic Society, Korea Branch.

Carson, Robert C.
   1969   *Interaction Concepts of Personality*. Chicago: Aldine Publishing Co.

Chang, Chu Keun
   1974   "Mu-sok—the Shaman Culture of Korea." In *Folk Culture in Korea*. Shin-Yong Chun, gen. ed. Seoul: International Cultural Foundation. (In Korean with English title and summary.)

Chang, Kyong Hak
   1965   *Outline of the Code of Civil Law*. Pp. 565-581. Seoul: Pŏbmun-sa. (In Korean.)

Chang, Shin Kyu, ed.
   1975   *Korea Statistical Yearbook, 22nd Edition*. Seoul: Bureau of Statistics, Economic Planning Board, Republic of Korea. (In Korean with title, table of contents, and subject headings in English.)

Chodorow, Nancy
   1974   "Family Structure and Feminine Personality." In *Woman, Culture, and Society*. M. Z. Rosaldo and Louise Lamphere, eds. Pp. 43-66. Stanford: Stanford University Press.

Ch'oe, Kil Sŏng (Chai Kil Sung)
   1968   "A Study in Korean Shamanism." *The Korean Journal of Cultural Anthropology* 1:35-43. (In Korean, with title in English.)

   1969   "A Study on the Transmission of Shamans." *Journal of Korean Folklore* 1:105-115. (In Korean, with title in English.)

   1970   "Research Activities on Korean Shamanism in the Past and the Present." *The Journal of the Korean Association of Cultural Anthropology* 3:125-141. (In Korean, with title in English.)

1971   "A Report on Decorations in the Shamanistic Shrine in Eastern Korea." *Cultural Anthropology* 4:135-147. (In Korean, with title in English.)

Ch'oe, Tŏkkyo (Sponsoring publisher)
1969   *Mother.* Seoul: Ch'angjo-sa. (In Korean.)

Choi, Jai Seuk
1963   "Process of Change in Korean Family Life." *Korea Journal* 3(10):10-15.

1964   "Traditional Values in Korean Family." *The Journal of Asiatic Studies* 7(2):19-47. (In Korean, with title and summary in English.)

1965   "Changes in Korean Family Values." *The Chin-tan Hakpo* 28:135-192. (In Korean, with title and summary in English.)

1966   *A Study of Korean Family.* Seoul: Minjung-sŏgwan. (In Korean, with title and summary in English.)

1967   "A Sociological Survey of Sindonae." *Transactions of the Korea Branch, Royal Asiatic Society* 43:104-155.

1969a "The Functions of Korean Rural Family." *Korean Classics Studies* 3:1-66 (In Korean, with title and summary in English.)

1969b "The Role Structure of Korean Rural Family." *The Chin-tan Hakpo* 32:239-258. (In Korean, with title in English.)

1969c "Family Power Structure in Korean Rural Area." *Journal of Asian Women* 8:1-180. (In Korean, with title and summary in English.)

Chun, Shin-Yong (ed.)
1974   *Folk Culture in Korea. Korean Culture Series 4.* Seoul: International Cultural Foundation.

Chung, Choon Ryang and Ho Chai Lee
1970   "A Study of the Life of Housewives of Urban Middle Class Families." *Journal of Korean Cultural Research Institute* 16:223-285. (In Korean, with title and summary in English.)

Clark, Charles Allen
  1929   *Religions of Old Korea.* 1961 ed. Seoul: The Chrisitian Literature
         Society of Korea.

Collier, Jane Fishburne
  1974   "Women in Politics." In *Women, Culture, and Society.* M. Z.
         Rosaldo and Louise Lamphere, eds. Pp. 89-96. Stanford: Stan-
         ford University Press.

Coser, Rose Laub
  1961   "Insulation from Observability and Types of Social Confor-
         mity." *American Sociological Review* 26:28-39.

Coutu, Walter
  1951   "Role-playing vs. Role-taking: an Appeal for Clarification."
         American Sociological Review 16:186-187.

Crane, Paul S.
  1967   *Korean Patterns.* Seoul: Hollym Corp.

  1972   "Some Reflections on *Korean Patterns." Transactions of the Korea
         Branch, Royal Asiatic Society* XLVII:41-57.

Dakin, Edwin F.
  1929   *Mrs. Eddy.* 1968 ed. Gloucester, Mass.: P. Smith.

Devereux, George
  1956   "The Origin of Shamanistic Powers as Reflected in a Neurosis:
         A Brief Clinical Communication." *Revue Internationale
         d'Ethnospsychologie Normale et Pathologique* 1:19-25.

  1961   "Shamans as Neurotics." *American Anthropologist* 63(5) Part 1:
         1088-1090.

East-West Population Institute
  1976   "Preliminary Census Results from Japan and Korea." *Asian
         and Pacific Census Newsletter* 2(3):1-2.

Edgerton, Robert B.
  1971   "A Traditional African Psychiatrist." *Southwestern Journal of
         Anthropology* Vol 27:3:259-278.

Ehrlich, Howard J. and J. W. Rinehart
    1962   "The Study of Role Conflict: Explorations in Methodology."
           Sociometry 25:85-97.

Erikson, Erik H.
    1958   *Young Man Luther: A Study in Psychoanalysis and History.* New
           York: W. W. Norton and Co.

Farber, Bernard
    1962   "Types of Family Organization: Child-oriented, Home-
           oriented, and Parent-oriented." In *Human Behavior and Social
           Processes.* A. M. Rose, ed. Pp. 285-306. Boston: Houghton
           Mifflin Co.

Febrega, Jr., Horacio and Daniel Silver
    1970   "Some Social and Psychological Properties of Zinacanteco
           Shamans." *Behavioral Science* 15(6):471-486.

Firth, Raymond
    1961   *Elements of Social Organization.* Boston: Beacon Press.

Foreign Areas Studies Division, Special Operations Research Office, The
American University
    1964   *U.S. Army Area Handbook for Korea.* Washington, D.C.: U.S.
           Government Printing Office.

Geertz, H.
    1971   "Religion as a Cultural System." In *Reader in Comparative Reli-
           gion.* W. A. Lessa and E. Z. Vogt, eds. Third ed. Pp. 167-178.
           New York: Harper and Row.

Getzels, J. W. and E. G. Guba
    1955   "Role, Role Conflict, and Effectiveness: An Empirical Study."
           American Sociological Review 19:164-175.

Glasser, Barney G. and Anselm L. Strauss
    1967   *The Discovery of Grounded Theory: Strategies for Qualitative Re-
           search.* Chicago: Aldine Co.

Goffman, Erving
    1959   *The Presentation of Self in Everyday Life.* Garden City, N.Y.:
           Doubleday and Co.

1961 "Role Distance." In *Encounters: Two Studies in the Sociology of Interaction*. Pp. 84-152. New York: The Bobbs-Merrill Co.

1962 "On Cooling the Mark Out: Some Aspects of Adaptation to Failure." In *Human Behavior and Social Processes: Interactionist Approach*. A. M. Rose, ed. Pp. 482-505. Boston: Houghton Mifflin Co.

1967 *Interaction Ritual: Essays on Face-to-face Behavior*. Garden City, N.Y.: Doubleday and Co.

Goode, William J.
1960 "A Theory of Role Strain." *American Sociological Review* 25:483-496.

1968 "Role Problems of the Divorce." In *Family Roles and Interaction: an Anthology*. Jerold Heiss, ed. Pp. 501-515. Chicago: Rand McNally and Co.

Goodenough, Ward H.
1969 "Rethinking 'Status' and 'Role': toward a General Model of the Cultural Organization of Social Relationships." In *Cognitive Anthropology*. S. A. Tyler, ed. New York: Holt, Rinehart and Winston.

Grajdanzev, Andrew J.
1944 *Modern Korea*. New York: The John Day Co.

Gross, Neal, et al.
1968 *Explorations in Role Analysis: Studies of the School Superintendency Role*. New York: John Wiley and Sons.

Ha, Hyŏn Kang
1972 "The Yi Dynasty." In *Han'guk Yŏsŏng-sa*. O. K. Kim et al, eds. Vol 2, Pp. 310-311, 503, 549-567. Seoul: Ewha University Press. (In Korean.)

Hahm, Pyong Choon
1967 *The Korean Political Tradition and Law: Essays in Korean Urban Society*. Seoul: Hollym Corp.

Han, Dong Se
1964 "A Clinical and Anthropological Study of Hysteria in Korean

Urban Society." *Neuropsychiatry* 3(4):9-21. (In Korean, with title and summary in English.)

Han, Woo Keun
1970   *The History of Korea.* Seoul: The Eul-yoo Publishing Co.

Handelman, Don
1967   "The Development of a Washo Shaman." *Ethnology* 6(4):444-464.

1968   "Shamanizing on an Empty Stomach." *American Anthropologist* 70(2):353-356.

Harvey, Youngsook Kim
1976   "The Korean *Mudang* as a Household Therapist." In *Culture-Bound Syndromes, Ethnopsychiatry, and Alternate Therapies.* W. P. Lebra, ed. Pp. 191-98. Vol. IV of *Mental Health Research in Asia and the Pacific.* Honolulu: The University Press of Hawaii.

Hatada, Takashi
1969   *A History of Korea.* Santa Barbara, Ca.: Clio Press.

Heiss, Jerold
1968   "An Introduction to the Elements of Role Theory." In *Family Roles and Interaction: an Anthology.* J. Heiss, ed., Chicago: Rand McNally.

Henry, Jules
1963   *Culture against Man.* New York: Random House, Vintage Books.

1965   *Pathways to Madness.* New York: Random House, Vintage Books.

1972   "Vulnerability in Education." In *Henry on Education.* Jules Henry, ed. Pp. 9-24. New York: Random House, Vintage Books.

Honigmann, John J.
1967   *Personality in Culture.* New York: Harper and Row.

Hsu, Francis L. K.
  1967   *Under the Ancestors' Shadow: Kinship, Personality and Social Mo-
          bility in Village China.* Garden City, N.Y.: Doubleday and Co.

Hulbert, Homer B.
  1906   *The Passing of Korea.* 1969 ed. Seoul: Yonsei University Press.

Izumi, Seiichi
  1970   "Korean Shamanism." *Chōsen Kakuhō* [Journal of the
          Academic Association of Koreanology in Japan] 56:1-12. (In
          Japanese, with title in English.)

Joe, Wanne J.
  1972   *Traditional Korea: a Cultural History.* Seoul: Chungang Univer-
          sity Press.

Kang, Yong Kwon
  1970   " 'Pyul Shin Gut' in Pusan District." *The Journal of the Korean
          Association of Cultural Anthropology* 3:79-91. (In Korean, with
          title in English.)

Kanter, Rosabeth Moss
  1968   "Commitment and Social Organization: a Study of Commit-
          ment Mechanisms in Utopian Communities." *American
          Sociological Review* 33(4):499-517.

  1972   "Commitment and the Internal Organization of Millennial
          Movements." *American Behavioral Scientist* 16(2):219-243.

Kiev, Ari, ed.
  1964   *Magic, Faith, and Healing: Studies in Primitive Psychiatry.* Glen-
          coe, Ill: The Free Press of Glencoe.

Kiev, Ari
  1968   *Curanderismo: Mexican-American Folk Psychiatry.* New York: The
          Free Press.

  1972   *Transcultural Psychiatry.* New York: The Free Press.

Killian, L. M.
  1952   "The Significance of Multiple-group Membership in Disas-
          ter." *American Journal of Sociology* 57:309-314.

Kim, Chong Un, trans.
  1974 "The True History of Queen In Hyŏn." In *Virtuous Women: Three Masterpieces of Traditional Korean Fiction*. R. Rutt and C. U. Kim, eds. Pp. 179-234. Seoul: Korean National Commission for UNESCO.

Kim, Kwang Iel
  1972a "Shamanism and Personality in Korea." A paper presented at the Oriental Convention on Shamanism, Wongwang University, Cholla-pukto, Korea, on October 6, 1972. (In Korean, with title in English.)

  1972b "New Religions in Korea: The Sociocultural Consideration." *Neuropsychiatry* 11(1):31-36.

  1972c "Psychoanalytic Consideration of Korean Shamanism." *Neuropsychiatry* 11(2):121-129. (In Korean, with title and abstract in English.)

  1972d " 'Sin-byung': a Culture-bound Depersonalization Syndrome." *Neuropsychiatry* 11(4):223-234. (In Korean, with title and abstract in English.)

  1972e "Traditional Concept of Disease in Korean Culture." *New Medical Journal* 15:49-51. (In Korean.)

  1973a "Shamanist Healing Ceremonies in Korea." *Korea Journal* 12(4):41-47.

  1973b "Traditional Concept of Disease in Korea." *Korea Journal* 13(1):12-18, 49.

  1974 "Psychodynamic Study on the Two Cases of Shaman in Korea." *Journal of Cultural Anthropology* 6:45-65. (In Korean.)

Kim, Kwang Iel and Tae Gon Kim
  1970 "The Psychological Function of a Shaman's Dreams during Initiation Process." *Neuropsychiatry* 9(1):47-56. (In Korean, with title and summary in English.)

Kim, Kwang Iel and H. T. Won
  1972 "Folk-psychiatry in Korea (1): Traditional Concept and Folk Treatment of Mental Illness among the Rural Peoples." *Neuropsychiatry* 11(2):85-99. (In Korean, with title and abstract in English.)

Kim, Ok Kil et al, eds.
1972 *History of Korean Women.* 3 vols. Seoul: Ewha University Press. (In Korean.)

Kim, Richard E.
1970 *Lost Names.* Seoul: The Sisayŏngŏ-sa Publishing Co.

Kim, Tae Gon
1967 "Shamanism in Korean Christianity—Influence of Shamanism on Korean Christianity." Pp. 182 ff. *Tongsŏ Ch'unch'u.* (In Korean, with title in English.)

1970 "The Tradition of Shamanistic Deities in Korea." *The Journal of the Korean Association of Cultural Anthropology* 3:69-78. (In Korean.)

1974 "Korean Shamanism and its Outlook on Future Life." *Journal of Social Sciences and Humanities* 39:83-104.

Kim, Tong Ni
1974 "Portrait of a Shaman," In *Flowers of Fire.* P. Lee, ed. Pp. 58-90. Honolulu: The University Press of Hawaii.

Kim, Tu Hŏn
1969 *A Study of Korean Family Structure.* Seoul: South National University Press. (In Korean.)

Kim, U-chang (Kim, U Ch'ang)
1976 "The Situation of the Writers under Japanese Colonialism." *Korea Journal* 16(5):4-15.

Knez, Eugene I. and Chang-su Swanson
1968 *A Selected and Annotated Bibliography of Korean Anthropology.* Seoul: National Assembly Library, Republic of Korea.

Koh, Hesung Chun
1975 "Yi Dynasty Korean Women in the Public Domain: a New Perspective on Social Stratification." *Social Science Journal* 3:7-19. Korean National Commission for UNESCO.

Komarovsky, Mirra
1946 "Cultural Contradictions and Sex Roles." *American Journal of Sociology* 52:184-189.

1973 "Presidential Address: Some Problems in Role Analysis."
      American Sociological Review 38(6):649-662.

Koo, Sang
  1972 "The Role of Women in Korean Culture." Thomas G. Mark-
        ham, trans. Paper presented at Korea Research Center Col-
        loquium, University of Hawaii.

Kroeber, Alfred L.
  1952 "Psychosis or Social Sanction." In *The Nature of Culture*. Pp.
        310-317. Chicago: University of Chicago Press.

Langness, L. L.
  1965 *The Life History in Anthropological Science*. New York: Holt,
        Rinehart and Winston.

Lebra, Takie Sugiyama
  1969 "Reciprocity and the Asymmetric Principle: an Analytical
        Reappraisal of the Japanese Concept of 'On'." *Psychologia*
        12:129-138.

  1970 "Religious Conversion as a Breakthrough for Transcultura-
        tion: a Japanese Sect in Hawaii." *Journal for the Scientific Study
        of Religion* 9:181-196.

  1973 "Millenarian Movements and Resocialization." *American Be-
        ‑havioral Scientist* 16:195-217.

  1976 "Taking the Role of the Supernatural 'Other': Spirit Posses-
        sion in a Japanese Healing Cult." In *Culture-bound Syndromes,
        Ethno-psychiatry, and Alternate Therapies*. W. P. Lebra, ed. Vol.
        IV of *Mental Health Research in Asia and the Pacific*. Honolulu:
        The University Press of Hawaii.

Lebra, William P.
  1964 "The Okinawan Shaman." In *Ryukyuan Culture and Society: A
        Survey*. Allen H. Smith, ed. Pp. 93-98. Honolulu: The Univer-
        sity Press of Hawaii.

  1966 *Okinawan Religion*. Honolulu: The University Press of Hawaii.

  1969 "Shaman and Client in Okinawa." In *Mental Health Research in
        Asia and the Pacific*. W. Caudill and T. Y. Lin, eds. Pp. 216-222.
        Honolulu: East-West Center Press.

n.d.   "Shamanism, Health, and the Moral Order in Okinawa."
       Manuscript in preparation.

Lederer, William J. and Don D. Jackson
   1968   *The Mirages of Marriage.* New York: W. W. Norton and Co.

Lee, Hae Yong
   1969   "Modernization of the Family Structure in an Urban
          Setting—with Special Reference to Marriage Relations." In
          Aspects of Social Change in Korea. E. Kim and C. Chee, eds. Pp.
          44-69. Kalamazoo, Mich.: The Korea Research and Publica-
          tions.

Lee, Hyo Chai
   1959   "A Sociological Study of the Urban Family in Seoul." Pp. 9-73.
          Seoul: Korean Cultural Research Institute, Ewha Woman's
          University. (In Korean.)

   1967   "Patterns of Changes Observed in the Korean Marriage In-
          stitution." *The Chin-tan Hakpo* 31:177-196. (In Korean, with
          title in English.)

   1971   *Kindred Relationships of Urban People.* Korea Research Institute,
          Korea Research Monograph No. 47. (In Korean, with title and
          summary in English.)

Lee, Jung Young
   1973   "The Seasonal Rituals of Korean Shamanism." *History of Reli-
          gions* 12(3):271-287.

Lee, Kwang-Kyu
   n.d.   "A Comparative Study of Chinese, Korean, and Japanese
          Family Systems." Manuscript.

Lee, Kwang-Kyu and Youngsook Kim Harvey
   1973   "Teknonymy and Geononymy in Korean Kinship Terminol-
          ogy." *Ethnology* 12(1):31-46.

Lee, Kyu Hwan
   1959   Early Status of Women's Education in Korea. Pp. 217-232.
          Seoul: Korean Cultural Research Institute, Ewha Woman's
          University.

Lee, O Young
    1967 *In this Earth and in that Wind: This is Korea.* David I. Steinberg,
          trans. Seoul: Hollym Corp.

Lewis, I. M.
    1971 *Ecstatic Religion: an Anthropological Study of Spirit Possession and
          Shamanism.* Middlesex, England: Penguin Books.

Lewis, Oscar
    1959 *Five Families.* New York: A Mentor Book.

Li, Dun J.
    1965 *The Ageless Chinese: a History.* New York: Charles Scribner's
          Sons.

Linton, Ralph
    1936 *The Study of Man: an Introduction.* New York: Appleton-
          Century-Crofts.

Lofland, John
    1966 *Doomsday Cult: a Study of Conversion, Proselytization, and
          Maintenance of Faith.* Englewood Cliffs, N.J.: Prentice-Hall.

    1971 *Analyzing Social Settings: a Guide to Qualitative Observation and
          Analysis.* Belmont, Calif: Wadsworth Publishing Co.

Martin, Samuel E., Yang Ha Lee, and Sung Un Chang
    1968 *New Korean-English Dictionary.* Seoul: Minjungseogwan.

Maruyama, Magoroh
    1968 "The Second Cybernetics: Deviation-amplifying Mutual
          Causal Processes." In *Modern Systems Research for the Behavioral
          Scientist.* Walter Buckley, ed. Pp. 304-313. Chicago: Aldine
          Publishing Co.

Merton, Robert K.
    1938 "Social Structure and Anomie." *American Sociological Review*
          3:672-682.

    1957 "The Role-set: Problems in Sociological Theory." *British Jour-
          nal of Sociology* 8:133 ff.

    1968 *Social Theory and Social Structure.* 1968 enlarged ed. New York:
          The Free Press.

Mischel, Walter and Frances Mischel
    1958 "Psychological Aspects of Spirit Possession." *American An-
          thropologist* 60(2) Part 1:249-260.

Moos, Felix
    1967 "Leadership and Organization in the Olive Tree Movement."
          Transactions of the Korea Branch Royal Asiastic Society 43:11-27.

    1970 "The New Women of Korea." A paper presented at the Third
          Conference on Korea, Western Michigan University. Manus-
          cript.

Moose, J. Robert
    1911 *Village Life in Korea.* Nashville, Tenn.: Publishing House of the
          M. E. Church, South.

Murphy, Jane M.
    1964 "Psychotherapeutic Aspects of Shamanism on St. Lawrence
          Island, Alaska." In *Magic, Faith, and Healing.* Ari Kiev, ed. Pp.
          53-83. Glencoe, Ill.: Free Press of Glencoe.

Nadel, S. F.
    1946 "A Study of Shamanism in the Nuba Mountains." *Journal of
          the Royal Anthropological Institute* 76:25-37.

    1957 *The Theory of Social Structure.* London: Cohen and West Ltd.

    1968 "Social Control and Self-Regulation." In *Modern Systems Re-
          search for the Behavioral Scientist.* Walter Buckley, ed. Pp. 401-
          408. Chicago: Aldine Publishing Co.

Nakane, Chie
    1970 *Japanese Society.* Berkeley: University of California Press.

Nelson, Sarah M.
    1975 "Han River Ch'ulmunt'ogi: a Study of Early Neolithic Korea."
          Occasional Paper No. 9. Program in East Asian Studies, West-
          ern Washington State College.

Opler, Marvin
    1961 "On Devereux's Discussion of Ute Shamanism." *American An-
          thropologist* 63(5) Part 1:1091-1093.

Osgood, Cornelius
  1951   *The Koreans and their Culture.* New York: Ronald Press Co.

Palmer, Spencer J.
  1967   *Korea and Christianity: the Problem of Identification with Tradition.*
         Seoul: Hollym Corp.

Park, Rae Young
  1966   "Fertility Control in Korea in View of Legal and Institutional
         Aspects." *Journal of Population Study* 3:129-142. (In Korean,
         with title and summary in English.)

Rhi, Bou Young
  1968   "Studies on the Dead in Korean Shamanism." *Neuropsychiatry*
         7(2):5-14. (In Korean, with title in English and title and
         abstract in German.)

  1970   "The Folk Psychiatry of Korea (1)." *Neuropsychiatry* 9(1):35-46.
         (In Korean, with title and summary in English.)

Rhi, Bou Young, Chul Kyu Lee, and Hwan Il Chang
  1970   "Mental Disorders Associated with Folk Religion." The Jour-
         nal of the Korean Association of Cultural Anthropology 3:5-
         32. (In Korean, with title and summary in English.)

Rinder, Irwin D.
  1964   "Toward an Integration of Sociological and Psychological
         Models of Personality through the Self-system." *Social
         Psychiatry, Section A: The International Journal of Social
         Psychiatry,* Special Edition 2: 32-37.

Ritchie, James
  1976   "A Generalized System of Socio-cultural Therapy amongst
         the Maori: or a Cultural Excuse for Time Out." In *Culture-
         bound Syndromes, Ethno-psychiatry, and Alternate Therapies.* W.
         P. Lebra, ed. Vol. IV of *Mental Health Research in Asia and the
         Pacific.* Honolulu: The University Press of Hawaii.

Roh, Chang Shub
  1969   "Family Life in Korea and Japan." *Silliman Journal,*
         XVI(2):200-215.

Rosaldo, Michelle Zimbalist
   1974   "Woman, Culture, and Society: a Theoretical Overview." In
          Woman, Culture, and Society. M. Z. Rosaldo and Louise Lam-
          phere, eds. Pp. 17-42. Stanford: Stanford University Press.

Rose, Arnold M.
   1962   *Human Behavior and Social Processes: Interactionist Approach.* Bos-
          ton: Houghton Mifflin Co.

Royal Asiatic Society, *Transations of the Korea Branch*
   1967   "The New Religions of Korea." *Royal Asiatic Society,* Vol. 43.
          (Edited with an introduction by Spencer J. Palmer.)

Ruesch, Jurgen and Gregory Bateson
   1968   *Communication: the Social Matrix of Psychiatry.* New York: W.
          W. Norton and Co.

Rutt, Richard
   1964   *Korean Works and Days.* Tokyo: Charles E. Tuttle Co. Inc.

Rutt, Richard and Kim Chong Un
   1974   *Virtuous Women: Three Masterpieces of Traditional Korean Fiction.*
          Seoul: Korean National Commission for UNESCO.

Ryu, Tongshik, ed.
   1972   *A Bibliography on Family and Religion in Korea. (1945-1970).* The
          Centre for East Asian Cultural Studies, Tokyo. Seoul: Kwang
          Moon Printing Co. (In Korean, with title in English.)

Sarbin, Theodore R.
   1968   "Role: Psychological Aspects." *International Encyclopedia of the
          Social Sciences* 13:546-552.

Sarbin, Theodore R. and Vernon L. Allen
   1968   "Role Theory." In *The Handbook of Social Psychology.* 2d ed. G.
          Lindzey and E. Aronson, eds. Pp. 488-567. Reading, Mass.:
          Addison-Wesley Publishing Co.

Sarbin, Theodore R. and B. G. Rosenbert
   1955   "Contributions to Role-taking Theory, IV: a Method for Ob-
          taining a Qualitative Estimate of the Self." *The Journal of Social
          Psychology* 42:71-81.

Sasaki, Yuji
  1969 "Psychiatric Study of the Shaman in Japan." In *Mental Health Research in Asia and the Pacific.* W. Caudill and T. Y. Lin, eds. Pp. 223-241. Honolulu: East-West Center Press.

Schein, Edgar H.
  1956 "The Chinese Indoctrination Program for Prisoners of War: a Study of Attempted 'Brain Washing'." *Psychiatry* 19:149-172.

Seo, Dae Seok
  1968 "A Study on [of] Korean Medicine Man [Men]." *The Korean Journal of Cultural Anthropology* 1:45-46. (In Korean, with title in English.)

Shibutani, Tomatsu
  1962 "Reference Groups and Social Control." In *Human Behavior and Social Processes.* A. M. Rose, ed. Pp. 128-147. Boston: Houghton Mifflin Co.

Shirokogoroff, S. M.
  1923 "General Theory of Shamanism among the Tungus." *Journal of the Royal Asiatic Society, North China Branch* 54:246-249.

Silverman, Julian
  1967 "Shamans and Acute Schizophrenia." *American Anthropologist* 69(1):21-31.

Sohn, Pow Key, Chol Choon Kim and Yi Sup Hong
  1970 *The History of Korea.* Seoul: Korean National Commission for UNESCO.

Son, Ch'ang Sŏp
  1962 *Husband and Wife.* Seoul: Chŏngmŭm-sa. (Fiction in Korean.)

Song, Un Sun
  1969 "Marriage and the Family in Korea." In *Marriage and Family in the Modern World: a Book of Readings. Third ed.* Ruth Shonle Cavan, ed. Pp. 92-98. New York: Thomas Y. Crowell Co.

Strauss, Anselm
  1962 "Transformations of Identity." In *Human Behavior and Social Processes.* A. M. Rose, ed. Pp. 63-85. Boston: Houghton Mifflin Co.

Stryker, Sheldon
    1962 "Conditions of Accurate Role-taking: a Test of Mead's
          Theory." In *Human Behavior and Social Processes*. A.M. Rose,
          ed. Pp. 41-62. Boston: Houghton-Mifflin Co.

T'ak Myŏng Hwan
    1971 "Life Styles of Female Founders of New Religions in Korea: its
          Analysis and Present Status." *Cultural Anthropology* 4:115-134.
          (In Korean.)

Takenob, Y. and K. Kawakami
    1911 *The Japan Year Book: Complete Cyclopaedia of General Information
          and Statistics on Japan for the Year 1911*. Tokyo: The Japan Year
          Book Office.

Thorton, Russell and Peter M. Nardi
    1975 "The Dynamics of Role Acquisition." *American Journal of
          Sociology* 80:870-885.

Toby, Jackson
    1952 "Some Variables in Role Conflict Analysis." *Social Forces*
          30:323-337.

Turner, Ralph H.
    1956 "Role-taking, Role Standpoint, and Reference-group Be-
          havior." *American Journal of Sociology* 61:316-328.

    1962 "Role-taking: Process vs. Conformity." In *Human Behavior and
          Social Processes*. A. M. Rose, ed. Pp. 20-41. Boston: Houghton
          Mifflin Co.

    1968 "Role: Sociological Aspects." *International Encyclopedia of the
          Social Sciences* 13:553-557.

Turner, Victor W.
    1969 *The Ritual Process: Structure and Anti-structure*. Chicago: Aldine
          Publishing Co.

Van Gennep, Arnold
    1960 *The Rites of Passage*. Chicago: University of Chicago Press.

Wallace, Anthony F.
    1956 "Revitalization Movements." *American Anthropologist* 58(2):
          264-281.

1969   *Culture and Personality.* New York: Random House.

Watzlawick, Paul, Janet Helmick Beavin and Don D. Jackson
 ⬧ 1967   *Pragmatics of Human Communication: a Study of Interactional Patterns, Pathologies, and Paradoxes.* New York: W. W. Norton and Co.

Weakland, John H.
   1968   "Shamans, Schizophrenia, and Scientific Unity." *American Anthropologist* 70(2):358.

Wheeler, Stanton
   1965   "The Structure of Formally Organized Socialization Settings." In *Socialization after Childhood.* O. G. Brim, Jr. and S. Wheeler, eds. Pp. 53-116. New York: John Wiley and Sons.

Wolf, Margery
   1972   *Women and the Family in Rural Taiwan.* Stanford: Stanford University Press.

Wolff, Kurt H.
   1950   *The Sociology of Georg Simmel.* 1967 edition. New York: The Free Press.

Yang, Key P. and Gregory Henderson
   1958- "An Outline History of Korean Confucianism, Part I: The
   1959   Early Period and Yi Factionalism." *Journal of Asian Studies* 18(1):81-105; "An Outline History of Korean Confucianism," Part II: The Schools of Yi Confucianism." *Journal of Asian Studies* 18(2):259-276.

INDEX

Akamatsu, Chijo, 10
Akiba, T., 10
Ancestral ghosts, as possessing spirits, 238
Animism, 10
Apprenticeship period, 269

Bishop, E. B., 9, 13
Brandt, V.S.R., 253, 269
Brother-sister conflicts, resolution of, 263
Buddhism, 8, 254, 273

Carpenter, F., 260
Ch'ach'aung, definition of, 7
Chang, C.K., 7, 10, 11
Chickens, used in chŏm, 132
Child groom, 258
Ch'ilsŏng, 75
Ch'oe, K.S., 12, 274
Choi, J.S., 256, 283
Chŏm, payment for, 22
Ch'ŏnmin, definition of, 10
Chŏndoism, 9, 274
Chōsen Sō Tokufu (The Korean Government-General), 12, 275

Christianity, identity with Korean tradition, 9
Christianity, influence of, in the lives of shaman informants, 7. See also Wangsimni-mansin; Deaconess Chang; Namsan-mansin; P'yŏng-yang-mansin; Suwŏm-mansin; and Ttongkkol-mansin
Ch'unhyang, 260
Clan exogamy, 256
Clapping of hands, 279
Clark, C.A., 7, 8, 11, 13
Colonization of Korea by Japan, 10
Concubinage, 46
Confucian values, in contemporary Korea, 253; in Yi Dynasty Korea, 254
Confucianism: Koreanization of, 8; Yi Dynasty, 282
Crane, P., 253
Curfew, 277

Daughters, selling of, 261
Deaconess Chang: birth of, 211; childhood, memories of early, 212; Christianity, conversion to, 209, 210, 229, 230, 231, 232, 233, 234; Christianity

317

†